#1877   l   7.50

John Barth:
A Bibliography

Garland Reference Library in the Humanities (Vol. 25)

John Barth:

*A Descriptive Primary and
Annotated Secondary Bibliography,
Including a Descriptive Catalog of
Manuscript Holdings in United States Libraries*

Joseph Weixlmann

Garland Publishing, Inc., New York & London

1976

Copyright © 1976

by Joseph Weixlmann

All Rights Reserved

Library of Congress Cataloging in Publication Data

Weixlmann, Joseph.
    John Barth : a descriptive primary and annotated secondary bibliography, including a descriptive catalog of manuscript holdings in United States libraries.

    (Garland reference library in the humanities ; v. 25)
    Includes indexes.
    1. Barth, John--Bibliography. 2. Barth, John --Manuscripts--Catalogs.
Z8076.7.W44   016.813'5'4   75-24076
ISBN 0-8240-9987-7

Printed in the United States of America

CONTENTS

Acknowledgments...vii

Preface..ix

Abbreviations and Symbols.......................................xi

Plates..[xiii]

    A1a   THE FLOATING OPERA [1956]....................[xiii]
    A2a   THE END OF THE ROAD 1958.....................[xiv]
    A2b   THE END OF THE ROAD [1960]....................[xv]
    A3a   THE SOT-WEED FACTOR 1960.....................[xvi]
    A4a   GILES GOAT-BOY 1966..........................[xvii]
    A5a   THE SOT-WEED FACTOR (REVISED) 1967..........[xviii]
    A6a   THE FLOATING OPERA (REVISED) 1967.............[xix]
    A7a   THE END OF THE ROAD (REVISED) 1967............[xx]
    A8a   LOST IN THE FUNHOUSE 1968....................[xxi]
    A9b   CHIMERA [1972].................................[xxii]

A. Separate Publications by John Barth.........................1

B. First Book Contributions by John Barth....................27

C. Barth's Contributions to Periodicals and to the Press....31

    Fiction..31
    Non-Fiction..32

D. Reprints of Short Works and Parts of Books by John
   Barth..35

    Fiction..35
    Non-Fiction..39

E. A Descriptive Catalog of the Barth Manuscripts Housed
   in United States Libraries...............................41

    The Library of Congress..................................41
    The Pennsylvania State University Library..............61
    The Johns Hopkins University Library...................62
    Washington University Library (St. Louis)..............63

F. Miscellanea..65

    Recordings by John Barth................................65
    Interviews with John Barth..............................65
    Panel Discussions Participated in by John Barth.......69

G. Biographical Commentary on John Barth....................71

    Unsigned Contributions..................................71
    Signed Contributions....................................79

H. Critical Commentary on Barth's Works.....................85

I. Reviews of Books by John Barth........................165
       The Floating Opera...................................165
       The End of the Road..................................167
       The Sot-Weed Factor..................................168
       Giles Goat-Boy.......................................171
       Lost in the Funhouse.................................175
       Chimera..177

J. Bibliographies of John Barth..........................181

Subject Index...183

Author Index..189

Title Index...195

Periodical Index..209

Publisher Index...213

ACKNOWLEDGMENTS

In any project of this size, there are many people to thank. I am particularly indebted to Fred H. Higginson, a tireless and inspirational teacher under whose direction I began this study and whose excellent bibliography of Robert Graves provided me with many good ideas. Without Jack Barth, this book would, of course, not exist, and it is in large measure owing to my correspondence and several meetings with him over the past four years that this study is as thorough as it is. Special thanks are also due to my wife Sher, who herself worked hard on this project and who has put up with more than most people would have in helping me see the book to press; Bill Brewer, who worked his magic on the photographs which grace these pages; Barth's literary agent Lurton Blassingame; and two super interlibrary loan librarians, Ellyn Taylor of Kansas State University and Gloria Lyerla of Texas Tech University, magicians in their own right, who made books from around the world materialize in a matter of days.

Also helpful have been Roger Mortimer, Holly Hall, and the rest of the staff at the Rare Book Room of the Washington University Library in St. Louis, John C. Broderick and his staff at the Manuscript Division of the Library of Congress, Charles Mann and his people at the Rare Book Room of the Pennsylvania State University Library as well as Lee Stout of the Library's Penn State Room, and Karl C. Gay and his staff at the Poetry Room of the Lockwood Memorial Library of the State University of New York at Buffalo; Marshall Bear (Doubleday & Co.), Peggy Bodkin (Farrar, Straus and Giroux), Leslie Byrne (Prentice-Hall, Inc.), Bridget Gasgoyne (Weidenfeld & Nicolson), Joseph Greene (Grosset & Dunlap), Pyke Johnson, Jr. (Doubleday & Co.), I. A. Looge (Rowohlt Verlag GmbH), Linda Marshall (Random House), Sheila Murphy (Andre Deutsch Ltd.), Margot Norton (Grosset & Dunlap), Lauri Olin (Literary Guild of America), Mary Grace Palmer (Doubleday & Co.), John M. Pickering (Pennsylvania State University Press), Lawrence H. Reed (Doubleday & Co.), Ruth Russ (The New American Library, Inc.), Evelyn M. Saccente (Fawcett Publications), Susan Mann Straub (Grosset & Dunlap), Tuulikki Tammenaho (Werner Söderström Osakeyhtiö), Victor Temkin (Bantam Books), Nick Webb (Panther Books), and Lee Wolfe (Doubleday & Co.); from Kansas State University, Walt Eitner, Ken Johnston, Paul Psilos, Harold Schneider, and Evan Williams; from Texas Tech University, George Hummasti, Chris Kloesel, Lynn Novak, and Wayne Storey; Joe David Bellamy (St. Lawrence Univ.), Peter C. Brunette (George Mason Univ.), Robert Murray Davis (Univ. of Oklahoma), Dorothy DeWitt (Johns Hopkins Univ.), Yukie Ebara (Lubbock, Tx.), Frank Gado (Union College), Marguerite Harkness (Virginia Commonwealth Univ.), Charles B. Harris (Illinois State Univ.), D. Allan Jones (Southwest Missouri State Univ.), Gary M. Lepper (Concordia, Calif.), and Jac Tharpe (Univ. of Southern Mississippi).

I am also grateful for the resources made available to me at the following libraries: the library of the Buffalo (N.Y.) Courier-Express, the library of the Buffalo (N.Y.) Evening News, the Buffalo Public Library, the Canisius College Library, the library of The Dorchester News (Cambridge, Md.), the Johns Hopkins University Library, the Kansas State University Library, the Library of Congress (which houses most of Barth's manuscripts), the Lubbock (Tx.) City-County Libraries, the Manhattan (Ks.) Public Library, the Norman (Okla.) Public Library, the Oklahoma State University Library, the Pennsylvania State University Library (which has a good collection of Barthiana), Lockwood Memorial Library of the State University of New York at Buffalo, the Texas Tech University Library, the Toronto Public Library, the University of Illinois at Urbana-Champaign Library, the University of Kansas Library, the University of Michigan Library, the University of Missouri at Columbia Library, the University of Oklahoma Library, the University of Toronto Library, and the Washington University Library in St. Louis (which houses the largest collection of Barth first editions in the world). The libraries that have responded to my numerous interlibrary loan requests are legion; I thank them all.

Just as an army marches on its stomach, scholars more often than not travel on the cold cash of their benefactors—forgoing food in the interests of academe. Without a sizable grant from Texas Tech University and some English department funding provided by my chairman at Tech, Marion C. Michael, and my former chairman at Kansas State, Fred Higginson, this bibliography would still be a long way from completion.

PREFACE

Three things are likely to be of particular interest to the user of the first section of this book. Solely the English language editions of Barth's separately published works are described in section A; translations are noted but not described. Secondly, when I was unable to obtain the number of published copies of one or more of the impressions of a given edition, I used one of three designations to indicate that fact: <u>unavailable</u> means that the publisher was unable to supply me with the figures that I requested, <u>undisclosed</u> means that he possessed the figures but was unwilling to release them, and <u>undetermined</u> means that the publisher never responded to my inquiry. Lastly, I have given two measurements, separated by a slash (/), to designate the bulk of the hardcover editions: the first indicates the thickness of the leaves and endpapers only, whereas the second indicates the thickness of the entire volume, including the binding.

Sections B through F are also devoted to primary materials: first book contributions are given in B, contributions to periodicals and to the press in C, reprints of short works and parts of books in D; Barth's manuscripts are catalogued in E; and his recordings and interviews are listed in F as are the published texts of panel discussions in which he participated. References to additional printed remarks made by Barth are noted at the end of the interview section. For the purposes of cataloging, I have considered those of Barth's <u>corrected</u> galley proofs which are housed in the Library of Congress as manuscripts, and I have listed them in section E; corrected and uncorrected galley and foundry proofs are mentioned in the "notes" sections throughout A. The reconstructed dates in the manuscript section have been arrived at with Barth's assistance. In compiling section C, I made no attempt to list the writings Barth published in his high school newspaper under the pseudonym "Ashcan Pete" (see G87), and I could not locate two stories, "Fox-Island Incident" and "Parnassus Approached," published—as Barth recalls—in <u>Harlequin</u> (Baltimore, Md.) in 1950 or shortly thereafter.

Sections G through J list the secondary materials devoted to Barth: biographical commentary is given in G, critical commentary in H, book reviews in I, and bibliographies in J. Section G contains a few items which are not exactly biographical in nature but which are of too little consequence to be listed in H (e.g., literary encyclopedia entries which tend toward plot summary). Numerous "mentions" as well as reviews of the separately published works devoted solely to Barth can be found in H. I have exercised considerable restraint in compiling section J; excluded are checklists by writers who, at the time their works were published, did not aspire to some degree of completeness. A fairly extensive subject index as well as author, title, periodical, and book publisher indexes round out the volume.

-ix-

All of the sections in this bibliography which deal with secondary materials, except the book review section, are annotated—as are sections C, E, and F. I trust that most users of this book will find the year-by-year arrangement of the criticism section preferable to a typological arrangement (i.e., separate publications, chapters of books, articles, dissertations and theses, mentions), since the chronological approach allows the trends which have developed in Barth criticism over the past decade and a half to emerge with considerable clarity.

Section E is, I suppose, a bonus: descriptive catalogs of manuscript holdings are not conventionally found in bibliographies. However, because almost no work has been done with Barth's manuscripts despite the fact that a massive collection of them has been housed in the Library of Congress for some years, I thought it worthwhile to demonstrate the vastness of this all but untapped resource. Barth's <u>Chimera</u> manuscripts comprise the only substantial body of papers not currently available to researchers. Additionally, there are a number of interesting documents in the various manuscript collections which Barth has chosen not to publish.

As I send this book to press, I do so with the realization that some materials from 1974 and 1975 have not found their way into the text. Hopefully, the primary sections are completely up-to-date, and no important biographical or critical study from the years preceding 1974 is missing. In concluding, let me note that the Pennsylvania State University Press plans to publish a book by David Morrell entitled <u>John Barth: An Introduction</u> in the fall of 1976, and let me ask that anyone whose work on Barth has not been included in this bibliography inform me of that fact—kindly, if possible.

Lubbock, Texas
10 September 1975

ABBREVIATIONS

FO	The Floating Opera
ER	The End of the Road
SWF	The Sot-Weed Factor
GGB	Giles Goat-Boy: or, The Revised New Syllabus
LF	Lost in the Funhouse: Fiction for Print, Tape, Live Voice

SYMBOLS

An asterisk (*) before the number of an entry indicates that the entry has not been examined.

A dagger (†) appears before the entry number of any dissertation which has been annotated solely on the basis of its abstract.

The

Floating

Opera

by JOHN BARTH

Appleton–
Century–
Crofts,
Inc.

NEW YORK

The Floating Opera, first edition (A1a)

By John Barth

The End of the Road

Doubleday & Company, Inc., Garden City, New York 1958

The End of the Road, first edition (A2a)

The first paperback edition of a Barth novel (A2b)

The SOT-WEED FACTOR

BY JOHN BARTH

DOUBLEDAY & COMPANY, INC., GARDEN CITY, NEW YORK

1960

The Sot-Weed Factor, first edition (A3a)

GILES GOAT-BOY
or,
THE REVISED
NEW SYLLABUS
by
JOHN BARTH

1966

DOUBLEDAY & COMPANY, INC., GARDEN CITY, NEW YORK

Giles Goat-Boy, first edition (A4a)

JOHN BARTH

THE SOT-WEED FACTOR

DOUBLEDAY & COMPANY, INC.
GARDEN CITY, NEW YORK
1967

The Sot-Weed Factor (Revised by the Author), first edition (A5a)

JOHN BARTH

THE
FLOATING
OPERA

DOUBLEDAY & COMPANY, INC.
GARDEN CITY, NEW YORK
1967

The Floating Opera (Revised by the Author), first edition (A6a)

JOHN BARTH

THE
END OF
THE ROAD

DOUBLEDAY & COMPANY, INC.
GARDEN CITY, NEW YORK
1967

The End of the Road (Revised by the Author), first edition (A7a)

JOHN BARTH

LOST IN THE FUNHOUSE

Fiction for print, tape, live voice

DOUBLEDAY & COMPANY, INC.
GARDEN CITY, NEW YORK
1968

Lost in the Funhouse, first edition (A8a)

Chimera, first edition (A9b)

A. SEPARATE PUBLICATIONS BY JOHN BARTH

A1   THE FLOATING OPERA   [1956]

a. First edition:

The | Floating [wavy line] | Opera | by JOHN BARTH | Appleton- | Century- | Crofts, | Inc. | [to the right of the publisher's name: publisher's emblem] | NEW YORK

Collation: [1]-[9]^{16}, 144 leaves.
p. [i] The | Floating [wavy line] | Opera; p. [ii] blank; p. [iii] title-page; p. [iv] publisher's disclaimer, copyright, publisher's, Library of Congress, and printing notices; p. [v] as p. [i]; p. [vi] blank; pp. 1-280 text; pp. [281]-[282] blank.
20.5 x 14.0 cm. Bulk: 2.1/2.7 cm. White wove paper; top-edge and tail cut, fore-edge trimmed. White wove endpapers. Bound in dull brown cloth; front and back blank; spine, stamped in black: [from top to bottom:] THE FLOATING OPERA · JOHN BARTH | APPLETON | CENTURY | CROFTS

Price: $3.95. Number of copies: 1,682. Published on 24 Aug. 1956 in a white, black, blue, and green dust-jacket lettered in black and white.

Notes: Printed in the U.S.A.
      The jacket design is by Charles W. North Studios.

Translation:
      <Finnish> Uiva ooppera. Trans. Pentti Saarikoski and Reijo Lehtonen. Helsinki: Werner Söderström, 1972. [Also includes a translation of Chs.27-29 of A6a]

b. Avon Books edition ([1965]):

[all within a single rule:] The Floating | Opera | John Barth | An Avon Library Book | [publisher's emblem]

Collation: 136 leaves, glued at spine.
p. [1] sixteen-line biographical sketch; p. [2] blank; p. [3] title-page; p. [4] publisher's disclaimer, publisher's, copyright, publication, Library of Congress, and printing notices; p. [5] The Floating | Opera; p. [6] blank; pp. 7-272 text.

-1-

18.0 x 10.5 cm. Bulk: 1.5 cm. White wove paper; all edges cut. Bound in paper covers printed in off-white, red, black, green, scarlet, grey, turquoise-blue, orange, yellow, and various shades of brown; fore-edge corners of paper and binding rounded.

Price: $0.75. Number of copies: undetermined. Published in Feb. 1965.

Notes: This book is Avon Library No. VS5.
Printed in the U.S.A.
Printing history undetermined: the book has twice changed numbers (NS40 and, more recently, YN326), and its impressions number approximately ten.

A2　　　　THE END OF THE ROAD　　　　1958

a. First edition:

The End of the Road | Doubleday & Company, Inc., Garden City, New York 1958

Collation: 120 leaves, glued at spine.
p. [i] The End of the Road; p. [ii] blank; p. [iii] By John Barth | The Floating Opera • The End of the Road; p. [iv] By John Barth; p. [v] title-page; p. [vi] publisher's disclaimer, Library of Congress, copyright, printing, and edition notices; pp. [vii] viii Contents; p. [ix] as p. [i]; p. [x] blank; p. [1] blank; pp. [2]-[3] 4-230 text, with pp. [9, 83, 107, 139, 181, 213] being blank and pp. [9-11, 26-27, 42-43, 60-61, 83-85, 107-109, 124-125, 139-141, 150-151, 181-183, 213-215] being unnumbered.

20.9 x 13.9 cm. Bulk: 1.8/2.3 cm. White wove paper; top-edge and tail cut, fore-edge trimmed. White wove endpapers. Bound in bright ultramarine cloth; front and back blank; spine, stamped in yellow: [from top to bottom:] John Barth | DOUBLEDAY | [from top to bottom:] The End of the Road

Price: $3.95. Number of copies: 3,500. Published on 17 July 1958 in a black, white, grey, blue, yellow, and brown dust-jacket lettered in yellow, black, blue, and white.

Notes: Printed in the U.S.A.
The jacket illustration is by Robert Watson.

Translations:
<Italian> Fine della strada. Trans. Aldo Buzzi. Milano:

Rizzoli, 1966.
<Finnish> Matkan pää. Trans. Antero Tiusanen. Helsinki: Werner Söderström, 1970.
<Hungarian> Az ut Vége. Trans. Gyula Tellér. Budapest: Európa Kiadó, 1970.

b. First Avon Books edition ([1960]):

[title, in white lettering, within a grey and black geometrical design:] THE | END | OF THE | ROAD | Complete and Unabridged | AVON BOOK DIVISION | The Hearst Corporation | 959 Eighth Avenue | New York 19, N.Y.

Collation: 80 leaves, glued at spine.
p. [1] nine-line blurb; p. [2] JOHN BARTH | [rule]; p. [3] title-page; p. [4] copyright, publisher's, and printing notices; pp. 5-158 text; p. [159] About the author; p. [160] publisher's advertisements.

18.0 x 10.7 cm. Bulk: 1.1 cm. White wove paper; all edges cut and stained green. Bound in paper covers printed in white, scarlet, salmon, magenta, slate-green, grey, and black.

Price: $0.35. Number of copies: undetermined. Published in Oct. 1960.

Notes: This book is Avon No. T-481.
Printed in the U.S.A.
Impressions: 2nd, Feb. 1964 (Avon Library No. GS2, number of copies undetermined); 3rd, Aug. 1966 (Avon Library No. GS2, number of copies undetermined).

c. Secker & Warburg impression (1962):

The End of the Road | Secker & Warburg, London, 1962

Collation: [1]-[4]^{16} [5]^{8} [6]-[8]^{16}, 120 leaves.
p. [i] The End of the Road | [thirty-three-line plot summary]; p. [ii] blank; p. [iii] By John Barth | The Floating Opera · The End of the Road | The Sot-Weed Factor; p. [iv] By John Barth; p. [v] title-page; p. [vi] publisher's, copyright, and printer's notices, publisher's disclaimer; pp. [vii] viii [ix]-[x] [1]-[3] 4-230 as A2a.

19.6 x 13.0 cm. Bulk: as A2a. White wove paper; all edges cut. Endpapers as A2a. Bound in black cloth; front and back blank; spine, stamped in silver: The End | of the | Road | [triple rule] | JOHN | BARTH | SECKER & | WARBURG

Price: 18s. Number of copies: 3,000. Published on 17 Sept.

1962 in a white dust-jacket with black, grey, and vermillion geometrical designs, lettered in black and vermillion.

Notes: Printed in England by A. Wheaton & Co. Ltd., Exeter. The jacket design is by Anne Hickmott.

d. Brown, Watson edition ([1964]):

THE END OF THE ROAD | By | JOHN BARTH | BROWN, WATSON, LIMITED LONDON

Collation: [EOR 1]^{16} EOR 2-EOR 7^{16}, 112 leaves. [The fact that the rectos of the fifth leaves of the gatherings are signed EOR 1*, EOR 2*, EOR 3*, EOR 4*, EOR 5*, EOR 6*, [EOR 7*] implies that this book is a 16° in 8's, although it is impossible to do more than infer this arrangement since the leaves are glued at the spine rather than sewn.]
p. [1] THE END OF THE ROAD | [eleven-line plot summary];
p. [2] publisher's advertisements; p. [3] title-page; p. [4] publisher's, publication, and copyright notices, publisher's disclaimer, publisher's, printing, and printer's notices; pp. 5-224 text.

17.8 x 10.8 cm. Bulk: 1.2 cm. White wove paper; all edges cu Bound in paper covers printed in white, greenish yellow, black, olive-bistre, magenta, orange, and various shades of olive, blue, brown, grey, flesh, and red.

Price: 3s.6d. Number of copies: undetermined. Published on 30 June 1964.

Notes: This book is Digit Books No. R871.
Made and printed in Great Britain by Thomson Printers Ltd., at Charles Birchall & Sons Ltd., Liverpool, and Withy Grove Press Ltd., Manchester.
Printing history undetermined.

e. Penguin Books edition ([1967]):

John Barth | The End of the Road | Penguin Books | in association | with Secker & Warburg

Collation: 96 leaves, glued at spine.
p. [1] Penguin Book 2691 | The End of the Road | [seventeen-line biographical sketch]; p. [2] blank; p. [3] title-page; p. [4] publisher's, publication, copyright, printer's, printing, and publisher's notices; pp. 5-190 [191] text, with pp. [9, 22, 35, 50, 70, 90, 104, 116, 124, 151, 177] being unnumbered; p. [192] blank.

-4-

18.0 x 11.1 cm. Bulk: 1.0 cm. White wove paper; all edges cut.
Bound in paper covers printed in black, pink, orange, white,
lemon, grey, and scarlet.

Price: 4s.6d. Number of copies: undetermined. Published in
Mar. 1967.

Notes: This book is Penguin Books No. 2691.
Printed in Great Britain by Cox & Wyman Ltd., London,
Reading, and Fakenham.
Set in Monotype Baskerville.
The cover design is by Peter Butler/David Jesson GDU.
Printing history undetermined.

f. Second Avon Books edition ([1967]):

[all within a single rule:] The | END | of the | ROAD | John
Barth | An Avon Library Book | [publisher's emblem]

Collation: 104 leaves, glued at spine.
p. [1] twenty-two-line biographical sketch; p. [2] blank;
p. [3] title-page; p. [4] publisher's, copyright, publisher's,
publication, design, trademark, and printing notices; pp. 5-
206 text; pp. [207]-[208] publisher's advertisements.

17.8 x 10.5 cm. Bulk: 1.4 cm. White wove paper; all edges cut
and stained red. Bound in paper covers printed in white,
black, and various shades of brown, green, and blue.

Price: $0.75. Number of copies: undetermined. Published in
Oct. 1967.

Notes: This book is Avon Library No. VS18.
Printed in the U.S.A.
The cover illustration is by Paul Bacon Studio.
Printing history undetermined.
This book is the second Avon edition of the novel from
a bibliographical standpoint despite the fact that
the publisher considers it the "Third Avon Library
Edition (Fourth Printing)."

A3   THE SOT-WEED FACTOR   1960

a. First edition:

The SOT-WEED | FACTOR | BY JOHN BARTH | DOUBLEDAY & COMPANY,

-5-

INC., GARDEN CITY, NEW YORK | 1960

Collation: 1-34^{12}, 408 leaves. [1 signed on 1^{12v}, 34 signed on 34^{12v}]
  pp. [i]-[ii] blank; p. [1] THE SOT-WEED FACTOR; p. [2] by John Barth; p. [3] title-page; p. [4] publisher's disclaimer, Library of Congress, copyright, printing, and design notices; pp. [5] 6-9 CONTENTS; p. [10] blank; pp. [11]-[13] 14-806 text, with pp. [12, 116, 504, 506, 790, 792] being blank and pp. [15, 22, 56, 115-117, 128, 173, 269, 327, 427, 479, 493, 504-507, 518, 543, 600, 650, 696, 774, 790-793] being unnumbered; pp. [807]-[814] blank.

23.2 x 15.3 cm. Bulk: 3.4/4.0 cm. White wove paper; all edges cut. White wove endpapers. Front and back blank, bound in blue cloth; spine bound in greenish yellow cloth overlapping approximately 3.5 cm. onto the front and back, stamped in blue: BARTH | [from top to bottom:] The SOT WEED FACTOR | DOUBLEDAY

Price: $7.50. Number of copies: 3,000. Published on 19 Aug. 1960 in a greyish blue, white, and greenish grey dust-jacket lettered in black, yellow, greyish blue, and greenish grey.

Notes: Printed in the U.S.A.
  Set in 10 on 13 Electra x 27 type.
  The cover design is by Charles Kaplan.
  The jacket design is by Edward Gorey.
  Impressions: 2nd, 30 Sept. 1960 (1,500 copies); 3rd, 2 Dec. 1960 (1,500 copies).
  The Manuscript Division of the Library of Congress houses a set of corrected final galley proofs of this edition (see E24) and an uncorrected, unbound set of foundry proofs.

Translations:
  <Italian> Il coltivatore del Maryland. 2 vols. Trans. Luciano Bianciardi. Milano: Rizzoli, 1968.
  <German> Der Tabakhändler. Trans. Susanna Rademacher. Reinbek b. Hamburg: Rowohlt, 1970.

b. Secker & Warburg impression (1961):

The SOT-WEED | FACTOR | BY JOHN BARTH | SECKER & WARBURG: LONDON 1961

Collation: [1]^{16} 2-24^{16} 25^4 26^{16}, 404 leaves.
  p. [1] THE SOT-WEED FACTOR | [twenty-four-line plot summary];
  p. [2] blank; p. [3] title-page; p. [4] publisher's disclaimer, printing, printer's, publication, and copyright notices; pp. [5 6-806 as A3a; pp. [807]-[808] blank.

21.3 x 13.9 cm. Bulk: 3.8/4.3 cm. White wove paper; all edges

cut. Endpapers as A3a. Bound in red cloth; front and back
blank; spine, stamped in silver: [book title in double cir-
cle:] The | Sot-Weed | Factor | JOHN | BARTH | SECKER & |
WARBURG

Price: 30s. Number of copies: 6,100. Published on 9 Oct. 1961
in a grey and white dust-jacket lettered in brick and black.

Notes: Printed in Great Britain by Morrison & Gibb Ltd.
The jacket design is by Owen Wood.

c. Grosset & Dunlap Universal Library impression ([1964]):

JOHN BARTH | THE | SOT-WEED | FACTOR | [publisher's emblem]
The Universal Library | GROSSET & DUNLAP | NEW YORK

Collation: 408 leaves, glued at spine.
p. [1] THE SOT-WEED FACTOR; p. [2] blank; p. [3] title-page;
p. [4] copyright and Library of Congress notices, publisher's
disclaimer, edition, publication, and printing notices; pp.
[5] 6-806 as A3a; pp. [807]-[808] blank; p. [809] seven-line
biographical sketch; p. [810] blank; pp. [811]-[813] publisher's advertisements; pp. [814]-[816] blank.

20.3 x 13.3 cm. Bulk: 2.7 cm. White wove paper; all edges cut.
Bound in paper covers printed in white, black, red, yellow,
pink, orange, and various shades of brown and green.

Price: $2.95 ($3.75 in Canada). Number of copies: 6,017. Published on 10 Jan. 1964.

Notes: This book is Grosset & Dunlap Universal Library No. 153.
Printed in the U.S.A.
Impressions: 2nd, 25 June 1964 (4,826 copies); 3rd, 18
June 1965 (3,138 copies); 4th, 7 Sept. 1965 (4,422
copies); 5th, 26 Jan. 1966 (7,724 copies); 6th, 15
Sept. 1966 (2,186 copies); 7th, 12 Feb. 1970 (18,085
copies).

d. Panther Books edition ([1965]):

John Barth | [rule] | THE SOT-WEED | FACTOR | [publisher's
emblem] | A PANTHER BOOK

Collation: 400 leaves, glued at spine.
p. [1] critical excerpts; p. [2] blank; p. [3] title-page;
p. [4] publisher's, publication, copyright, publisher's,
design, printing, printer's, and publisher's notices; pp.
[5]-[10] CONTENTS; p. [11] THE | SOT-WEED | FACTOR; p. [12]
blank; pp. 13-795 text, with p. [496] being blank and pp.

-7-

[495-496, 781] being unnumbered; pp. [796]-[800] publisher's advertisements.

18.0 x 11.0 cm. Bulk: 3.2 cm. White wove paper; all edges cut. Bound in paper covers printed in white, grey, lake-brown, and black.

Price: 9s.6d. Number of copies: 30,000. Published on 1 Aug. 1965.

Notes: This book is Panther Books No. 1892.
Printed in Great Britain by C. Nicholls & Company Ltd., The Philips Park Press, Manchester.
The cover design is by Owen Wood.
Impressions: 2nd, June 1966 (20,000 copies); 3rd, Jan. 1970 (12,500 copies); 4th, Jan. 1972 (15,000 copies).

e. Grosset & Dunlap Special impression ([1966]):

JOHN BARTH | THE | SOT-WEED | FACTOR | A Grosset Special | GROSSET & DUNLAP | NEW YORK

Collation: 407 leaves, glued at spine.
pp. [1]-[2] blank; p. [3] title-page; p. [4] copyright and Library of Congress notices, publisher's disclaimer, edition and printing notices; pp. [5] 6-806 as A3a; p. [807] seven-line biographical sketch; pp. [808]-[814] blank.

20.3 x 13.8 cm. Bulk: 3.5 cm. White wove paper; all edges cut. Bound in paper covers printed in olive-yellow, brown-red, white, and black.

Price: $1.50. Number of copies: unavailable. Published in Sept. 1966.

Notes: This book is Grosset & Dunlap No. 1096.
Printed in the U.S.A.
Printing history unavailable.

A4 GILES GOAT-BOY 1966

a. First edition:

GILES GOAT-BOY | or, | THE REVISED | NEW SYLLABUS | by | JOHN BARTH | 1966 | DOUBLEDAY & COMPANY, INC., GARDEN CITY, NEW YORK

Collation: $1-31^{12}$, 372 leaves. [1 signed on 1^{12V}]

-8-

p. [i] GILES GOAT-BOY; p. [ii] Books by John Barth; p. [iii] title-page; p. [iv] Library of Congress, copyright, and printing notices; pp. [v] vi-vii Contents; p. [viii] blank; pp. [ix] x-xvi [xvii] xviii-xxxi [xxxii]-[xxxiv] [1]-[5] 6-710 text, with pp. [xxxii, xxxiv, 2, 4, 74, 76, 202, 204, 386, 388, 528, 644, 698] being blank and pp. [10, 14, 21, 27, 36, 46, 74-77, 107, 113, 130, 152, 167, 184, 202-205, 226, 248, 265, 318, 339, 353, 385-389, 423, 440, 462, 481, 502, 513, 527-529, 552, 573, 588, 602, 617, 635, 643-645, 654, 660, 667, 674, 680, 688, 697-699, 709] being unnumbered.

23.2 x 15.3 cm. Bulk: 3.1/3.7 cm. White wove paper; top-edge and tail cut, fore-edge trimmed. Mustard wove endpapers, inner sides white. Bound in black cloth; front and back blank; spine, stamped in gold except as indicated: JOHN | BARTH | [silver rule] | GILES | GOAT- | BOY | DOUBLEDAY

Price: $6.95. Number of copies: 15,000. Published on 31 May 1966 in a mottled cream and white dust-jacket lettered in bistre-brown and black with a black-and-white photo by Alex Gotfryd.

Notes: Printed in the U.S.A.
Set in 10 on 13 Electra x 27 type.
The jacket design is by Lorellie Stubbs.
Impressions: 2nd, 22 July 1966 (10,000 copies); 3rd, 12 Aug. 1966 (15,000 copies); 4th, 23 Sept. 1966 (10,000 copies); 5th, 14 Oct. 1966 (10,000 copies). This book was a Mid-Century Book Society selection in 1966.
The Manuscript Division of the Library of Congress houses both corrected (see E51) and uncorrected, unbound copies of the final galley proofs of this edition as well as a set of uncorrected foundry proofs and a set of foundry proofs with editorial notations.
The Rare Book Room of the Washington University Library (St. Louis) houses an uncorrected, bound copy of the final galley proofs of this edition; accompanying it is a note from Douglas Andrews, publicity manager at Doubleday & Company.

Translation:
<French> L'Enfant-Bouc ou Version revue et corrigée du Nouveau Syllabus. 2 vols. Trans. Maurice Rambaud. Paris: Gallimard, 1970. [The prefatory and posttape sections of the novel have been deleted.]

b. Limited first edition (1966):

Title-page as A4a.

Collation: π^1 1-31^{12}, 373 leaves. [1 signed on 1^{12V}]
p. [π^r] [limited edition notice, the fifth and last line ending in a single rule where the number in the series is entered in black ink] | [signature, in black ink:] John Barth; p. [π^v] blank; pp. [i]-[v] vi-vii [viii]-[ix] x-xvi [xvii] xviii-xxxi [xxxii]-[xxxiv] [1]-[5] 6-710 as A4a.

Size, bulk, paper, edges, and endpapers as A4a. Bound in buff cloth; front, blind stamped except as indicated: JOHN | BARTH | [gold rule] | GILES | GOAT- | BOY; back blank; spine, stamped in brick except as indicated: JOHN | BARTH | [gold rule] | GILES | GOAT- | BOY | DOUBLEDAY

Price: $25.00. Number of copies: 250. Published on 31 May 1966 in a mottled brown slip case with a lilac-brown label, stamped in off-white: [all within a single rule:] JOHN | BARTH | [full rule] | GILES | GOAT- | BOY | [full rule] | Limited Edition

Note: Printed in the U.S.A.

c. Literary Guild impression (1966):

Title-page as A4a.

Collation and contents as A4a.

Size, bulk, paper, edges, and endpapers as A4a. Bound in charcoal-grey cloth; front, back, and spine as A4a.

Price: $3.50. Number of copies: 10,000 (printed in July 1966). Released in Nov. 1966 by the Literary Guild of America in a mottled ochre and white dust-jacket lettered in sepia and black with a black-and-white photo by Alex Gotfryd.

Notes: Printed in the U.S.A.
       The jacket design is by Lorellie Stubbs.
       Impressions: 2nd, Oct. 1966 (10,000 copies); 3rd, Dec. 1966 (15,000 copies); 4th, Feb. 1967 (10,000 copies).

d. Secker & Warburg impression ([1967]):

GILES GOAT-BOY | or, | THE REVISED | NEW SYLLABUS | by | JOHN BARTH | London • SECKER & WARBURG

Collation: [1]-[21]^{16} [22]^{20} [23]^{16}, 372 leaves.
pp. [i]-[ii] as A4a; p. [iii] title-page; p. [iv] publication, copyright, and printer's notices; pp. [v] vi [vii] Contents; pp. [viii]-[ix] x-xvi [xvii] xviii-xxxi [xxxii]-[xxxiv] [1]-[5] 6-710 as A4a.

-10-

22.4 x 14.9 cm. Bulk: 3.7/4.4 cm. White wove paper; all edges
cut. White wove endpapers. Bound in deep crimson cloth;
front and back blank; spine, stamped in gold: GILES | GOAT-BOY |
[rule] | JOHN | BARTH | SECKER & | WARBURG

Price: 42s. Number of copies: 8,500. Published on 30 Mar. 1967
in a black, blue, scarlet, and white dust-jacket lettered in
white and black with a black-and-white photo by Alex Gotfryd.

Notes: Printed by Fletcher & Sons Ltd., Norwich.
The jacket design is by Kenneth Reilly.

e. Penguin Books edition ([1967]):

John Barth | Giles Goat-Boy | or, The Revised New Syllabus |
Penguin Books | in association | with Secker & Warburg

Collation: 408 leaves, glued at spine.
p. [1] Penguin Book 2728 | Giles Goat-Boy | [sixteen-line biographical sketch]; p. [2] blank; p. [3] title-page; p. [4] publisher's, publication, copyright, printer's, printing, and publisher's notices; pp. [5]-[6] Contents; pp. 7-812 [813] text, with pp. [16, 34, 36, 38, 464] being blank and pp. [16, 33-38, 112, 250, 462-464, 619, 747, 800, 811] being unnumbered; p. [814] blank; pp. [815]-[816] publisher's advertisements.

18.0 x 11.3 cm. Bulk: 2.5 cm. White wove paper; all edges cut.
Bound in paper covers printed in orange, black, white, and
scarlet.

Price: 8s.6d. Number of copies: undetermined. Published in
mid-1967.

Notes: This book is Penguin Books No. 2728.
Printed in Great Britain by Hazell Watson & Viney Ltd.,
    Aylesbury, Bucks.
Set in Linotype Plantin.
Printing history undetermined.

f. Fawcett Crest edition ([1967]):

GILES | GOAT-BOY | or, | THE REVISED | NEW SYLLABUS | by | JOHN
BARTH | A FAWCETT CREST BOOK | Fawcett Publications, Inc.,
Greenwich, Conn. | Member of American Book Publishers Council,
Inc.

Collation: 384 leaves, glued at spine.
p. [i] critical excerpts; p. [ii] blank; p. [iii] title-page;
p. [iv] publisher's, copyright, Library of Congress, publication,

book club, publication, and publisher's notices; pp. [v]-[vii] Contents; p. [viii] blank; p. [ix] Giles Goat-Boy; p. [x] blank; pp. xi-xxxvi [37]-[40] 41-766 text, with pp. [38, 40, 112, 246, 430, 432, 702, 754] being blank and pp. [112, 246, 430-432, 702, 754] being unnumbered; pp. [767]-[768] publisher's advertisements.

18.0 x 10.7 cm. Bulk: 3.0 cm. White wove paper; all edges cut and stained orange-red. Bound in paper covers printed in white, black, red, and gold.

Price: $1.25. Number of copies: 250,000. Published on 15 Aug. 1967.

Notes: This book is Fawcett Crest No. P1052.
Printed in the U.S.A.
Impressions: 2nd, Nov. 1967 (35,000 copies); 3rd, July 1968 (75,000 copies); 4th, Oct. 1971 (50,000 copies); 5th, Oct. 1972 (20,000 copies); 6th, Jan. 1974 (20,00 copies); 7th, Mar. 1975 (10,000 copies).

A5   THE SOT-WEED FACTOR (REVISED BY THE AUTHOR)   1967

a. First edition:

JOHN BARTH | THE | SOT-WEED | FACTOR | DOUBLEDAY & COMPANY, INC. | GARDEN CITY, NEW YORK | 1967

Collation: $1-32^{12}$, 384 leaves. [1 signed on 1^{12v}]
p. [i] THE SOT-WEED FACTOR; p. [ii] by John Barth; p. [iii] title-page; p. [iv] publisher's disclaimer, edition, Library of Congress, copyright, and printing notices; p. [v] Forewor to the Second Edition; p. [vi] blank; pp. vii-x Contents; pp. [1]-[2] 3-756 text, with pp. [2, 100, 102, 478, 742] being blank and pp. [100-102, 477-478, 741-742] being unnumbered; pp. [757]-[758] blank.

23.2 x 15.3 cm. Bulk: 3.2/3.8 cm. White wove paper; top-edge and tail cut, fore-edge trimmed. Lemon wove endpapers, inne sides white. Bound in black cloth; front and back blank; spine, stamped in gold except as indicated: JOHN | BARTH | [silver rule] | THE | SOT-WEED | FACTOR | [in silver:] Revised Edition | DOUBLEDAY

Price: $7.50. Number of copies: 8,000. Published on 6 Jan. 1967 in a brown and white dust-jacket lettered in black and red with a black-and-white photo by Alex Gotfryd.

-12-

Notes: Printed in the U.S.A.
Set in 10 on 12 Electra x 26 type.
The jacket design is by Lorellie Stubbs.
Impressions: 2nd, 29 Nov. 1968 (2,000 copies); 3rd,
23 June 1972 (2,000 copies).

b. Bantam Books edition ([1969]):

JOHN BARTH | [rule] | THE SOT-WEED FACTOR | [publisher's emblem]

Collation: 416 leaves, glued at spine.
pp. [i]-[iii] critical excerpts; p. [iv] Books by John Barth; p. [v] title-page; p. [vi] publisher's disclaimer, printing, publisher's, publication, copyright, publisher's, trademark, and printing notices; p. [vii] Foreword to the Second Edition; p. [viii] blank; pp. [ix]-[xii] Contents; pp. [1]-[2] 3-819 text, with pp. [2, 112, 514, 516, 802, 804] being blank and pp. [111-112, 514-516, 802-804] being unnumbered; p. [820] ABOUT THE AUTHOR.

17.9 x 10.4 cm. Bulk: 2.6 cm. White wove paper; all edges cut and stained lemon. Bound in paper covers printed in white, black, red-brown, red, orange, yellow-orange, turquoise-blue, scarlet, and slate-violet.

Price: $1.25. Number of copies: 130,600. Published in Mar. 1969.

Notes: This book is Bantam Books No. 04692.
Printed in the U.S.A.
There are typesetting errors on p. 314, line 2 ('goden' should read 'golden'); p. 456, line 11 (which should be indented); and p. 559, line 44 ('wet.' should read 'wet,').
Impressions: 2nd, 20 Apr. 1970 (30,000 copies); 3rd, 19 Apr. 1971 (25,000 copies); 4th, 24 Apr. 1972 (25,000 copies); 5th, 30 July 1973 (25,000 copies); 6th, 8 July 1974 (25,000 copies); 7th, 19 May 1975 (25,000 copies).

A6   THE FLOATING OPERA (REVISED BY THE AUTHOR)   1967

a. First edition:

JOHN BARTH | THE | FLOATING | OPERA | DOUBLEDAY & COMPANY, INC. | GARDEN CITY, NEW YORK | 1967

Collation: 1-11¹², 132 leaves. [1 signed on 1¹²ᵛ]
    p. [i] THE FLOATING OPERA; p. [ii] Books by John Barth; p.
    [iii] title-page; p. [iv] publisher's disclaimer, publica-
    tion, Library of Congress, copyright, and printing notices;
    p. [v] Prefatory Note to the Revised Edition; p. [vi] blank;
    p. [vii] Contents; p. [viii] blank; p. [ix] as p. [i]; p. [x]
    blank; pp. [1] 2-252 text, with pp. [9,19, 43, 49, 52, 57,
    71, 73, 84, 109, 112, 117, 125, 142, 145, 152, 162, 170, 172,
    182, 196, 204, 214, 217, 229-230, 246, 251] being unnumbered;
    pp. [253]-[254] blank.

23.3 x 15.3 cm. Bulk: 1.8/2.4 cm. White wove paper; top-edge
and tail cut, fore-edge trimmed. Light blue wove endpapers,
inner sides white. Bound in black cloth; front and back
blank; spine, stamped in gold except as indicated: JOHN |
BARTH | [silver rule] | THE | FLOAT- | ING | OPERA | [in
silver:] REVISED EDITION | DOUBLEDAY

Price: $4.95. Number of copies: 4,500. Published on 19 May
    1967 in a mottled grey and white dust-jacket lettered in
    black and blue with a black-and-white photo by Alex Gotfyrd.

Notes: Printed in the U.S.A.
    Set in 11 on 14 Janson x 25 type.
    The initial press run of this edition resulted in the
        production of some volumes which have a duplicate set
        of pages numbered 171-174 sewn in the middle of the
        eighth gathering. All the copies of this state were
        supposedly destroyed, but some still exist.
    Impressions: 2nd, 24 Nov. 1967 (2,000 copies); 3rd, 28
        Dec. 1973 (2,000 copies).

Translations:
    <Italian> L'opera galleggiante. Trans. Henry Furst. Milano:
        Longanesi, 1968.
    <French> L'Opéra flottant. Trans. Henri Robillot. Paris:
        Gallimard, 1968.

b. Secker & Warburg edition ([1968]):

John Barth | The Floating | Opera | Secker & Warburg | London

Collation: [1]-[8]¹⁶, 128 leaves.
    p. [i] THE FLOATING OPERA | [five-line blurb]; p. [ii] also by
    John Barth; p. [iii] title-page; p. [iv] publication, publish-
    er's, copyright, printing, and printer's notices; p. [v]
    Prefatory Note to the | Revised Edition; p. [vi] blank; p. [vii
    Contents; p. [viii] blank; pp. 1-247 text; p. [248] blank.

20.9 x 13.5 cm. Bulk: 1.8/2.4 cm. White wove paper; all edges
cut. White wove endpapers. Bound in maroon paper overboards;
front and back blank; spine, stamped in gold: JOHN | BARTH |
[from top to bottom, wavy:] The Floating Opera | S&W

-14-

Price: 30s. Number of copies: 4,000. Published on 30 Sept. 1968 in a black, white, brick, and olive dust-jacket lettered in white, black, and brick.

Notes: Printed in Great Britain by Western Printing Services Ltd., Bristol.
Set in 11 on 13 Caledonia type.
The jacket design is by Kenneth Reilly.
British spellings have been adopted.

c. Penguin Books edition ([1970]):

John Barth | The Floating Opera | Penguin Books | in association with Secker & Warburg

Collation: 120 leaves, glued at spine.
p. [1] Penguin Books | The Floating Opera | [ten-line biographical sketch]; p. [2] blank; p. [3] title-page; p. [4] publisher's, publication, copyright, printer's, printing, and publisher's notices; p. [5] Prefatory Note to the Revised Edition; p. [6] blank; p. [7] Contents; p. [8] blank; pp. 9-233 [234] text, with pp. [15, 24, 46, 51, 54, 58, 70, 81, 103, 105, 110, 118, 133, 136, 143, 152, 160, 162, 171, 184, 192, 201, 203, 213-214, 228, 232] being unnumbered; p. [235] publisher's advertisement; p. [236] blank; pp. [237]-[240] publisher's advertisements.

18.1 x 11.0 cm. Bulk: 1.1 cm. White wove paper; all edges cut. Bound in paper covers printed in orange, grey, black, white, and various shades of blue.

Price: £0.30 (6s.). Number of copies: undetermined. Published in Jan. 1970.

Notes: Printed in Great Britain by C. Nicholls & Company Ltd.
Set in Linotype Plantin.
The cover illustration is by Mike McInnery.
British spellings have been adopted.
Printing history undetermined.

d. Bantam Books edition ([1972]):

john barth | THE FLOATING OPERA | [publisher's emblem] | A NATIONAL GENERAL COMPANY

Collation: 128 leaves, glued at spine.
p. [i] thirteen-line blurb; p. [ii] Bantam Books by John Barth; p. [iii] title-page; p. [iv] publisher's disclaimer, printing, publisher's, publication, copyright, publisher's, trademark, and printing notices; p. [v] prefatory note to the revised

-15-

edition; p. [vi] blank; p. [vii] contents; p. [viii] blank;
pp. [1] 2-247 text, with pp. [8, 18, 42, 48, 51, 56, 69, 71,
76-80, 82, 106, 109, 114, 122, 138, 141, 148, 158, 166, 168,
178, 192, 200, 210, 213, 224, 226, 241, 246] being unnumbered; p. [248] ABOUT THE AUTHOR.

17.9 x 10.7 cm. Bulk: 1.5 cm. White wove paper; all edges cut and stained lemon. Bound in paper covers printed in bright pink, white, black, pink, rose, scarlet, and various shades of brown.

Price: $1.25. Number of copies: 55,000. Published in July 1972.

Notes: This book is Bantam Books No. Q7459.
Printed in the U.S.A.
Impressions: 2nd, 14 May 1973 (25,000 copies); 3rd, 11 Mar. 1974 (25,000 copies); 4th, 12 May 1975 (25,000 copies).

A7   THE END OF THE ROAD (REVISED BY THE AUTHOR)   1967

a. First edition:

JOHN BARTH | THE | END OF | THE ROAD | DOUBLEDAY & COMPANY, INC. GARDEN CITY, NEW YORK | 1967

Collation: $1-4^{12}$ $[5]-[8]^{12}$, 96 leaves. [1 signed on 1^{12V}]
p. [i] THE END OF THE ROAD; p. [ii] Books by John Barth;
p. [iii] title-page; p. [iv] publisher's disclaimer, Library of Congress, copyright, printing, and edition notices; pp. 1-188 text.

23.2 x 15.3 cm. Bulk: 1.3/1.9 cm. White wove paper; top-edge and tail cut, fore-edge trimmed. Greenish yellow wove endpapers, inner sides white. Bound in black cloth; front and back blank; spine, stamped in gold except as indicated: JOHN | BARTH | [silver rule] | THE | END | OF | THE | ROAD | [in silver:] REVISED | [in silver:] EDITION | Doubleday

Price: $4.95. Number of copies: 4,500. Published on 8 Sept. 1967 in a black, grey, and white dust-jacket lettered in black and yellow with a black-and-white photo by Alex Gotfryd.

Notes: Printed in the U.S.A.
Set in 11 on 13 Fairfield x 25 type.
The Manuscript Division of the Library of Congress houses

both corrected (see E58) and uncorrected, unbound copies of the final galley proofs of this edition; the uncorrected copy bears the following holographic notation by Barth: "The End of the Road—uncorrected galleys of revised D'day edition." The Library also houses two copies of the foundry proofs of this edition; one is uncorrected, and the other has numerous editorial markings.

b. Grosset & Dunlap Universal Library impression ([1969]):

JOHN BARTH | THE | END OF | THE ROAD | [publisher's emblem] | The Universal Library | GROSSET & DUNLAP • NEW YORK

Collation: [1]-[12]^8, 96 leaves.
  p. [i] THE | END OF | THE ROAD; p. [ii] Other Books by John Barth; p. [iii] title-page; p. [iv] publisher's notice, publisher's disclaimer, copyright, printing, and edition notices; pp. 1-188 as A7a.

20.2 x 13.5 cm. Bulk: 1.6 cm. White wove paper; all edges cut. Bound in paper covers printed in grey, black, yellow-orange, and white.

Price: $2.45 ($3.25 in Canada). Number of copies: 5,067. Published on 29 July 1969.

Notes: This book is Grosset & Dunlap Universal Library No. UL240.
  Printed in the U.S.A.
  Impressions: 2nd, 2 Dec. 1970 (5,122 copies); 3rd, 20 Dec. 1973 (2,692 copies); 4th, 10 Apr. 1974 (2,676 copies).

c. Bantam Books edition ([1969]):

The | End of | the Road | [rule] | by | John | Barth | [publisher's emblem]

Collation: 104 leaves, glued at spine.
  p. [i] critical excerpts; p. [ii] Books by John Barth; p. [iii] title-page; p. [iv] publisher's disclaimer, printing, publisher's, publication, copyright, publisher's, trademark, and printing notices; p. [v] The | End of | the Road; p. [vi] blank; pp. 1-198 text; p. [199] ABOUT THE AUTHOR; pp. [200]-[202] publisher's advertisements.

17.7 x 10.7 cm. Bulk: 1.4 cm. White wove paper; all edges cut and stained lemon. Bound in paper covers printed in white, black, slate-blue, rose, buff, light blue, turquoise-blue, light green, turquoise-green, drab, and scarlet.

Price: $0.95. Number of copies: 138,300. Published in Oct. 1969.

Notes: This book is Bantam Books No. N4775.
Printed in the U.S.A.
There is a typesetting error on p. 29, line 26—'sport:' should read 'sport)'.
Impressions: 2nd, 9 Feb. 1970 (25,000 copies); 3rd, 14 Sept. 1970 (25,000 copies); 4th, 11 Oct. 1971 (20,000 copies); 5th, 7 Feb. 1972 (35,000 copies); 6th, 27 Nov. 1972 (35,000 copies); 7th, 14 Jan. 1973 (25,000 copies); 8th, 8 Oct. 1974 (25,000 copies); 9th, 24 Mar. 1975 (25,000 copies).

A8   LOST IN THE FUNHOUSE   1968

a. First edition:

JOHN BARTH | LOST | IN THE | FUNHOUSE | Fiction for print, tape, | live voice | DOUBLEDAY & COMPANY, INC. | GARDEN CITY, NEW YORK | 1968

Collation: $1-5^{12}$ [6]-[9]^{12}, 108 leaves. [1 signed on 1^{12V}] p. [i] LOST IN THE FUNHOUSE; p. [ii] blank; p. [iii] Other Books by John Barth; p. [iv] blank; p. [v] title-page; p. [vi] publication, Library of Congress, copyright, printing, and edition notices; p. [vii] Contents; p. [viii] blank; pp. [ix] x Author's Note; p. [xi] as p. [i]; p. [xii] blank; pp. [1]-[3] 4-201 text, with pp. [14, 35, 40, 58, 72, 98, 104-105, 114, 116, 130, 168] being unnumbered; pp. [202]-[204] blank.

23.2 x 15.3 cm. Bulk: 1.5/2.1 cm. White wove paper; top-edge and tail cut, fore-edge trimmed. Red wove endpapers, inner sides white. Bound in black cloth; front and back blank; spine, stamped in gold: [from top to bottom:] JOHN BARTH Lost in the Funhouse   Doubleday

Price: $4.95. Number of copies: 25,000. Published on 27 Sept. 1968 in a black, yellow, red, and white dust-jacket lettered in black and red with a black-and-white photo by Don Glena Photos.

Contents: Frame-Tale——Night-Sea Journey——Ambrose His Mark——Autobiography——Water-Message——Petition——Lost in the Funhouse——Echo——Two Meditations——Title——Glossolalia——Life-Story——Menelaiad——Anonymiad

Notes: Printed in the U.S.A.

Set in 11 on 14 Janson x 25 type.
The jacket design is by George Giusti.
The Manuscript Division of the Library of Congress houses a set of corrected final galley proofs of this edition (see E70) as well as a set of uncorrected foundry proofs and a set of foundry proofs with editorial markings.
The Rare Book Room of the Washington University Library (St. Louis) houses both bound and unbound, uncorrected copies of the final galley proofs of this edition; the unbound copy bears the signature of H. Crosby.

Translations:
<Portuguese> Perdido no túnel do terror. Trans. Edilson Alkmin. Rio de Janeiro: Lidador, 1970.
<French> Perdu dans le Labyrinthe. Trans. Maurice Rambaud. Paris: Gallimard, 1972.

b. Limited first edition (1968):

Title-page as A8a.

Collation: π^1 1-5^{12} [6]-[9]^{12}, 109 leaves. [1 signed on 1^{12v}] p. [π^r] [limited edition notice, the second and last line ending in a single rule where the number in the series is entered in black ink] | [signature, in black ink:] John Barth; p. [π^v] blank; pp. [i]-[ix] x [xi]-[xii] [1]-[3] 4-201 [202]-[204] as A8a.

Size, bulk, paper, and edges as A8a. Mustard wove endpapers, inner sides white. Bound in buff cloth; front, blind stamped except as indicated: JOHN | BARTH | [gold rule] | LOST | IN THE | FUNHOUSE; back blank; spine, from top to bottom, stamped in brick except as indicated: [gold rule] | JOHN BARTH   LOST IN THE FUNHOUSE   Doubleday | [gold rule]

Price: $25.00. Number of copies: 250. Published on 27 Sept. 1968 in a mottled brown slip case with a lilac-brown label, stamped in off-white: [all within a single rule:] JOHN | BARTH | [full rule] | LOST | IN THE | FUNHOUSE | [full rule] | Limited Edition

Contents: As A8a.

Note: Printed in the U.S.A.

c. Grosset & Dunlap Universal Library impression ([1969]):

JOHN BARTH | LOST | IN THE | FUNHOUSE | Fiction for print, tape, | live voice | [publisher's emblem] | The Universal Library |

GROSSET & DUNLAP • NEW YORK

Collation: [1]-[14]⁸, 112 leaves.
  p. [i] LOST | IN THE | FUNHOUSE; p. [ii] blank; p. [iii] Other Books by John Barth; p. [iv] blank; p. [v] title-page; p. [vi] publication, copyright, and printing notices; pp. [vii]-[ix] x as A8a; p. [xi] as p. [i]; pp. [xii] [1]-[3] 4-201 as A8a; pp. [202]-[212] blank.

20.3 x 13.6 cm. Bulk: 1.9 cm. White wove paper; all edges cut. Bound in paper covers printed in yellowish orange, black, and brownish grey.

Price: $2.45 ($3.25 in Canada). Number of copies: 5,062. Published on 29 July 1969.

Contents: As A8a.

Notes: This book is Grosset & Dunlap Universal Library No. UL239.
  Printed in the U.S.A.
  Impressions: 2nd, 1 Feb. 1971 (3,233 copies); 3rd, 23 June 1973 (number of copies unavailable).

d. Bantam Books edition ([1969]):

Lost In | The | Funhouse | [rule] | by | John | Barth | [rule] Fiction for Print, Tape, Live Voice | [publisher's emblem]

Collation: 104 leaves, glued at spine.
  pp. [i]-[iii] critical excerpts; p. [iv] Books by John Barth; p. [v] title-page; p. [vi] printing, publisher's, publication copyright, publisher's, trademark, and printing notices; p. [vii] Contents; p. [viii] blank; p. [ix] Author's Note; pp. x-xi Seven Additional Author's Notes; p. [xii] blank; pp. [1]-[3] 4-194 text, with pp. [13, 33, 38, 55, 69, 95, 101-102, 111, 113, 127, 163] being unnumbered; p. [195] ABOUT THE AUTHOR; p. [196] publisher's advertisements.

17.8 x 10.5 cm. Bulk: 1.4 cm. White wove paper; all edges cut and stained lemon. Bound in paper covers printed in white, black, orange, light blue, lilac, and various shades of green red, and brown.

Price: $0.95. Number of copies: 155,000. Published in Sept. 1969.

Contents: As A8a.

Notes: This book is Bantam Books No. N4718.
  Printed in the U.S.A.
  Impressions: 2nd, 21 Sept. 1970 (14,000 copies); 3rd,

-20-

8 Sept. 1971 (25,000 copies); 4th, 17 July 1972 (20,000 copies); 5th, 25 June 1973 (25,000 copies); 6th, 6 Jan. 1975 (25,000 copies).

e. Secker & Warburg impression ([1969]):

JOHN BARTH | LOST | IN THE | FUNHOUSE | Fiction for print, tape, | live voice | LONDON | SECKER & WARBURG

Collation: [A]^8 B-F^{16} G^4 H^{16}, 108 leaves.
pp. [i]-[iv] as A8a; p. [v] title-page; p. [vi] publication, copyright, printing, and printer's notices; pp. [vii]-[viii] as A8a; pp. [ix] x-xi Author's Note, SEVEN ADDITIONAL AUTHOR'S NOTES; pp. [xii] [1]-[3] 4-201 [202]-[204] as A8a.

21.6 x 13.7 cm. Bulk: as A8a. White wove paper; all edges cut. White wove endpapers. Bound in black cloth; front and back blank; spine, stamped in gold: LOST | IN THE | FUN- | HOUSE | John | Barth | S&W

Price: 42s. Number of copies: 1,800. Published on 22 Sept. 1969 in a brilliant rose and white dust-jacket lettered in black, green, and rose with a black-and-white photo by Don Glena Photos.

Contents: As A8a.

Notes: Reproduced by photolithography and bound in Great Britain by Bookprint Ltd., Crawley, Sussex.
The jacket design is by Bernard Higton.

f. Penguin Books edition ([1972]):

John Barth | Lost in the Funhouse | Fiction for print, tape, live voice | Penguin Books | in association with Secker & Warburg Ltd.

Collation: 100 leaves, glued at spine.
p. [1] Penguin Books | Lost in the Funhouse | [seventeen-line biographical sketch]; p. [2] blank; p. [3] title-page; p. [4] publisher's, publication, copyright, printer's, printing, and publisher's notices; p. [5] Contents; p. [6] blank; p. [7] Author's Note; pp. 8-9 Seven additional Author's notes; p. [10] blank; pp. [11]-[13] 14-198 text, with pp. [23, 43, 48, 64, 77, 102, 108-109, 118, 120, 133, 168] being unnumbered; pp. [199]-[200] publisher's advertisements.

18.1 x 11.2 cm. Bulk: 0.9 cm. White wove paper; all edges cut. Bound in paper covers printed in yellow, orange, blue, cerise, red-orange, black, and white.

Price: £0.30. Number of copies: undetermined. Published in Nov. 1972.

Contents: As A8a.

Notes: Printed in Great Britain by Hazell Watson & Viney Ltd., Aylesbury, Bucks.
Set in Linotype Plantin.
The cover design is by Eduardo Paolozzi.
Printing history undetermined.

A9   CHIMERA   [1972]

a. Limited first edition:

Title-page as A9b.

Collation: 163 leaves, sewn at spine.
p. [πr] [six-line limited edition notice] | [on a single rule in black ink: number in series] | [signature, in black ink:] John Barth; p. [πv] blank; pp. [i]-[x] [1]-[3] 4-308 [309]-[314] as A9b.

20.8 x 13.9 cm. Bulk: 2.3/3.0 cm. White wove paper; all edges cut, top-edge stained black. Olive-yellow laid endpapers. Bound in brick-red cloth; front, stamped in silver: [in mirror-impression stenciled letters:] EMIHC [in regular letters:] CHIMERA; back blank; spine, stamped in silver except as indicated: [from top to bottom, in gold:] CHIMERA | [double wavy line] | John | Barth | [double wavy line] | [from top to bottom, in gold:] RANDOM HOUSE | [in gold: publisher's emblem]

Price: $15.00. Number of copies: 300. Published in July 1972 in a clear, plasticine dust-jacket within a slate-blue slip case, with the series number in black ink near the bottom of the spine of the case.

Contents: As A9b.

Notes: Printed in the U.S.A. by The Book Press, Brattleboro, Vt. There is a typesetting error on p. 60, line 12: 'dip' should read 'sip'.

b. First edition ([1972]):

CHIMERA | by John Barth | [double wavy line] | RANDOM HOUSE [publisher's emblem] NEW YORK

-22-

Collation: 162 leaves, glued at spine.
 pp. [i]-[iii] blank; p. [iv] <u>Books by John Barth</u>; p. [v] CHIMERA; p. [vi] CHIMERA appears twice in stenciled letters—first upside down, then as a mirror-impression (the C and half of the H of the mirror-impression overlapping onto the title-page); p. [vii] title-page; p. [viii] copyright, publisher's, Library of Congress, publication, printing, printer's, and edition notices; p. [ix] CONTENTS; p. [x] blank; pp. [1]-[3] 4-308 text, with pp. [2, 58, 136] being blank and pp. [57-59, 135-137] being unnumbered; p. [309] ABOUT THE AUTHOR; pp. [310]-[314] blank.

20.7 x 14.1 cm. Bulk: 2.3/2.9 cm. White wove paper; all edges cut. Red wove endpapers. Bound in dull gold cloth; front blind stamped: CHIMERA; back blank; spine, stamped in silver: [from top to bottom:] CHIMERA | [double wavy line] | <u>John</u> | <u>Barth</u> | [double wavy line] | [from top to bottom:] <u>RANDOM</u> <u>HOUSE</u> | [publisher's emblem]

Price: $6.95. Number of copies: 24,982. Published in Sept. 1972 in a white dust-jacket with a black, yellow, orange, deep pink, and red-orange design, lettered in black with a black-and-white photo by Hal Jopp.

Contents: Dunyazadiad——Perseid——Bellerophoniad

Notes: Printed in the U.S.A. by The Book Press, Brattleboro, Vt.
 The jacket design is by George Giusti.
 There is a typesetting error on p. 60, line 12: 'dip' should read 'sip'.
 This book was a Saturday Review Book Club selection in Sept. 1972, a Time Inc. Book Club selection in Oct. 1972, and an American Journal Book Club selection in Mar. 1973.
 Impression: 2nd, 16 Nov. 1972 (5,144 copies).

<u>c</u>. <u>Fawcett Crest edition</u> ([<u>1973</u>]):

John Barth | [apostrophes over scalloped line] | CHIMERA | A FAWCETT CREST BOOK | Fawcett Publications, Inc., Greenwich, Connecticut

Collation: 160 leaves, glued at spine.
 p. [1] critical excerpts; p. [2] Fawcett Crest Books | by John Barth: | GILES GOAT-BOY | CHIMERA | [fourteen-line publisher's notice within a single rule]; p. [3] title-page; p. [4] publisher's, copyright, and publisher's notices, publisher's disclaimer, copyright, publication, book club, Library of Congress, and printing notices; p. [5] <u>Contents</u>; p. [6] blank; p. [7] [apostrophes over scalloped line] | CHIMERA | [apostrophes over scalloped line]; p. [8] blank; pp. [9]-[11]

-23-

12-320 text, with pp. [10, 66, 144] being blank and pp. [47, 65-67, 143-145, 302, 307] being unnumbered.
17.7 x 10.4 cm. Bulk: 1.7 cm. White wove paper; all edges cut and stained yellow. Bound in paper covers printed in white, black, grey, yellow, orange, deep pink, and red-orange
Price: $1.50. Number of copies: 175,000. Published in Oct. 1973.

Contents: As A9b.

Notes: This book is Fawcett Crest No. Q1984.
Printed in the U.S.A.
The cover design is by George Giusti.
There is a typesetting error on p. 68, line 2: 'dip' should read 'sip'.
Impression: 2nd, Jan. 1975 (20,000 copies).

d. Andre Deutsch impression ([1974]):

CHIMERA | by John Barth | [double wavy line] | [publisher's emblem] | ANDRE DEUTSCH

Collation: [1]-[10]¹⁶, 160 leaves.
pp. [i]-[ii] blank; p. [iii] CHIMERA; p. [iv] Also by John Barth; p. [v] title-page; p. [vi] publication, publisher's, copyright, printing, printer's, and publication notices; p. [vii] CONTENTS; p. [viii] blank; pp. [1]-[3] 4-308 as A9b; pp. [309]-[312] blank.

19.7 x 12.7 cm. Bulk: 2.8/3.4 cm. White wove paper; all edges cut. White wove endpapers. Bound in red paper overboards; front and back blank; spine, stamped in gold: John Barth | CHIMERA | [publisher's emblem] | ANDRE | DEUTSCH

Price: £2.75. Number of copies: 2,500. Published on 18 July 1974 in a white dust-jacket with yellow, orange, scarlet, henna-red, and black designs, lettered in black, scarlet, and carmine with a black-and-white photo by Diane Kilmer.

Contents: As A9b.

Notes: Printed in Great Britain by Lowe & Brydone Ltd., Thetford, Norfolk.
The jacket illustrations are by Meg Rutherford.

A10 NATIONAL BOOK AWARD REMARKS 1973

JOHN BARTH | NATIONAL BOOK AWARD IN | FICTION, 1973-- for
CHIMERA | ACCEPTANCE REMARKS | 6:00 PM, April 12, 1973 |
Alice Tully Hall, Lincoln Center

One white, 8½ x 11" Xeroxed leaf, verso blank. Twenty-seven
lines of text follow the heading.

Not for sale; distributed gratis. Number of copies: undetermined. Published on 11 Apr. 1973.

Notes: Printed privately in New York, N.Y.
This broadside is an advance release of Barth's 1973
NBA remarks.

B. FIRST BOOK CONTRIBUTIONS BY JOHN BARTH

B1   THE ADVENTURES OF RODERICK RANDOM   [1964]

THE ADVENTURES OF | Roderick Random | TOBIAS SMOLLETT | WITH AN AFTERWORD BY | JOHN BARTH | [publisher's emblem] | A SIGNET CLASSIC | Published by THE NEW AMERICAN LIBRARY

Collation: 240 leaves, glued at spine.
 p. [i] portrait, biographical sketch; p. [ii] blank; p. [iii] title-page; p. [iv] publisher's, copyright, publication, trademark, publisher's, and printing notices; pp. v-xiv CONTENTS; pp. xv-xx 21-468 text; pp. 469-479 AFTERWORD; p. 480 SELECTED BIBLIOGRAPHY, A NOTE ON THE TEXT.

17.9 x 10.7 cm. Bulk: 1.7 cm. White wove paper; all edges cut. Bound in paper covers printed in white, blue, black, grey-green, and red.

Price: $0.75. Number of copies: 56,470. Published on 1 July 1964.

Notes: Barth's contributions are the biographical sketch (p. [i]) and the afterword (pp. 469-479). This book is Signet Classics No. CT255. Printed in the U.S.A.
Impressions: 2nd, 1 Sept. 1964 (Canadian printing: 2,397 copies); 3rd, Mar. 1972 (16,070 copies).

B2   MODERN OCCASIONS   [1966]

a. First edition:

MODERN | OCCASIONS | Selected and edited by | Philip Rahv [slash, publisher's emblem] | FARRAR, STRAUS AND GIROUX | NEW YORK

-27-

Collation: [1]-[12]¹⁶, 192 leaves.
  pp. [i]-[ii] blank; p. [iii] MODERN OCCASIONS; p. [iv] blank;
  p. [v] title-page; p. [vi] copyright, Library of Congress,
  publication, printing, and printer's notices; pp. [vii]-[ix]
  Contents; p. [x] blank; pp. [xi]-[xii] Foreword; p. [1] as
  p. [iii]; p. [2] blank; pp. [3] 4-366 text, with pp. [60,
  72, 102, 107, 123, 139, 144, 178, 181, 202, 222, 226, 247,
  264, 267, 285, 309, 327, 341, 346] being unnumbered; pp.
  [367] 368-369 Notes on Contributors; pp. [370]-[372] blank.

20.3 x 14.0 cm. Bulk: 2.4/3.0 cm. White wove paper; all edges
  cut, top-edge stained orange-red. Red wove endpapers. Bound
  in blue-green cloth; front and back blank; spine, from top to
  bottom: [stamped in silver:] MODERN OCCASIONS | [stamped in
  black:] Selected and edited by Philip Rahv [slash] FARRAR,
  STRAUS & GIROUX

Price: $6.95. Number of copies: 3,500. Published on 30 June
  1966 in a red and white dust-jacket lettered in red, white,
  and black.

Notes: Barth's contribution is a piece entitled "Test Borings"
  (pp. 247-263), "fragments," in Barth's words, "written
  as trial-starts for Giles Goat-Boy before its hero,
  attitude, and viewpoint were clearly conceived."
  These fragments, with their narrative point of view
  altered, appear in GGB.
  Printed in the U.S.A. by H. Wolff.

b. Noonday Press impression ([1966]):

MODERN | OCCASIONS | Selected and edited by | Philip Rahv
[slash, publisher's emblem] | THE NOONDAY PRESS [slash] a
division of | FARRAR, STRAUS and GIROUX, INC. | NEW YORK

Collation: 192 leaves, glued at spine.
  Contents as B2a.
20.0 x 13.7 cm. Bulk: 2.7 cm. White wove paper; all edges
  cut. Bound in paper covers printed in white, black, red,
  and rose.

Price: $2.45. Number of copies: 4,000. Published on 15 Nov.
  1966.

Notes: This book is Noonday No. N300.
  Other notes as B2a.

c. Weidenfeld and Nicolson impression ([1967]):

MODERN | OCCASIONS | Selected and edited by | Philip Rahv

[slash] | WEIDENFELD AND NICOLSON | 20 NEW BOND STREET | LONDON W1

Collation: [1]-[12]¹⁶, 192 leaves.
 pp. [i]-[iv] as B2a; p. [v] title-page; p. [vi] copyright, Library of Congress, and printing notices; pp. [vii]-[xii] [1]-[3] 4-366 [367] 368-369 [370]-[372] as B2a.

20.4 x 13.8 cm. Bulk: as B2a. White wove paper; all edges cut, top-edge stained bright purple. Endpapers as B2a. Bound in black cloth; front and back blank; spine, stamped in gold: MODERN|OCCASIONS | [rule] | Edited by | Philip Rahv | Weidenfeld | & Nicolson

Price: 45s. Number of copies: 1,500. Published in Feb. 1967.

Notes: Barth's contribution is a piece entitled "Test Borings" (pp. 247-263). Printed in the U.S.A.

B3   WRITER'S CHOICE   [1974]

a. First edition:

WRITER'S CHOICE | [leaf decoration] BY [leaf decoration] | John Barth   James Jones | Donald Barthelme   Norman Mailer | Hortense Calisher   Arthur Miller | Truman Capote   Reynolds Price | R. V. Cassill   James Purdy | Evan S. Connell, Jr.   Philip Roth | Stanley Elkin   Terry Southern | George P. Elliott   John Updike | Bruce Jay Friedman   Thomas Williams | Herbert Gold   Richard Yates | [rule] | Edited with an introduction by | RUST HILLS | David McKay Company, Inc. | NEW YORK

Collation: 224 leaves, glued at spine.
 p. [i] WRITER'S CHOICE; p. [ii] blank; p. [iii] title-page; p. [iv] publisher's, copyright, Library of Congress, publisher's, and printing notices; p. [v] CONTENTS; p. [vi] blank; pp. [vii] viii-xii INTRODUCTION; p. [xiii] as p. [i]; p. [xiv] blank; pp. [1] 2-432 text, with pp. [34, 50, 68, 124, 152, 186, 222, 226, 250, 252, 278, 280, 312, 338, 350, 352, 412] being blank and pp. [3, 25, 27, 34-35, 37, 49-51, 68-69, 71, 87, 89, 124-125, 127, 152-153, 155, 186-187, 189, 195, 197, 222-223, 226-227, 250-253, 278-281, 309, 312-313, 338-339, 341, 350-353, 371, 373, 391, 393, 397, 399, 412-413, 415] being unnumbered; pp. [433]-[434] blank.

-29-

21.0 x 13.5 cm. Bulk: 2.6/3.1 cm. White wove paper; all edges cut. White wove endpapers. Bound in red cloth; front and back blank; spine, stamped in black: [from top to bottom:] WRITER'S CHOICE | [from top to bottom:] Rust Hills, Editor | [publisher's emblem] | McKay

Price: $9.95. Number of copies: undisclosed. Published on 25 Nov. 1974 in a white and blue dust-jacket lettered in blue, red, and yellowish green.

Notes: Barth's contribution is a statement about his current predilection for short fiction and his "sentimental" attachment to "Lost in the Funhouse," the story he asks to be printed as his favorite (pp. 1-2); "Lost in the Funhouse" is reprinted on pp. 3-24. Printed in the U.S.A.
The jacket design is by Janet Halverson.

b. McKay paperback impression ([1975]):

Title-page as B3a.

Collation and contents as B3a.

Size as B3a. Bulk: 2.6 cm. Paper and edges as B3a. Bound in paper covers printed in white, blue, red, and yellowish green.

Price: $4.95. Number of copies: undisclosed. Published on 13 Feb. 1975.

Notes: Barth's contribution is a statement about his current predilection for short fiction and his "sentimental" attachment to "Lost in the Funhouse," the story he asks to be printed as his favorite (pp. 1-2); "Lost in the Funhouse" is reprinted on pp. 3-24. Printed in the U.S.A.
The cover design is by Janet Halverson.

*B4   WESTERN WIND, EASTERN SHORE   1975

Western Wind, Eastern Shore: A Sailing Cruise Around the Eastern Shore of Maryland, Delaware and Virginia by Robert DeGast. Baltimore: Johns Hopkins University Press, 1975 (forthcoming).

Note: Barth's contribution is the foreword.

C. BARTH'S CONTRIBUTIONS TO PERIODICALS AND TO THE PRESS

FICTION

C1 "Lilith and the Lion." The Hopkins Review, 4 (Fall 1950), 49-53.

C2 "The Remobilization of Jacob Horner." Esquire, 50 (July 1958), 55-59.

Shortened version of Ch. 6 of ER.

C3 "Landscape: The Eastern Shore." The Kenyon Review, 22 (Winter 1960), 104-10.

C4 "Ambrose His Mark." Esquire, 59 (Feb. 1963), 97, 122-24, 126-27.

Collected, after revision, in LF.

C5 "Water-Message." Southwest Review, 48 (Summer 1963), 226-37.

Collected, after revision, in LF.

C6 "Night-Sea Journey." Esquire, 65 (June 1966), 82-83, 147-48.

Collected, after some minor changes, in LF.

C7 "Lost in the Funhouse." The Atlantic Monthly, 220 (Nov. 1967), 73-82.

Collected, after revision, in LF.

C8 "Title." The Yale Review, 57 (Winter 1968), 213-21.

Collected in LF.

C9 "Autobiography: A Self-Recorded Fiction." New American Review, No. 2 (Jan. 1968), pp. 72-75.

Collected, after some minor changes, in LF.

C10 "Petition." Esquire, 70 (July 1968), 68-71, 135.

Collected, after revision, in LF.

C11 "Help! A Stereophonic Narrative for Authorial Voice." Esquire, 72 (Sept. 1969), 108-09.

C12 "Dunyazadiad." Esquire, 77 (June 1972), 136-42, 158, 160, 162, 164, 166, 168.

C13 "Bellerophoniad." Fiction, Fall 1972, pp. 16-19.
 An excerpt from what was to become the third novella in Chimera (cf. pp. 148-66 and 213-20 of A9b).

C14 "Perseid." Harper's Magazine, 245 (Oct. 1972), 79-96.
 Collected, after some minor changes, in Chimera.

NON-FICTION

C15 "My Two Muses." The Johns Hopkins Magazine, 12 (Apr. 1961), 9-13.
 Barth discusses the demands of his two muses, the muse of the classroom and the muse of the writing table.

C16 "The Revolving Bookstand." The American Scholar, 34 (Summer 1965), 474, 476, 478, 480, 482, 484, 486, 488, 490, 492, 494, 496. [p. 474]
 Barth, asked to mention the book or books published between 1955 and 1965 which he finds himself going back to—or thinking about—most often, replies that, aside from his own Maryland trilogy, the books he reflects upon most frequently are Hawkes' Second Skin, Nabokov's Pale Fire, and Borges' Ficciones.

C17 "Muse, Spare Me." Book Week, 26 Sept. 1965, pp. 28-29.
 Barth formally dissociates himself from the school of Black Humor and proclaims his love affair with Scheherazade.

C18 "A Gift of Books." Holiday, 40 (Dec. 1966), 171-72, 174, 177. [p. 171]
 Barth was one of seven distinguished authors asked to recommend a book with Christmas giving in mind. He chose Borges' Labyrinths and gave his reasons for having selected it.

C19 "The Literature of Exhaustion." The Atlantic Monthly, 22 (Aug. 1967), 29-34.
 Barth discusses intermedia art, Borges, and his personal response to the notion that narrative literature "has b this hour of the world just about shot its bolt." This essay has become widely regarded as one of the most important aesthetic statements about post-Modern fiction.

C20 Letter to the Editor. The Dorchester News (Cambridge, Md.), 9 Aug. 1967, p. 2.

Barth, "sickened" by accounts of the irresponsibility of the police chief and the fire department of his native Cambridge during a 24 July 1967 racial disturbance in the city, lets his feelings be known.

C21 A Tribute to Vladimir Nabokov. TriQuarterly, No. 17 (Winter 1970), p. 350. Released in book form as Nabokov: Criticism, Reminiscences, Translations and Tributes, ed. Alfred Appel, Jr., and Charles Newman (Evanston: Northwestern Univ. Press, 1970), p. 350.

A letter from Barth to Nabokov on his seventieth birthday.

C22 "A Tribute to John Hawkes." The Harvard Advocate, 104 (Oct. 1970), 11.

Barth discusses the originality, difficulty, and beauty of Hawkes' works and singles Hawkes out as the contemporary writer he most admires.

C23 "What One Person Can Do." World, 1 (10 Oct. 1972), 48.

An attack on America's destructive involvement in Vietnam.

-33-

D. REPRINTS OF SHORT WORKS AND PARTS OF BOOKS BY JOHN BARTH

FICTION

<"AMBROSE HIS MARK">

D1   In The Naked I: Fiction for the Seventies. Ed. Frederick R. Karl and Leo Hamalian. Greenwich, Conn.: Fawcett (Fawcett Premier Books), 1971. Pp. 122-40.

<"AUTOBIOGRAPHY">

D2   In Black and White: Stories of American Life. Ed. Donald B. Gibson and Carl Anselment. New York: Washington Square Press, 1971. Pp. 36-39.

D3   In Innovative Fiction: Stories for the Seventies. Ed. Jerome Klinkowitz and John Somer. New York: Dell (A Laurel Original), 1972. Pp. 220-24.

D4   In Scenes from American Life: Contemporary Short Fiction. Ed. Joyce Carol Oates. New York: Random House, 1973. Pp. 268-71.

<THE END OF THE ROAD, Chapter 6>

D5   In The Esquire Reader. Ed. Arnold Gingrich, L. Rust Hills, and Gene Lichtenstein. New York: Dial Press, 1960. Pp. 171-90.

D6   In How We Live: Contemporary Life in Contemporary Fiction. Ed. Penney Chapin Hills and L. Rust Hills. New York: Macmillan, 1968. Pp. 21-36.

<THE FLOATING OPERA, Chapter 10>

D7   In The Single Voice: An Anthology of Contemporary Fiction. Ed. Jerome Charyn. New York: Macmillan, 1969. Pp. 265-86.

<THE FLOATING OPERA, Chapters 27-29>

D8   In The World of Black Humor: An Introductory Anthology of Selections and Criticism. Ed. Douglas M. Davis. New York: E. P. Dutton, 1967. Pp. 278-93.

<"LIFE-STORY">

D9   In Anti-Story: An Anthology of Experimental Fiction. Ed. Philip Stevick. New York: The Free Press, 1971. Pp. 3 15.

D10 In Literature in America: The Modern Age. Ed. Charles Kaplan. New York: The Free Press, 1971. Pp. 601-11.

D11 In The Modern Tradition: An Anthology of Short Stories. 2nd ed. Ed. Daniel Howard. Boston: Little, Brown and Company, 1972. Pp. 556-65.

<"LOST IN THE FUNHOUSE">

D12 In American Literature. Ed. Richard Poirier and William L. Vance. Boston: Little, Brown and Company, 1970. II, 1111-27.

D13 In The American Tradition in Literature. 4th ed. Ed. Scully Bradley, Richard Croom Beatty, E. Hudson Long, and George Perkins. New York: Grosset & Dunlap, 1974. II, 1781-1801.

D14 In The Art of Fiction: A Handbook and Anthology. 2nd ed. Ed. R. F. Dietrich and Roger H. Sundell. New York: Holt, Rinehart and Winston, 1974. Pp. 434-52.

D15 In Introduction to Fiction. Ed. Paul J. Dolan and Joseph T. Bennett. New York: John Wiley and Sons, 1974. Pp. 427-46.

D16 In The Literature of America: Twentieth Century. Ed. Mar Schorer. New York: McGraw-Hill, 1970. Pp. 1029-48.

D17 In The Literature of the United States. 3rd ed. Ed. Walt Blair, Theodore Hornberger, Randall Stewart, and James Miller, Jr. Glenview, Ill.: Scott, Foresman, 1969. II 644-59.

D18 In Major American Short Stories. Ed. A. Walton Litz. Ne

York: Oxford Univ. Press, 1975. Pp. 735-55.

D19 In The Modern Tradition: An Anthology of Short Stories. 2nd ed. Ed. Daniel F. Howard. Boston: Little, Brown and Company, 1972. Pp. 538-55.

D20 In Prize Stories 1969: The O. Henry Awards. Ed. William Abrahams. Garden City, N.Y.: Doubleday, 1969. Pp. 63-85.

D21 In The Process of Fiction: Contemporary Stories and Criticism. 2nd ed. Ed. Barbara McKenzie. New York: Harcourt Brace Jovanovich, 1974. Pp. 561-81.

D22 In Writer's Choice. Ed. Rust Hills. New York: McKay, 1974. Pp. 3-24.

<"MENELAIAD">

D23 In Stories from the Sixties. Ed. Stanley Elkin. New York: Doubleday, 1971; New York: Anchor Books, 1971. Pp. 363-400.

<"NIGHT-SEA JOURNEY">

D24 In American Poetry and Prose. 5th ed. Ed. Norman Foerster, Norman S. Grabo, Russel B. Nye, E. Fred Carlisle, and Robert Falk. Boston: Houghton Mifflin, 1970. Pp. 1554-58.

D25 In Anthology of American Literature. Ed. George McMichael. New York: Macmillan, 1974. II, 1886-93.

D26 In Elements of Fiction: Introduction to the Short Story. Ed. Jack Carpenter and Peter Neumeyer. Dubuque, Iowa: William C. Brown, 1974. Pp. 118-25.

D27 In The Fact of Fiction: Social Relevance in the Short Story. Ed. Cyril M. Gulassa. San Francisco: Canfield Press, 1972. Pp. 381-89.

D28 In Four Modes: A Rhetoric of Modern Fiction. Ed. James M. Mellard. New York: Macmillan, 1973. Pp. 392-98.

D29 In How We Live: Contemporary Life in Contemporary Fiction. Ed. Penney Chapin Hills and L. Rust Hills. New York: Macmillan, 1968. Pp. 974-81.

D30 In The Process of Fiction: Contemporary Stories and Criticism. 2nd ed. Ed. Barbara McKenzie. New York: Harcourt Brace Jovanovich, 1974. Pp. 592-600.

D31 In Short Stories: Classic, Modern, Contemporary. Ed. Marcus Klein and Robert Pack. Boston: Little, Brown and Company, 1967. Pp. 598-606.

D32 In Studies in Short Fiction: Five Short Novels & Thirty Stories. 2nd. ed. Ed. Douglas A. Hughes. New York: Holt, Rinehart and Winston, 1974. Pp. 487-94.

D33 In Three Stances of Modern Fiction: A Critical Anthology of the Short Story. Ed. Stephen Minot and Robley Wilson, Jr. Cambridge, Mass.: Winthrop, 1972. Pp. 213-21.

<THE SOT-WEED FACTOR, Part I, Chapter 1>

D34 In Multimediate: Multi Media and the Art of Writing. Ed. Warren L. Clare and Kenneth J. Ericksen. New York: Random House, 1972. Pp. 179-80.

<THE SOT-WEED FACTOR, Part I, Chapters 6-7>

D35 In Black Humor. Ed. Bruce Jay Friedman. New York: Bantam Books, 1965. Pp. 108-26.

<THE SOT-WEED FACTOR, Part II, Chapter 16>

D36 In American Literature: The Makers and the Making. Ed. Cleanth Brooks, R. W. B. Lewis, and Robert Penn Warren. New York: St. Martin's Press, 1973. II, 2907-15.

<THE SOT-WEED FACTOR, Part III, Ch. 21>

D37 In 12 from the Sixties. Ed. Richard Kostelanetz. New York: Dell (Laurel Books), 1967. Pp. 71-90.

<"TITLE">

D38   In Fiction 100: An Anthology of Short Stories. Ed. James
       H. Pickering. New York: Macmillan, 1974. Pp. 38-42.

NON-FICTION

<"THE LITERATURE OF EXHAUSTION">

D39   In The American Novel Since World War II. Ed. Marcus
       Klein. Greenwich, Conn.: Fawcett (Fawcett Premier
       Books), 1969. Pp. 267-79.

D40   In Surfiction: Fiction Now . . . and Tomorrow. Ed. Ray-
       mond Federman. Chicago: Swallow Press, 1975. Pp. 19-
       33.

D41   New Society, 11 (1968), 718-19. [lengthy excerpt]

<"MUSE, SPARE ME">

D42   In The Sense of the Sixties. Ed. Edward Quinn and Paul
       J. Dolan. New York: The Free Press, 1968. Pp. 440-44.

D43   In The Would-Be Writer. 3rd ed. Ed. Clinton S. Burhans,
       Jr. Lexington, Mass.: Xerox College Publishing, 1971.
       Pp. 182-85.

E. A DESCRIPTIVE CATALOG OF THE BARTH MANUSCRIPTS HOUSED IN UNITED STATES LIBRARIES

THE LIBRARY OF CONGRESS

E1 Title: "The Floating Opera" (holograph)
Date: Jan.-Mar. 1955
Contents: First draft of FO.
Description: 236 leaves of regular white, 8½ x 11" loose-leaf paper; 2 leaves of white, 8½ x 11" loose-leaf paper torn from a spiral notebook (the sides of which are numbered 407-410); 1 whole leaf and 5 partial leaves of poor quality, white, unruled, 8½ x 11" loose-leaf paper of the type which serves as a cover sheet on new packages of loose-leaf paper; and one-half of 1 leaf of yellow, unruled, 8½ x 11" paper with a row of holes down each side. Holograph, with some emendations. Sides of ruled loose-leaf paper numbered 1-146 [insertion on partial leaf of unruled, white paper; verso blank] 147-236 [insertion on partial leaf of unruled, white paper; verso blank] 237-318 [insertion on partial leaf of unruled, white paper; verso blank] 319-332 [insertion on half-leaf of yellow paper, verso blank] 333-349 349-357 357 359-380 [380a blank] 381-446 [446a-446b blank] 447-448 [insertion on partial leaf of unruled, white paper; verso blank] 449-460 [insertion on partial leaf of unruled, white paper; verso blank] 461-468 [insertion on whole leaf of unruled, white paper; recto blank] 469-472.
Publication: See Ala

E2 Title: "THE FLOATING OPERA" (initial typescript)
Date: [Mar. 1955, Apr.-Sept. 1955, 1965 or 1966]
Contents: The story surrounding the publication of Barth's first novel is widely known. Five publishers turned the book down before Appleton-Century-Crofts decided to accept it. Unfortunately, they were only willing to publish the book on the condition that Barth agree to make some major changes in his manuscript, including a complete alteration of the book's ending. He did so in order to get into print. Subsequently, he was given the opportunity to return the book to its original design. The resultant "revised" edition of the novel was issued by Doubleday in 1967.
    This manuscript reflects the entire literary evolution outlined above. Basically, it is a typescript, produced on yellow paper during Mar. 1955 and subsequently emended, of the first draft of the novel. But there are also some leaves of typescript, on white paper, which Barth rejected as he endeavored to please Appleton-

-41-

Century-Crofts, as well as holographic leaves, on loose-leaf paper, dating from mid-1955 and 1965/6, the period during which Barth worked on the "revised" edition of the book. Many of the holographic notations on the typescript were done in 1955, but some were added in 1965/6. I have attempted to account for the latter in my description.

Description: 327 leaves of yellow, unruled, 8½ x 11" paper with a row of holes down each side and perforations running widthwise across the middle of each leaf; 15 leaves of white, 8½ x 11" loose-leaf paper; 15 leaves of white, 8½ x 11" typing paper; and 2 partial leaves of yellow, ruled paper. The yellow typescript has many holographic emendations; the white typescript has some holographic emendations; the loose-leaf paper leaves are holographic and have a few emendations; the yellow, ruled inserts are holographic. The yellow typescript leaves are numbered [i] 1-102 [103]-[166] 11-12 [169] 14 [171] 16 [173] 18 [175] 20 [177]-[326]. There are holographic notations on the versos of pp. [i], 14, 19-20, 69, 88, [163], 18 (the second), [192], [204], [225], [298], [315], and [319]; other versos blank. The 1955 loose-leaf paper leaves are unnumbered: 3 are between pp. [219] and [220], the verso of the third being blank; 3 are between pp. [296] and [297]; 5 are between pp. [317] and [318]; and 3 follow p. [326], the third having a 2½ x 4" piece cut out of it and a blank verso. The 1966 loose-leaf paper leaf ("While finally my cigar . . . ") is unnumbered; it is inserted between pp. [323] and [324]. The white typescript leaves which postdate the yellow by several months, appear at the end of the manuscript and are numbered 308 (number typed) 309 (number typed), 302 (298), 303 (299), 305 (301), 306 (302), 303, 306-308, 312-316; versos blank. The partial yellow leaves (1965/6) are unnumbered, versos blank: 1 is between pp. [133] and [134], and 1 is between pp. [140] and [141]. 1965/6 notations are in red ink and occur on the following pages of the yellow typescript: [134]-[135] [141]-[142], [220]-[221], [223], [297]-[298], [298^V], [314]-[315], [315^V], [316]-[319], [324]-[326].
Publication: See Ala and A6a

E3 The Floating Opera (final typescript)
Date: [Sept. 1955]
Contents: The typescript from which the galley proofs of the Appleton-Century-Crofts edition of FO were set, with some penned-in authorial emendations and some penciled-in editorial markings.
Description: 319 leaves of white, 8½ x 11" typing paper; typescript, with some holographic emendations by the author and some editorial markings; leaves numbered [1] 2-49 49a 50-121 121a 122-143 144/5 146-167 167a-167b 168-281 281a 282-315 (the publisher has renumbered the leaves 5-323 in a blue stamp); figuring on the verso of p. 162, other versos blank.
Publication: See Ala

E4 Title: "What to Do Until the Doctor Comes" (holograph)
    Date: Oct.-Dec. 1955
    Contents: First draft of ER
    Description: 194 leaves of regular white, 8½ x 11" loose-leaf paper and 5 leaves of white, 8½ x 11" loose-leaf paper torn from a spiral notebook (the sides of which are numbered 357-366); holograph, with some emendations; sides numbered [i] [ii blank] [1] 2-11 [11a blank] 12-238 [238a blank] 239-253 [253a blank] 254-288 [288a-288b blank] 289-348 350-392.
    Publication: See A2a

E5 Title: "What to Do Until the Doctor Comes" (initial typescript)
    Date: [early 1956]
    Contents: Typescript of the first draft of ER, with holographic emendations.
    Description: 253 whole leaves and 1 half-leaf of yellow, unruled, 8½ x 11" paper with a row of holes down each side and widthwise perforations running across the middle of each whole leaf; typescript, with relatively few holographic emendations; leaves unnumbered, the half-leaf inserted between the twenty-seventh and twenty-eighth whole leaves; there is typing on the verso of the one hundred fifty-second whole leaf. The last thirteen leaves are pages rejected in the process of revision; two of them have holographic notations on the versos. The remaining versos are blank.
    Publication: See A2a

E6 Title: "WHAT TO DO UNTIL THE DOCTOR COMES" (final typescript)
    Date: [early 1956]
    Contents: Carbon copy of the typescript from which the galley proofs of the 1958 Doubleday edition of ER were set and the story "The Remobilization of Jacob Horner" was produced.
    Description: 215 leaves of white, 8½ x 11" typing paper and 25 leaves of white, 8½ x 11" reproduction quality paper; carbon copy of typescript (except p. 59, which is an original, and pp. 82-106, which are photoreproductions prepared by Esquire), with autograph emendations; leaves numbered [i blank] [ii] [1] 2-54 54a 55-233 233a 234-235 [236 blank], versos blank.
    Publication: See A2a and C2

E7 Title: "Characters, etc." THE SOT-WEED FACTOR"
    Date: [1956 or 1957]
    Contents: Cards containing, in the main, brief biographical sketches, in note form, of the characters Barth intended to use in SWF; many of the cards include references to the novel's major documentary source, the Archives of Maryland.
    Description: 171 off-white-and-brown cards measuring 3¼ x 5" (these are book charge cards from the Pennsylvania State

-43-

University Library; all but the first, which serves as a
title card, and the last, which is merely protective, are
used rather than new); holograph; cards unnumbered, last
card blank.
Publication: None

E8   Character Lists for The Sot-Weed Factor
     Date: [1956 or 1957]
     Contents: Lists labeled "Men," "Indians," and "Women,"
       which indicate the political affiliations, if any, of
       the characters in SWF as well as the tribal affiliations
       of the Indians; working guide.
     Description: 3 leaves of white, 8½ x 11" loose-leaf paper;
       holograph, with a few emendations; sides numbered 1 [1a]
       2 [2a] [3] [3a].
     Publication: None

E9   Game and Book List for The Sot-Weed Factor
     Date: [1956 or 1957]
     Contents: A preliminary list of the games the Cooke twins
       played as children and the books they read; working guide
       for Part I, Ch. 2 of SWF.
     Description: 1 leaf of white, 8½ x 11" typing paper; holo-
       graph, with several emendations; leaf unnumbered, verso
       blank.
     Publication: None

E10 A Chronology for The Sot-Weed Factor
     Date: [1956 or 1957]
     Contents: A breakdown of the major events related in SWF
       for the years 1688-1700; working guide.
     Description: 13 leaves (one for each year) of white, 8½ x
       11" loose-leaf paper; holograph, with several emendations
       sides unnumbered, none blank.
     Publication: None

E11 Notes for The Sot-Weed Factor
     Date: [1957]
     Contents: A permutation chart for folio-quarto-cardboard-
       leather-unruled-ruled-thin-fat (the problem faced by
       Ebenezer Cooke as he attempts to select a notebook in
       Part II, Ch. 1 of SWF) and a character list for SWF.
     Description: 1 leaf of white, 8½ x 11" typing paper and 1
       leaf of white, 8½ x 11" loose-leaf paper torn from a spi-
       ral notebook; holograph, with a few emendations; both
       leaves are folded in half; the halves of the typing paper
       leaf are numbered 43-44, and those of the loose-leaf pap
       leaf are numbered 45-46.
     Publication: None

E12 Geminology Lists for The Sot-Weed Factor
     Date: [1958]
     Contents: Lists of twins which Barth used in composing Pa
       III, Ch. 2 of SWF; also the definitions of converse, ob-

-44-

verse, reverse, inverse, and vice-versa.
Description: 1 leaf of white, 8½ x 11" typing paper, ac-
 cordian-folded in quarters; holograph; sides unnumbered,
 neither blank.
Publication: None

E13 The Russecks Coat of Arms
Date: [late 1958]
Contents: A sketch of the Russecks family's coat of arms
 (see Part III, Ch. 12 of SWF).
Description: A scrap of unruled, white paper measuring ap-
 proximately 3 x 5"; holograph; leaf unnumbered, verso
 blank.
Publication: None

E14 Title: "The Song of Algol" (holograph)
Date: 18-19 Nov. 1958
Contents: Early draft of "Landscape: The Eastern Shore,"
 adapted from one of Barth's unpublished Dorchester
 Tales (1954).
Description: 7 leaves of white, 8½ x 11" loose-leaf paper;
 holograph, with numerous emendations; sides numbered [1]
 2-6 6-12 [13].
Publication: See C3

E15 Title: "The Invulnerable Castle"
Date: 19-20 Nov. 1958
Contents: Rewritten version of one of Barth's unpublished
 Dorchester Tales (1954).
Description: 9 leaves of white, 8½ x 11" loose-leaf paper;
 holograph, with numerous emendations; sides numbered [1]
 2-18.
Publication: Used in Part III, Ch. 17 of SWF

E16 Title: "The Song of Algol" (typescript)
Date: [early 1959]
Contents: Final draft of what was to become "Landscape: The
 Eastern Shore," a revised version of one of Barth's un-
 published Dorchester Tales (1954).
Description: 7 leaves of white, 8½ x 11" typing paper; car-
 bon copy of typescript, with several autograph notations
 and emendations; leaves numbered [1] 2-7, versos blank.
Publication: See C3

E17 Map for The Sot-Weed Factor
Date: [1956-1959]
Contents: A map of Ebenezer Cooke's travels in America as
 well as a list of the American characters in SWF by coun-
 ty.
Description: 1 leaf of white, 18 x 18" paper; holograph;
 sides unnumbered, verso blank.
Publication: None

-45-

E18 Title: "The Sot-Weed Factor: PLOT"
     Date: [1956-1959]
     Contents: A lengthy sketch, in note form, of the plot of
       SWF; working guide.
     Description: 2 leaves of white, 8½ x 11" loose-leaf paper
       followed by 2 leaves of white, 8 x 10½" loose-leaf paper;
       holograph, with some emendations; sides numbered 1-8.
     Publication: None

E19 Title: "The Sot-Weed Factor" (holograph)
     Date: 1955-3 Mar. 1959
     Contents: First draft of SWF.
     Description: 816 leaves of regular white, 8½ x 11" loose-
       leaf paper; 41 leaves of white, 8½ x 11" loose-leaf paper
       torn from a spiral notebook; 172 leaves of white, 8 x 10½"
       loose-leaf paper; 4 leaves of white, 8½ x 11" typing paper
       (pp. [3ab^r]/[3ab], [173a]/[173a^v], 1229a/[1229a^v], and
       1593a/[1593a^v]); 3 leaves of yellow, ruled, 8½ x 11" paper
       (pp. 168-173); 2 leaves of poor quality, white, unruled,
       8½ x 11" loose-leaf paper of the type used as a cover
       sheet on new packages of loose-leaf paper (pp. 31/[31^v]
       and 134a/[134a^v]); 1 leaf of yellow, unruled, 8½ x 11"
       paper with a row of holes down each side and widthwise
       perforations across the middle (pp. 5/[5^v]); 1 leaf of
       white, unruled, 5½ x 8½" paper; and 1 leaf of white, 8 x
       10" loose-leaf paper torn from a spiral notebook. Holo-
       graph, with numerous emendations. Sides numbered [i]-[x]
       3a [3aa] [3ab^r blank] [3ab] 3b-3i 3ia 3ja-3jc 3j-3k 31
       [31^v blank] 3m [3m^v blank] 5 [5^v blank] 5a-5z 5aa-5gg
       5dd-5ee [second 5ee^v blank] 5ff-5kk 5kka [5kka^v blank]
       5ll-5vv [5vva] 5ww-5zz 5aaa-5lll 6 6a-6m 1-9 [9a] 10-19
       20a-20c [20c^v blank] 20-47 36a-36j 48-52 52a-52c 53-106
       77a-77b 107-134 134a [134a^v blank] 135-156 156 156a 157-
       160 [160a]-[160b] 161 [161a] 162-173 [173a] [173a^v blank]
       174-289 [289a] 290-291 [291^v blank] 292-304 [304^v blank]
       305-308 [308a] 309-336 [336^v blank] 337-405 [405^v blank]
       [405a] [405a^v blank] 406-412 [412a]-[412b] 413-416 416a
       417-428 [428a] 429-444 [444^v blank] 445-484 [white, 5½ x
       8½" insert; verso blank] 485-525 525a 526-566 [566a]
       567-623 [623^v blank] 624-656 [656^v blank] 657-695 [695^v
       blank] 696-764 [764^v blank] 765-791 [791^v blank] 792-859
       859a-859b [white, 8 x 10" insert in a hand other than
       Barth's; it contains translations of French phrases which
       Barth used in SWF in lieu of his own translations, which
       appear on pp. 859a-859b] 860-862 [862^v blank] 863-883
       [883a] 884-911 [911a] [911a^v blank] 912-948 [948^v blank]
       949-1061 [1061^v blank] 1062-1128 [1128^v blank] 1129-1155
       [1155^v blank] [1155a] [1155a^v blank] 1156-1182 [1182^v
       blank] 1183 1183a 1184-1229 1229a [1229a^v blank] 1230-
       1242 [1242^v blank] 1243-1320 [1320a^r blank] 1320a 1321-
       1323 [1323^v blank] 1324-1362 [1362a] 1363-1387 [1387^v
       blank] 1388-1416 [1416^v blank] 1417-1443 [1443^v blank]
       1444-1512 [1512^v blank] 1513-1536 1536a [1536b] 1537-
       1563 [1563a] 1564 [1564^v blank] 1565-1587 [1587^v blank]

1588-1593 1593a [1593a^v blank] 1594-1620 [1620a] 1621-1657 [1657a] 1658-1688 [1688^v blank] 1689-1837 [1837a] 1838-1840 [1840a] 1841-1872 [1873-1874 blank].
Publication: See A3a

E20 Title: "The Sot-Weed Factor" (final typescript)
Date: [1959]
Contents: Typescript, with authorial emendations (including name changes for several characters) and editorial markings, from which the galley proofs of the 1960 Doubleday edition of SWF were set.
Description: Following a layout of the title-page and 4 leaves of front matter prepared by Doubleday are 5 leaves of Barth's typescript (pp. [i]-[v]), an additional leaf of front matter, and the body of Barth's text. 1069 leaves of white, 8½ x 11" typing paper; typescript, with some emendations in Barth's hand and numerous editorial markings; leaves numbered [i]-[v] 1-1064; versos blank, although there is a typescript emendation on a piece of white, unruled paper measuring 1 x 5" stapled to the lower left-hand margin on p. 293.
Publication: See A3a

E21 Title: "John Barth: The Sot-Weed Factor—synopsis"
Date: [1959 or 1960]
Contents: A chapter-by-chapter summary of Parts I and II of SWF, prefaced by a paragraph about the historical Ebenezer Cooke and his poem "The Sot-Weed Factor."
Description: 6 leaves of white, 8½ x 11" loose-leaf paper; holograph, with some emendations; sides unnumbered, none blank.
Publication: None

E22 Title: "IT WAS BILL BELL"
Date: 28 Jan.-4 Feb. 1960
Contents: First draft of the magazine version of "Water-Message."
Description: 17 leaves of white, 8½ x 11" loose-leaf paper; holograph, with numerous emendations; sides numbered 5-38.
Publication: See C5

E23 Title: "Water-message"
Date: [early to mid-1960]
Contents: Revised draft of the magazine version of "Water-Message."
Description: 20 leaves of white, 8½ x 11" typing paper; typescript, with numerous holographic emendations; leaves numbered [1] 2-20; text on the verso of p. 15, other versos blank.
Publication: See C5

E24. Corrected Final Galley Proofs of the 1960 Doubleday Edition of The Sot-Weed Factor
Date: [Corrected in May 1960]

-47-

Contents: Final galley proofs of the first edition of SWF, which contain numerous substantive changes and a large number of corrections in Barth's hand as well as numerous editorial markings.
Description: 297 leaves of pale green, 6 x 24" galley sheets numbered 1-296 (pieces of [297] are missing, including the place where the page number once was; all of [298] is missing); 62 has a holographic note on a scrap of white, unruled, 2 x 3" paper clipped to it on the upper lefthand margin; emendations in Barth's hand appear on sheets 3, 7-13, 15-32, 34, 37-42, 45-110, 112-116, 119, 121-138, 140-151, 153-157, 159-208, 210-215, 217-222, 224-225, 227-230, 233-241, 244-245, 247-252, 254-271, 273-279, 281, 283-291, 293-296, [297].
Publication: See A3a

E25 Title: "Characteristics of the ritual hero"
Date: 1-6 June 1960
Contents: A detailed listing, in note form, of ritual heroic patterns; proved useful in the composition of GGB.
Description: 2 leaves of white, 8½ x 11" loose-leaf paper; holograph, with several emendations; sides unnumbered, none blank.
Publication: None

E26 Title: "THE HERO'S LIFE AND ADVENTURES"
Date: 8 June 1960
Contents: A step-by-step account of what it takes to become a hero, with copious examples; a distillation of E25.
Description: 3 leaves of white, 8½ x 11" loose-leaf paper; holograph, with several emendations; leaves unnumbered, versos blank.
Publication: None

E27 Title: "AMBROSE HIS MARK"
Date: [1960-1961]
Contents: Revised typescript of the magazine version of "Ambrose His Mark," with numerous revisions—chiefly deletions made to satisfy the editorial staff at Esquire.
Description: 28 leaves of white, 8½ x 11" onionskin typing paper and 3 leaves of standard weight white, 8½ x 11" typing paper (pp. [1], new 6, and 23a); carbon copy of typescript (except for the standard weight leaves which are original typescripts), with numerous autograph emendations; leaves numbered [1] 1a 2-5 new 6 6-23 23a 24-28, versos blank.
Publication: See C4

E28 Letter to Mr. [Rust] Hills, 10 Oct. 1961. Letter concerning the changes made in the manuscript of the magazine version of "Ambrose His Mark" in order to please the editorial staff at Esquire; holograph, with several emendations; 1 leaf of yellow, ruled, 8½ x 11" paper; signed Jack Barth. "'Ambrose His Mark' was written as part

-48-

of . . . . "
Publication: None

E29 Test-Borings for Giles Goat-Boy (holograph)
Date: 20 Dec. 1961-15 Jan. 1962
Contents: First draft of "Test-Borings."
Description: 15 leaves of white, 8½ x 11" loose-leaf paper and 1 leaf of yellow, ruled, 8½ x 11" paper (pp. [17a^r]/17a); holograph, with numerous emendations; sides numbered [1a^r] 1a [1] 2-16 [17a^r] 17a 17-23 23-27.
Publication: See pp. 247-263 of B2a

E30 Title: "The Goat-Boy: Politics & Graduation"
Date: 9-14 Mar. 1962
Contents: An interesting essay that delves into the epistemology of paradox which informs GGB.
Description: 5 leaves of white, 8½ x 11" loose-leaf paper; holograph, with some emendations; sides numbered [1] 2-10.
Publication: None

E31 Prospectus for Giles Goat-Boy and Introduction to "Test-Borings" (holograph)
Date: 7 Sept. 1962
Contents: A prospectus for GGB, written at the time that Barth had nearly completed the First Reel of the novel, and an introduction written to accompany "Test-Borings" (see B2a).
Description: 4 leaves of white, 8½ x 11" loose-leaf paper with 1 leaf of white, unruled, 5 x 8" paper stapled to the front of the first loose-leaf sheet (leaf unnumbered, verso blank); holograph, with some emendations; sides of the loose-leaf paper unnumbered, none blank.
Publication: None

E32 Title: "'There is one way to raise a cow.'" (typescript)
Date: [1962]
Contents: Typescript of the logical diagram which, after revision, was used in "Test-Borings" and Volume Two, First Reel, Ch. 1 of GGB; presumably this typescript served as a layout for the ditto copy of the diagram which was used as a handout at a Penn State University reading (see E72).
Description: 1 leaf of white, 8½ x 11" typing paper; typescript, with penciled-in typing instructions; leaf unnumbered, verso blank.
Publication: See A4a and B2a

E33 "Prospectus" and "TEST-BORINGS" for Giles Goat-Boy (typescript)
Date: [Sept. 1962]
Contents: Final typescript of E29 and E31.
Description: 26 leaves of white, 8½ x 11" typing paper; 4 leaves of poor quality, yellow, unruled, 8½ x 11" paper;

-49-

and 1 double-leaf of paper used for musical scoring, measuring 8 x 18½". Typescript, with a few holographic emendations. Typing paper leaves numbered [i]-[viii] [1] 2-19, versos blank. Pp. 4 and 14 have been cut roughly in half and scotch taped to the yellow leaves. The two inner sides of the scoring paper contain holographic lyrics and music; the leaf is paper clipped to the top of p. 8.
Publication: Song "Wander we down College Mall" used in variant form in Volume One, Second Reel, Ch. 7 of GGB; "Test-Borings" published in B2a and used in variant form in GGB.

E34 Title: "Biographical Sketch"
Date: Dec. 1963
Contents: Final version of Barth's biographical sketch of Tobias Smollett, prepared for the Signet edition of The Adventures of Roderick Random.
Description: 1 leaf of white, 8½ x 11" typing paper; carbon copy of typescript, with an autograph note at the top of the recto; leaf unnumbered, verso blank.
Publication: See p. [i] of B1

E35 Title: "Afterword to Roderick Random"
Date: Dec. 1963
Contents: Final version of Barth's critical afterword to the Signet edition of The Adventures of Roderick Random.
Description: 13 leaves of white, 8½ x 11" typing paper; carbon copy of typescript, with one reproduced holographic emendation and one autograph addition; leaves numbered [1] 2-13, versos blank.
Publication: See pp. 469-479 of B1

E36 Title: "Publish or Perish" (holograph)
Date: June 1965
Contents: Early—and lengthy—draft of "Muse, Spare Me," much of which was cut before the essay assumed its final shape.
Description: 9 leaves of white, 8½ x 11" loose-leaf paper; holograph, with numerous emendations; sides numbered [1] 2-15 [15a blank] 16 [16a].
Publication: See C17

E37 Title: "Publish or Perish" (typescript)
Date: June 1965
Contents: Final draft of what was to become "Muse, Spare Me." Barth read this text at Ball State University on 1 July 1965.
Description: 7 leaves of poor quality, yellow, 8½ x 11" paper; carbon copy of typescript, with a few reproduced typed emendations and some autograph emendations and notations; leaves numbered [1] 2-7; figuring on the verso of p. 6, other versos blank.
Publication: See C17

-50-

E38 Title: "Final Droppings from Giles Goat-Boy—Introduction"
Date: [July 1965]
Contents: Prepared text designed to introduce a reading of the "Publisher's Disclaimer" and the "Cover-Letter to the Editors and Publisher" which preface GGB at a Penn State English Colloqium on 13 July 1965, just prior to Barth's departure for SUNY-Buffalo. At the time, Barth was considering deleting these prefatory sections from the novel. His introduction briefly discusses the writer's block which he experienced in the early 1960's, and he claims that the J. B. of GGB was given his name because "his imperfect patience with fate" corresponded to Job's.
Description: 2 leaves of white, 8½ x 11" loose-leaf paper; holograph, with a few emendations; sides unnumbered, none blank.
Publication: None

E39 Plot Outline for Giles Goat-Boy
Date: [1962-1965]
Contents: A detailed outline, in note form, of GGB; working guide.
Description: 10 leaves of white, 8½ x 11" loose-leaf paper; holograph, with numerous emendations; sides numbered [1] 2 1-18.
Publication: None

E40 Title: "Giles Goat-Boy, or, The Revised New Syllabus" (holograph)
Date: 5 Feb. 1962-21 July 1965
Contents: First draft of GGB.
Description: 735 leaves of white, 8½ x 11" loose-leaf paper; 11 full leaves and 1 partial leaf of white, 5 x 8" Pennsylvania State University letterhead stationery; 7 leaves of white, unruled, 5 x 8" note paper (inserts and the leaf numbered 76a/[76b]); 3 leaves of white, 8 x 10½" loose-leaf paper (pp. [586a]/[586b], [588a]/[588b], and [590a]/[590b]); 2 full leaves (pp. [703a]/[703b] and [447a]/[447b]) and 1 partial leaf (measuring 3 x 8½" and stapled to the right-hand margin of p. 347, second series) of yellow, ruled, 8½ x 11" paper; 1 leaf of white, 8½ x 11" typing paper (pp. [i]/[ii], first series); 1 leaf of poor quality, dull blue, 8½ x 11" loose-leaf paper of the type used as a cover sheet on new packages of loose-leaf paper (pp. [76la]/[76lb]); and 1 leaf of music paper, measuring 5 x 8¼". Holograph, with numerous emendations. Sides numbered [i]-[vi] 1-30 [note paper insertion, recto blank] 31-36 [note paper insertion] 37-47 [48 blank] [i] [ii blank] 1-76 76a [76b] 77-85 [85a] 86-111 [note paper insertion, recto blank] 112-152 [152a] 153-154 154a [154b blank] 155-302 [302a]-[302b] 303-308 [note paper insertion, verso blank] 309-314 [note paper insertion, recto blank] 315-344 [letterhead insertion; 2" torn off of bottom, verso blank] 345-397 [figuring on 397a] [397b] [397c blank] 398-445 [note paper insertion, verso blank] 446-451

-51-

[music paper insertion] 452-479 [letterhead insertion, verso blank] 480-511 [letterhead insertion, verso blank] 512-519 [letterhead insertion, verso blank] 520-577 [letterhead insertion, verso blank] 578-585 [letterhead insertion, recto blank] 586-625 [letterhead insertion, verso blank] 626-675 [letterhead insertion, recto blank] 676-687 [letterhead insertion, verso blank] 688-703 [703a]-[703b] 704-749 [letterhead insertion, verso blank] 750-761 [762-763 blank] [i] [ii blank] [1] 2 [3]-[5] [6 blank] 1-221 223-261 [letterhead insertion, recto blank] 262-273 [273a] [273b blank] [273c] [273d blank] 274-447 [447a] [447b blank] 448-450 [450a] 451-504 [504a] [504b blank] 505-566 [letterhead insertion, recto blank] 567-586 [586a] [586b blank] 587-588 [588a blank] [588b] 589-590 [590a blank] [590b] 591-605 [605a blank] [605b] [figuring on 605c] 606-609 609a [609b blank] 610-629.
Publication: See A4a

E41 Title: "Giles Goat-Boy, or, The Revised New Syllabus" (final typescript)
Date: [late 1965 or early 1966]
Contents: Typescript, with numerous authorial emendations and numerous editorial markings, from which the galley proofs of the 1966 Doubleday edition of GGB were set.
Description: Barth's typescript follows 4 leaves of front matter prepared by the publisher (and numbered i-iv) as well as a layout of the title-page. 972 leaves of white, 8½ x 11" typing paper, with layouts prepared by the publisher stapled or paper clipped to pp. v, xxxv/xxxvi, 1/2, 3/4, and 5. Typescript, with numerous emendations in Barth's hand and numerous editorial markings. Leaves numbered v-vi vii/viii ix-xviii xviiia-xviiid xix-xxxiv xxxiva-xxxive xxxv/xxxvi 1/2 3/4 5 2-94 94a 95-282 282a 283-312 312a 313-318 318a 319-328 328a 329-420 421/422 423-506 507/508 509-535 535a-535b 536-708 708a 709-848 848a 849-908 908a 909-923. Holographic notations on the versos of pp. 23, 38, 139, 399, 460, 520, 570, 736, 774, and 831; typescript notation on the verso of p. 851; other versos blank. The six musical inserts prepared for and originally attached to pp. 273-275, 320, and 750 are missing; a black ink stamp, Barth, prefaces the page numbers on the typescript. A 5½ x 8½" note on blue Doubleday letterhead paper from the copy editor to the compositor and the printer's proofreader is stapled to the recto of p. ix; it warns that Barth has "a highly individual style" and that "what looks like inconsistency at first glance is usually intentional."
Publication: See A4a

E42 Carbon Copy of the Final Typescript of Giles Goat-Boy
Date: [late 1965 or early 1966]
Contents: Carbon copy of E41 (beginning with the "Publisher's Disclaimer"), with autograph emendations.
Description: 657 leaves of white, 8½ x 11" typing paper;

314 leaves of poor quality, yellow, unruled, 8½ x 11"
paper; and 6 partial leaves of paper used for musical
scoring (inserts scotch taped to pp. 273-275, 320, and
750; all but the last are autographs rather than carbon
copies). Carbon copy of typescript (except p. xl, which
is a Xerox copy, and p. 556, which is merely a numbered
leaf inserted in place of the missing carbon copy), with
autograph emendations. Leaves numbered iva v-xix xx/xxi
xxii-xlii 1-94 94a 95-282 282a 283-312 312a 313-318 318a
319-328 328a 329-421 423-506 508-535 535a-535b 536-708
708a 709-848 848a 849-908 908a 909-923 [924·925 blank].
Autograph notations on the versos of pp. 95 and 915, figuring on the verso of p. xvii, and a typescript notation
on the verso of p. 851; three full-page sketches, presumably done by Barth, are on the versos of pp. 547-549;
other versos blank. A black ink stamp, Barth, prefaces
the page numbers on the typescript; reading times for the
"Publisher's Disclaimer" (27 min.), the "Cover-Letter"
(40 min.), and Volume One, First Reel, Ch. 1 (12 min.)
are noted; reading keys are given for the voices of three
of the editors in the "Publisher's Disclaimer" (A—
"Churchill," B—"young & brisk," C—"cynical, level,
businesslike").
Publication: See A4a

E43 Setting Copy for the Revised Doubleday Edition of The Sot-
Weed Factor
Date: [1965 or 1966]
Contents and Description: In preparing the text for the revised edition of SWF, Barth simply emended a copy of the
Grosset & Dunlap Universal Library impression of the novel
(see A3c) and added a foreword on 1 leaf of white 8½ x 11"
typing paper (unnumbered, verso blank). Barth's emendations in the paperback consist almost wholly of deletions
from the original. The typescript of the foreword is interesting, because it too contains numerous deletions—
147 words of them. The manuscript is laden with editorial
markings.
Publication: See A5a

E44 Letter to (editor), [1965 or 1966]. Draft of a letter to an
unspecified editor at Doubleday regarding the changes in
Doubleday's revised edition of FO; holograph, with several
emendations; 1 leaf of white, 8½ x 11" loose-leaf paper;
the verso of this leaf contains E45. "Here is the revised
version of The Floating Opera."
Publication: None

E45 Title: "The Floating Opera Prefatory note to the revised
edition" (holograph)
Date: [1965 or 1966]
Contents: First draft of the prefatory note which appears in
Doubleday's revised edition of FO.
Description: 1 leaf of white, 8½ x 11" loose-leaf paper;

-53-

holograph, with numerous emendations; leaf unnumbered; the recto of this leaf contains E44.
Publication: See p. [v] of A6a

E46 Addenda to the Revised Edition of The Floating Opera
Date: [1965 or 1966]
Contents: Carbon copy of the typescript containing the prefatory note to Doubleday's revised edition of FO as well as the major changes to be made in the revised edition; also included is a holographic note identifying the typescript.
Description: 17 leaves of white, 8½ x 11" typing paper and 1 partial leaf of yellow, unruled paper. Carbon copy of typescript, with a few reproduced emendations and some autograph emendations and notations, to which is appended the yellow leaf (holograph, unnumbered, neither side blank). Typescript labeled: prefatory note (1 leaf, unnumbered), Insert XI-A (1 leaf, unnumbered), Insert XII-A (1 leaf, unnumbered), Insert XX-A (3 leaves, numbered [1] 2-3), Insert XXVI (1 leaf, unnumbered), Insert XXVII-A (3 leaves, numbered [1] 2-3), Insert XXVIII-A (5 leaves, numbered [1] 2-5), Insert XXIX-A (2 leaves, numbered [1] 2); versos blank.
Publication: These changes were incorporated in A6a.

E47 Setting Copy for Doubleday's Revised Edition of The Floating Opera
Date: [1965 or 1966]
Contents and Description: Barth indicated the minor textual changes which he wanted made in the revised edition of FO by marking them in a copy of the Avon Books edition of the novel (see A1b); the major changes were indicated on typescript inserts (the carbon copies of these original typescripts are described in E46). There are far more deletions than additions. Both the paperback and the inserts are laden with editorial markings. 7 leaves of front matter prepared by Doubleday and a 14 x 22" offprint accompany Barth's manuscript.
Publication: See A6a

E48 Setting Copy for the Revised Doubleday Edition of The End of the Road
Date: [1965 or 1966]
Contents and Description: Barth indicated the changes he wanted made in the revised Doubleday edition of ER by marking them in a copy of the first Avon Books edition of the novel (see A2b). There are far more deletions than additions. The paperback is filled with editorial markings. 5 leaves of front matter prepared by Doubleday accompany Barth's manuscript.
Publication: See A7a

E49 Figures for Giles Goat-Boy
Date: [early 1966]

-54-

Contents: Offprints of the musical scores, PASS ALL FAIL
ALL symbols, and mirror-image Q.E.D.'s which appear in
GGB as well as the "There is one way to raise a cow."
diagram.
Description: 1 whole leaf (music, PASS ALL FAIL ALL,
Q.E.D.'s) and 2 half-leaves (music) of white, 14 x 19³/₄"
paper; 1 leaf of white, unruled, 8½ x 11" paper (Xerox
copy of final galley proof of logical diagram); versos
blank.
Publication: Figures used in A4a

E50 Correction Notes for Giles Goat-Boy
Date: [early 1966]
Contents: A "style sheet" constructed by Barth to regu-
larize the capitalization and spelling of approximately
fifty of the terms in GGB; a sheet of questions from a
proofreader, with responses by Barth; two sheets of
changes, suggested by one of Barth's readers and responded to by the author; and a second carbon copy of
the title-page and the table of contents of the final
typescript of the novel.
Description: Stapled together are 1 leaf of white, 8 x
10½" loose-leaf paper (the "style sheet": holograph,
with several emendations; unnumbered, verso blank); 1
leaf of white, 8½ x 11" typing paper (the question sheet:
publisher's typescript, with some holographic notations
and emendations by the author; unnumbered, neither side
blank); and 2 leaves of white, 8 x 10" typing paper (the
suggested changes: publisher's typescript, with numerous
holographic emendations and notations by the author; unnumbered, verso of the first leaf blank). Paper clipped
to the front of this gathering is a dittoed sheet from
the publisher and clipped to the rear of the gathering
are the following leaves: 1 leaf of white, 8½ x 11" typing paper, with the holographic notation "1st 55 pages
not finally copyedited" (other notations, emendation;
unnumbered, verso blank); a second leaf of white, 8½ x
11" typing paper (second carbon copy of the title-page:
carbon copy of typescript, with autograph notations; unnumbered, verso blank); and 3 leaves of poor quality,
yellow, unruled, 8½ x 11" paper (second carbon copy of
the table of contents: carbon copy of typescript, with
autograph additions; leaves numbered ii-iv, versos
blank).
Publication: None

E51 Corrected Final Galley Proofs of the 1966 Doubleday Edition
of Giles Goat-Boy
Date: [Corrected in Feb.-Mar. 1966]
Contents: The final galley proofs of the first edition of
GGB, which contain some emendations in Barth's hand as
well as numerous editorial markings.
Description: 289 leaves of pale green, 6 x 24" galley sheets,
numbered 1-289; with a layout of the title-page stapled to

the upper left-hand margin of 2. Emendations in Barth's
hand appear on sheets 3, 7-8, 10-11, 13, 15-17, 21-23,
25-26, 28-30, 32, 35-38, 40, 42, 44, 46-47, 49-51, 53,
56, 58, 60-63, 68, 72-76, 78-80, 83-84, 86, 88, 90-91,
95, 97-98, 101-102, 105, 107-110, 113-116, 118-125, 130-
135, 138, 140-141, 145, 149-152, 154-157, 160-161, 165-
166, 168-170, 173, 175-176, 179, 184, 189-190, 194, 196-
200, 204, 206-216, 220-222, 225-227, 230, 232-238, 240,
242, 244-245, 247-251, 253-254, 256, 258-259, 261-262,
265-268, 274-277, 279-280, 282-283, 287-289.
Publication: See A4a

E52 Title: "Jorge Luis Borges and the Literature of Exhaustion"
(holograph)
Date: 28 Feb. 1966
Contents: First draft of Barth's "Literature of Exhaustion"
essay.
Description: 11 leaves of white, 8½ x 11" loose-leaf paper;
holograph, with many emendations; sides numbered [1] 2-11
[11^v blank] 11a 12-19 [19^v blank].
Publication: See C19

E53 Title: "JORGE LUIS BORGES AND THE LITERATURE OF EXHAUSTION"
(typescript)
Date: Mar. 1966
Contents: Second draft of Barth's essay, "The Literature of
Exhaustion." This version was read at the University of
Virginia, the University of Chicago, Stanford University,
Canisius College, and SUNY-Buffalo.
Description: 14 leaves of white, 8½ x 11" typing paper,
with 1 leaf of white, 4 x 6" note paper following p. [1]
and 2 partial leaves of yellow, ruled paper inserted following pp. 8 and 10 respectively. 14 leaves of typescript;
the 3 inserted leaves are holographs. Numerous holographic
emendations. Typewritten pages numbered [1] 2-14. There
are holographic notations on the versos of pp. 8 and 14,
the verso of the 4 x 6" leaf, and the verso of the first
of the yellow leaves ("and one way to handle . . . ");
other versos blank.
Publication: See C19

E54 Letter to Anne [Freedgood], 9 Mar. 1966. Photoreproduction
of a letter to one of Barth's Doubleday editors regarding
alterations in the galley proofs of GGB; typescript; 1
leaf of 8½ x 11" onionskin paper; unsigned. "Thanks for
the final GILES jacket."
Publication: None

E55 Title: "Labyrinths, by Jorge Luis Borges (New Directions)"
Date: 28 July 1966
Contents: First draft of Barth's contribution to "A Gift
of Books" in the Dec. 1966 Holiday, in which he praises
Borges' Labyrinths.
Description: 1 leaf of yellow, ruled, 8½ x 11" paper;

holograph, with numerous emendations; sides unnumbered, neither blank.
Publication: See C18

E56 Title: "Jorge Luis Borges: LABYRINTHS (New Directions Paperback 186, 1964. $1.90)"
Date: 28 July 1966
Contents: Final draft of Barth's contribution to "A Gift of Books" in the Dec. 1966 Holiday.
Description: 1 leaf of white, 8½ x 11" typing paper; carbon copy of typescript, with one autograph emendation and two autograph notations; leaf unnumbered, verso blank.
Publication: See C18

E57 Title: "Intro. for Buffalo 3/8/67"
Date: [Feb. or Mar. 1967]
Contents: Several paragraphs used to preface an 8 Mar. 1967 reading of the second draft of "Jorge Luis Borges and the Literature of Exhaustion" (see E53) at SUNY-Buffalo.
Description: 2 leaves of white, 8½ x 11" typing paper; typescript, with several holographic emendations; leaves unnumbered, versos blank.
Publication: Barth employed a small segment of this introduction in his "Literature of Exhaustion" essay (see C19).

E58 Corrected Final Galley Proofs of the Revised Doubleday Edition of The End of the Road
Date: [Corrected in Feb. or Mar. 1967]
Contents: Final galley proofs of the 1967 revised Doubleday edition of ER, with some authorial emendations and numerous editorial markings.
Description: 68 leaves of pale green, 6 x 24" galley sheets, numbered 1-68; emendations in Barth's hand appear on sheets 4, 6, 8-9, 11-17, 19, 22, 24, 26-27, 31-36, 38, 43, 47-48, 51-53, 55, 57.
Publication: See A7a

E59 Title: "JOSEPH HELLER—INTRODUCTION—MARCH 30, 1967 (SUNY/Buffalo)"
Date: [Mar. 1967]
Contents: Prepared text which Barth used on 30 Mar. 1967 to introduce a five-novelist lecture series at SUNY-Buffalo as well as the series' first speaker, Joseph Heller. Barth suggests that the thesis of Catch-22 is that war is "not only atrocious but demented, and . . . horridly comic."
Description: 2 leaves of white, 8½ x 11" typing paper; carbon copy of typescript, with a few reproduced holographic emendations and one autograph addition; leaves numbered [1] 2, versos blank.
Publication: None

E60 Title: "JOHN UPDIKE—INTRODUCTION—APRIL 6, 1967 (SUNY/Buffalo)"

Date: [Mar. or Apr. 1967]
Contents: Prepared text which Barth used on 6 Apr. 1967 to
 introduce John Updike, the last speaker in a five-novelist
 lecture series at SUNY-Buffalo. Barth sees Updike as a
 writer of "'magic realism.'"
Description: 2 leaves of white, 8½ x 11" typing paper; carbon copy of typescript, with a few reproduced holographic
 emendations and one autograph addition; leaves numbered
 [1] 2, versos blank.
Publication: None

E61 Letter to Mr. Wensburg, 24 Apr. 1967, Buffalo, N.Y. Carbon
 copy of a letter sent to the New York Times in response
 to an inquiry from Wensburg concerning the book of Barth's
 which Barth would reread during the summer of 1967 had he
 the time; carbon copy of typescript, with several autograph notations; 1 leaf of white, 8½ x 11" typing paper;
 unsigned. "It's easier to recognize another's identity,
 personal and literary, than one's own."
Publication: Response published, see F11

E62 Title: "Introduction for Library of Congress Reading, May 1,
 1967"
Date: 25-27 Apr. 1967
Contents: Prepared text designed to introduce and accompany
 a performance of "Title" and "Autobiography" at a 1 May
 1967 Library of Congress reading.
Description: 3 leaves of white, 8 x 10½" loose-leaf paper;
 holograph, with some emendations; sides unnumbered, verso
 of the last leaf blank.
Publication: None

E63 Title: "Intro. for U. of Md. Reading 5/10/67 (Lost in the
 Funhouse)"
Date: [May 1967]
Contents: Prepared text designed to introduce a reading of
 "Lost in the Funhouse" at the University of Maryland on
 10 May 1967.
Description: 1 leaf of white, 8 x 10½" loose-leaf paper;
 holograph, with some emendations; sides unnumbered, nei-
 ther blank.
Publication: None

E64 Title: "Intro. for Harvard reading"
Date: 13 Aug. 1967
Contents: Prepared text designed to introduce and accompany
 a performance of "Echo," "Title," and "Autobiography" at
 a 1967 Harvard reading.
Description: 2 leaves of white, 8½ x 11" loose-leaf paper;
 holograph, with numerous emendations; sides numbered [1]
 2-4.
Publication: None

E65 Title: "JORGE LUIS BORGES: introduction—SUNY/Buffalo, Nov. 13 & 14, 1967"
Date: [Nov. 1967]
Contents: A largely factual, highly laudatory text, which Barth, on behalf of the Department of English at SUNY-Buffalo, used to introduce Borges, who gave two lectures at SUNYAB on 13 and 14 Nov. 1967.
Description: 2 leaves of white, 8½ x 11" typing paper; typescript, with a few holographic emendations and the holographic note "slowly, voice down"; leaves numbered [1] 2, versos blank.
Publication: None

E66 Title: "Intro. for Petition and Life-Story reading"
Date: [late 1967 or early 1968]
Contents: Introduction to "Petition" for a reading at the University of Michigan.
Description: 1 leaf of white, 7½ x 10½" University of Michigan letterhead stationery; holograph, with several emendations; leaf unnumbered, recto blank.
Publication: None

E67 Title: "Lost in the Funhouse" (holograph)
Dates: "Night-Sea Journey" (Nov. 1965), "Petition" (Dec. 1965), "Title" (15-17 June 1966), "Two Meditations" ("Lake Erie," 1965-1967; "Niagara Falls," 1965-1966), "Autobiography" (first draft of tape version, 9 Jan. 1966; second draft of script version, 11 Jan. 1967), "Glossolalia" (first draft, n.d.; second draft, 1-4 Feb. 1967), "Echo" (25 Jan.-10 Feb. 1967), "Lost in the Funhouse" (20 Feb.-21 Mar. 1967), "Frame-Tale" (21 Apr. 1967), "Life-Story" (24 Apr.-26 May 1967), "Menelaiad" (13 June-12 Oct. 1967), "Foreword" (25 Oct.-6 Nov. 1967), "Anonymiad" (second version of the first draft, 8 Dec. 1967-19 Jan. 1968)
Contents: With several exceptions, the first drafts of the Funhouse pieces; plot notes for "Echo," "Lost in the Funhouse," and "Menelaiad"; brief notes on the revision of "Water-Message" and "Ambrose His Mark"; alternate table of contents ("Autobiography," "Petition," and all of the fictions following "Two Meditations" had their positions in the collection altered at least once). See E22, E23, and E27 for the manuscripts of the early fictions, "Water-Message" and "Ambrose His Mark."
Description: 129 leaves of white, 8½ x 11" loose-leaf paper; 35 leaves of white, 8 x 10½" loose-leaf paper (pp. 1/[1a], 2-5, and 12-31 of "Life-Story"; pp. [1]/1a, [1b]/2, 3-6, 6a/[6b], 7-20, 21/[21a], and 22-33 of "Menelaiad"; and the "Menelaiad" notes); 3 leaves of white, 5½ x 8½" note paper (pp. [i]/[ii] of the "Contents" and the inserts in "Anonymiad"); 2 leaves of white, 5 x 8" loose-leaf paper (pp. [iii]/[iv] and [4a]/[4b] of the "Foreword"); and 1 leaf of white, ruled, 8½ x 11" paper with 1½" torn off of the bottom (pp. [3]/[4] of the second draft of "Glossolalia").

-59-

Holograph, with at least as many words altered as left
intact. Sides numbered: <CONTENTS> [i] [ii blank] <CON-
TENTS, WATER-MESSAGE AND AMBROSE HIS MARK NOTES> [iii]-
[iv] <TITLE-PAGE> [i] [ii blank] <FOREWORD> [1] 2-6
<NIGHT-SEA JOURNEY> [1] 2-4 4a [4b blank] 5-17 [18 blank]
<PETITION> [1] 2-23 [24 blank] <TITLE> [1] 2-4 [4a] [4b
blank] 5-15 [16 blank] <AUTOBIOGRAPHY (first draft of the
tape version)> [1] 2-8 <AUTOBIOGRAPHY (second draft of
the script version)> [1] 2-8 <GLOSSOLALIA (first draft)>
[1] 2-12 <GLOSSOLALIA (second draft)> [1]-[3] [4 blank]
<ECHO> [1] [1a] 2-14 [15 blank] <ECHO: NOTES> [1]-[2]
<TWO MEDITATIONS> 1 [1a blank] 2 [2a blank] <LOST IN THE
FUNHOUSE> [1] 2-46 <LOST IN THE FUNHOUSE: NOTES> [1]-[2]
<FRAME-TALE> [1]-[2] <LIFE-STORY> 1 [1a] 2-31 <MENELAIAD>
[1] 1a [1b blank] 2-6 **6a** [6b] 7-21 [21a blank] 22-37 48-
61 64-67 72-76 [77 blank] <MENELAIAD: NOTES> [1]-[6]
<ANONYMIAD (second version of the first draft)> [1] 2-16
[note paper insertion] 17-20 [note paper insertion] 21-24
37-65 [66 blank].
Publication: See A8a

E68 Title: "LOST IN THE FUNHOUSE" (final typescript)
    Date: [early 1968]
    Contents: Ribbon and Xerox copy of the final typescript of
    LF, with some autograph and some reproduced emendations
    in Barth's hand and numerous editorial markings; the
    manuscript from which the galley proofs of the 1968
    Doubleday edition of LF were set.
    Description: Following 7 leaves of front matter prepared
    by the publisher (including a layout of the title-page),
    there appear 2 leaves of Barth's typescript (pp. v/vi and
    vii/viii), an eighth leaf of front matter, and then the
    remainder of the typescript. 216 leaves of white, 8½ x
    11" typing paper; ribbon and Xerox copy of typescript,
    with some autograph and some reproduced emendations in
    Barth's hand as well as numerous editorial markings;
    leaves numbered (underlining indicates Xerox copy) v/vi
    vii/viii 1/2 3-13 14-41 42-59 60 61-102 103-111 112-215,
    versos blank.
    Publication: See A8a

E69 Title: "LOST IN THE FUNHOUSE" (copy of the final typescript)
    Date: [early 1968]
    Contents: Carbon and Xerox copy of the final typescript of
    LF, with some autograph and some reproduced holographic
    emendations.
    Description: 217 leaves of white, 8½ x 11" typing paper;
    carbon and Xerox copy of typescript, with some autograph
    and some reproduced holographic emendations; leaves num-
    bered (underlining indicates Xerox copy) [i] iii ii 2 3-
    60 61-76 77-178 179-215; figuring on the verso of p. 11
    and an autograph notation on the verso of p. 102, other
    versos blank. Reading time noted for "Petition" (25

min.), "Lost in the Funhouse" (75 min.), and "Life-Story" (36 min.).
Publication: See A8a

E70 Corrected Final Galley Proofs of the 1968 Doubleday Edition of Lost in the Funhouse
Date: [Corrected in May 1968]
Contents: Final galley proofs of the first edition of LF, which contain some minor emendations in Barth's hand as well as numerous editorial markings.
Description: 76 leaves of pale green, 6 x 24" galley sheets, numbered 1-76; with a white, 8½ x 11" sheet of copyright material to be added to the verso of the title-page paper clipped to the lower left-hand margin of 2. Emendations in Barth's hand appear on sheets 2-4, 7-10, 12, 17, 19-25, 28-29, 33, 36-37, 39-42, 46-48, 50-51, 53, 57-58, 60-62, 64-68, 70, 72-73, 75-76.
Publication: See A8a

↠See also the notes to A3a, A4a, A7a, and A8a for the uncorrected galley proofs and foundry proofs housed in the Manuscript Division of the Library of Congress.

THE PENNSYLVANIA STATE UNIVERSITY LIBRARY

E71 Title: "SAMS' SON AGONISTES"
Date: [Sept. 1961]
Contents: A twenty-four line poem by "E.C., Gent, P^t & L^t of M^{d}" presented by Barth to his then English department chairman at Penn State; the lyric was occasioned by the upcoming birth of the Sams' "son"—who turned out to be a girl.
Description: 1 leaf of white, 8½ x 11" typing paper; typescript; leaf unnumbered, verso blank.
Publication: None

E72 Title: "'There is one way to raise a cow.'"
Date: [1962]
Contents: Ditto copy of the typescript of the logical diagram which, after revision, was used in "Test-Borings" and Volume Two, First Reel, Ch. 1 of GGB; this ditto was handed out at a Pennsylvania State University reading.
Description: 1 leaf of white, 8½ x 11" reproduction quality paper; ditto copy of typescript; unnumbered; verso has a holographic note on it in a hand other than Barth's.
Publication: See A4a and B2a

E73 Letter to Charlie [Mann], [1965]. Note thanking Mann, the

Chief of the Rare Book Room at the Pennsylvania State
University Library, for pointing out a reference to a
fictional John Barth in Edgar Pangborn's novel Davy;
holograph; 1 leaf of white, 5 x 8" Pennsylvania State
University letterhead stationery; signed Jack. "A nutty happenstance, faintly ominous."
Publication: None

E74 Restricted File
Date: Apr. 1953-1 Dec. 1965
Contents and Description: A departmental file of correspondence by and relating to John Barth, placed in
the Rare Book Room of the Pennsylvania State University
Library by Henry Sams, Barth's English department chairman at Penn State. 40 of the 56 leaves in this file are
typescripts or holographs composed by Barth. I have not
examined the file, since it is restricted, but biographers
may find it useful at some later date if the restrictions
concerning its use are lifted. The file begins with
Barth's application for a teaching position at Penn State
and ends following his move to SUNY-Buffalo.
Publication: None

E75 Letter to Charles W. Mann, 29 Jan. 1968, Buffalo, N.Y. Letter to the Chief of the Rare Book Room at the Pennsylvania
State University Library concerning one Vincent Godfrey
Burns, the self-proclaimed "Poet and Laureate of Maryland"
typescript, with a few holographic emendations; 1 leaf of
white, 8½ x 11" SUNY-Buffalo letterhead stationery; signed
Jack. "I've had dealings with this bird before . . . . "
Publication: None

E76 Title: "AUTOBIOGRAPHY"
Date: [early 1968]
Contents: Photoreproduction of the final typescript of
"Autobiography," with instructions for reading and the
notation "13-15 min."
Description: 5 leaves of white, 8½ x 11" reproduction quality paper; photoreproduction of typescript, with several
reproduced holographic emendations and numerous reproduced
notations; leaves numbered [1] 2-5, versos blank.
Publication: See A8a

THE JOHNS HOPKINS UNIVERSITY LIBRARY

*E77 Title: "Shirt of Nessus"
Date: 1952
Contents: A novel-in-progress, Barth's MA project at Johns
Hopkins University.

Description: Unable to examine, missing from library.
Publication: None

WASHINGTON UNIVERSITY LIBRARY (St. Louis)

→→See the notes to A4a and A8a for the uncorrected final galley proofs housed in the Rare Book Room of the Washington University Library.

F. MISCELLANEA

RECORDINGS BY JOHN BARTH

F1   John Barth Reads from Giles Goat-Boy. New York: CMS Records, 1968. [LP disc: No. 551]
Barth reads from the "Cover-Letter to the Editors and Publisher"; Volume One, First Reel, Ch. 1; Volume Two, Third Reel, Ch. 7; and the "Posttape" to GGB.
Review:
F2   Lask, Thomas. "The 30's and the 60's—A Parallel." The New York Times, 9 Feb. 1969, p. D31.

F3   Prose Readings by John Barth. Intro. by John Hawkes. New York: McGraw-Hill, 1970. [Tape: cassette No. 81575, reel-to-reel No. 75988]
Barth reads "Test Borings" (see B2a).

*F4   Two Narratives for Tape and Live Voice. New York: McGraw-Hill, 1970. [Tape: cassette No. 81673, reel-to-reel No. 78162]

INTERVIEWS WITH JOHN BARTH

F5   Michaels, Rochelle. "Teaching Next Best To Rich Wife—Barth." The (Pennsylvania State University) Daily Collegian, 20 Feb. 1962, p. 3.
Barth discusses the virtues of the teaching profession.

F6   "John Barth: An Interview." With John J. Enck. Wisconsin Studies in Contemporary Literature, 6 (Winter-Spring 1965), 3-14.   Rpt. in The Contemporary Writer: Interviews with Sixteen Novelists and Poets, ed. with an intro. by L. S. Dembo and Cyrena N. Pondrom (Madison: Univ. of Wisconsin Press, 1972), pp. 18-29.
Barth speaks about the writers he admires, his increasing popularity, his compositional methodology, philosophy, his four novels, the demands of academe, the sociological dimension in his fiction, and allegory.

F7   Cooper, Arthur. "An In-Depth Interview With: John
      Barth . . . A Young Novelist With Exciting Ideas."
      The (Harrisburg, Pa.) Patriot, 30 Mar. 1965, p. 6.

      Barth discusses his beginnings as a writer, Joyce,
      book reviewing, his disdain for the label "Black Hu-
      morist," teaching, and his compositional methodology.

F8   Meras, Phyllis. "John Barth: A Truffle No Longer." The
      New York Times Book Review, 7 Aug. 1966, p. 22.

      Barth discusses the myth of the hero as it relates to
      GGB, farce, the literature of exhaustion, university
      life, and his reaction to securing a wider reading
      public.

F9   Anon. "Heroic Comedy." Newsweek, 68 (8 Aug. 1966), 81-
      82. [p. 82]

      Barth comments on Buffalo, Joyce, Kafka, Beckett,
      Borges, the artificial element in art, and GGB.

F10   Brady, Karen. "Barth Enjoys Teaching Youth; Finds Buffalo
      Culturally Alive." Buffalo Evening News Magazine, 3
      Sept. 1966, p. B-10.

      Barth comments on his favorite pastimes (jazz and ten-
      nis), Buffalo's favorable cultural atmosphere, his fa-
      vorite writers, and his creative writing classes at
      SUNY-Buffalo.

F11   Anon. "Reading Your Own." The New York Times Book Review
      4 June 1967, p. 6.

      Barth, asked which of his novels he would reread for
      pleasure during the summer of 1967 if he were so in-
      clined, answers GGB—if it were not for the fact that
      he already knows the book by heart.

F12   Anon. "Censorship—1967: A Series of Symposia." Arts in
      Society, 4 (Summer 1967), 265-358. [p. 294]

      Barth expresses a general distaste for censorship and
      adds: " . . . my British publishers and certain of my
      American paperback publishers have altered words in my
      books which they apparently considered offensive . . .
      The American firm, at my request, restored the correct
      wording in subsequent editions; the British firm I've
      not bothered to protest to as yet."

F13   Smith, H. Katherine. "Professor Welcomes Winter—Then He
      Writes." Buffalo Courier-Express, 12 Nov. 1967, p. 10.

      Barth comments on the effect of environment on his writ-
      ing, Borges, the literature of exhaustion, creative
      writing classes, and his compositional methodology.

-66-

F14 Prince, Alan. "An Interview With John Barth." Prism (Sir George Williams University, Montreal; Spring 1968), pp. 42-62.

Barth discusses his college years at Johns Hopkins, the influence of music on his work, Marshall McLuhan, FO, ER, SWF, GGB, Borges, the French New Novel, his use of the love triangle, the myth of the hero, and the tape medium.

F15 "L'ombra di Sheherazade: Conversazione con John Barth." With Romano Giachetti. La Fiera Letteraria, 18 July 1968, pp. 2-3.

Barth discusses his undergraduate days at Johns Hopkins, the realistic aspects of FO and ER, the relationship between Jacob Horner and Joe Morgan in ER, his use of plot and history in SWF, history and tragic vision in GGB, parodic elements in FO, his favorite writers (Kafka, Joyce, Mann, Beckett, Borges), the preference among young writers (e.g., Dino Buzzati) for "irrealistic" fiction, the influence of various old masters on his work, LF, the cinema, war and poverty, the ineffectiveness of political demonstrations, and his own silent role in social and political affairs.

F16 Davis, Douglas M. "The End Is a Beginning for Barth's 'Funhouse.'" The National Observer, 16 Sept. 1968, p. 19.

Barth comments on the tape and live voice media as they relate to LF as well as the book's cyclical structure, McLuhan, and the importance of technique.

F17 Kaufman, Michael T. "The Buffalo Strike: High Spirits and Cloudy Issues." The New York Times, 18 Mar. 1970, p. 30.

Barth's comments on the 1970 student strike at SUNY-Buffalo.

F18 Tempest, Timothy. "Latest Barth Book Is 'Untaped Print.'" Buffalo Courier-Express Focus, 29 Aug. 1971, p. 1.

Barth discusses the auditory aspects of LF, the tape conceit of GGB, Buffalo, and the English department at SUNY-Buffalo.

F19 Bellamy, Joe David. "Exclusive Interview with John Barth." In Writer's Yearbook '72. Cincinnati: F and W Publishing, 1972. Pp. 70-72, 120-21. A fuller version of this interview appears in The Falcon, No. 4 (Spring 1972), pp. 5-15, as "Algebra and Fire: An Interview with John Barth."

Barth discusses his use of "received stories," Black Humor, his contemporaries, his use of autobiographical details, his compositional methodology, FO, ER, SWF, GGB, and Chimera.

F20 "Having It Both Ways: A Conversation between John Barth and Joe David Bellamy." New American Review, No. 15 (Apr. 1972), pp. 134-50. Rpt. in The New Fiction: Interviews with Innovative American Writers, ed. Joe David Bellamy (Urbana: Univ. of Illinois Press, 1974), pp. 1-18.

Barth comments on twentieth-century novelists, innovative fiction, the origins of SWF, parody, the "death" of the novel, myth and authorial voice and artificiality in LF, the "obsolescence" of plot, and the function of imitatio in fiction writing.

F21 Shenker, Israel. "Complicated Simple Things." The New York Times Book Review, 24 Sept. 1972, pp. 35-38.

Barth discusses his use of complicated narration, the gnomon as a metaphor for his work, FO, ER, SWF, GGB, the ways in which his thoughts have changed since turning forty, Chimera, and writer's block.

F22 "A Conversation with John Barth." With Frank Gado. The Idol (Union College), 49, No. 2 (Fall 1972), 1-36. Rpt with a longer introduction and five "typos" corrected, i First Person: Conversations on Writers & Writing, ed. Frank Gado (Schenectady, N.Y.: Union College Press, 1973 pp. 110-41.

Barth comments on his life in Eastern Maryland and at Johns Hopkins, his decision to become a writer, the form tive impressions made on him by Faulkner's work, the com position of his Maryland trilogy, the importance of the short story genre, the financial concerns of the novelis aesthetic distance in LF, his literary development (with special reference to Chimera), his general dislike for engagé literature, his use of the frame-tale in "Menela-iad," the importance of paralysis and choice in his work and "secular news reporting" versus innovation in contem porary fiction.

F23 Simon, Jeff. "Prize-Winning Writer Reflects on Buffalo." Buffalo Evening News, 1 June 1973, p. 35.

Barth comments on his decision to leave SUNY-Buffalo in favor of Johns Hopkins and the controversy surrounding the 1973 National Book Award for fiction.

F24 Bowden, Mark. "Return of The Native." Biography News, 1 (May 1974), 491-92.

Barth discusses the benefits which the academic life affords the writer, the books he read during his pre-University days, his undergraduate years at Johns Hopkins, his decision to become a writer, his compositional methodology, the fact that writing becomes more complicated for him as he grows older, and his favorite contemporary writers.

→→See also comments by Barth in G5, G12, G35, G76, G80, G88, G97, H23, H97, H149, H153, H285, I37.

PANEL DISCUSSIONS PARTICIPATED IN BY JOHN BARTH

F25 Henkle, Roger. "Symposium Highlights: Wrestling (American Style) with Proteus." Novel, 3 (Spring 1970), 197-207. See also Ann Banks' analysis of the symposium in "Symposium Sidelights," Novel, 3 (1970), 208-11.

Barth, as a panel member in a 1969 symposium at Brown University on "The Relevance of Contemporary Forms" in American fiction, discusses the shifting nature of reality and the effects of time on literary form.

F26 [Barth, John]. "John Barth Dissects 'Prosaic.'" Buffalo Evening News Lively Arts, 18 Sept. 1970, p. 66.

A transcript of Barth's remarks at a 1970 panel discussion on "The Prosaic in Fiction." Barth explains the ways in which post-realistic fiction writers transmute the "prosaic" into art: through the use of irrealistic conceits, through "radical unprosaicizing of the prose," and through "radical manipulation of narrative viewpoint or dramatic form or content."

F27 Shenker, Israel. "Whither the Short Story (Or Is It Wither)?" The New York Times, 21 Nov. 1970, p. 33.

Barth speaks of his conversion from novel writing to short story writing.

G. BIOGRAPHICAL COMMENTARY ON JOHN BARTH

UNSIGNED CONTRIBUTIONS

G1 "About John Barth." In The Sounder Few: Essays from the Hollins Critic. Ed. R. H. W. Dillard, George Garrett, and John Rees Moore. Athens: Univ. of Georgia Press, 1971. Pp. 209-10.

Several-paragraph biographical sketch.

G2 "Author John Barth Leaving UB Staff." Buffalo Courier-Express, 25 Jan. 1973, p. 30.

Briefly sketches Barth's literary and teaching accomplishments and announces his decision to join the faculty at Johns Hopkins.

G3 "Author Talks to Self in 'Oral Literature.'" Buffalo Courier-Express, 29 Nov. 1967, p. 1.

Report of a reading at SUNY-Buffalo's Norton Union in which Barth presented "Autobiography," "Echo," and "Title."

G4 "Authors Barth, Fiedler Appointed To UB Endowed Chairs in English." Buffalo Evening News, 12 Oct. 1972, p. 41.

Gives a brief biography of Barth and notes that he has been awarded the Edward H. Butler Professorship of English Literature at SUNY-Buffalo.

G5 "Backstage with Esquire." Esquire, 50 (July 1958), 16.

A few paragraphs describing Barth's Maryland trilogy and a brief statement by Barth about "intellectuality" in the modern American novel.

G6 "Backstage with Esquire." Esquire, 59 (Feb. 1963), 52.

A brief description of each of Barth's first three novels and his work-in-progress.

G7 "Backstage with Esquire." Esquire, 72 (Sept. 1969), 60.

Identifies Barth as the author of ER and LF as well as "two underground best sellers," SWF and GGB, and indicates that eminent designer Rudolph de Harak did the graphic work for Barth's narrative "Help."

G8 "Backstage with Esquire." Esquire, 77 (June 1972), 12,

-71-

14, 16. [p. 16]
Praise for "Dunyazadiad" and a brief literary history of Barth.

G9 "Barth Authors 'End of Road.'" State College and Bellefonte, Pa., Centre Daily Times, 8 July 1958, p. 5.
Announces the pending publication of ER.

G10 A Barth Chronology, 1930-68. In American Literature. Ed. Richard Poirier and William L. Vance. Boston: Little, Brown and Company, 1970. II, 1111.

G11 "Barth, John." In Who's Who in the East. X (Chicago: Marquis, 1965), 66.

G12 "Barth, John 1930—." In Contemporary Authors: The International Bio-Bibliographical Guide to Current Authors and Their Works. Ed. James M. Ethridge. I (Detroit: Gale Research Co., 1962), 24.

Gives some basic biographical facts about Barth, a sketchy primary bibliography, and a few excerpts from one of Barth's letters.

G13 "Barth, John (Simmons)." Current Biography, 30 (May 1969), 3-6. Rpt. in Current Biography Yearbook 1969 (New York: H. W. Wilson, 1970), pp. 30-33.

The most thorough biographical treatment of Barth, save that written by Morrell (see G96). The biography is interlaced with numerous remarks excerpted from interviews, reviews, and critiques.

G14 "Barth, John Simmons." In Who's Who in America. XXXIV (Chicago: Marquis, 1966), 123.

G15 "Barth, John Simmons." In Who's Who in America. XXXV (Chicago: Marquis, 1968), 152.

G16 "Barth, John Simmons." In Who's Who in America. XXXVI (Chicago: Marquis, 1970), 120.

G17 "Barth, John Simmons." In Who's Who in America. XXXVII (Chicago: Marquis, 1972), 170.

G18 "Barth, John Simmons." In Who's Who in America. XXXVIII (Chicago: Marquis, 1974), 172.

G19 "Barth, John Simmons." In Who's Who in the East. XI (Chicago: Marquis, 1967), 75.

G20 "Barth, John (Simmons)." In World Authors, 1950-1970. Ed John Wakeman. New York: H. W. Wilson, 1975. Pp. 117-1

Biographical paragraphs frame brief examinations of Barth's work from FO to Chimera—provides a good overview.

G21 "Barth, John (Simmons) 1930—." In Contemporary Authors: A Bio-Bibliographical Guide to Current Authors and Their Works. Rev. ed. Ed. James M. Ethridge and Barbara Kopala. I (Detroit: Gale Research Co., 1967), 54. Rpt. in 200 Contemporary Authors: Bio-Bibliographies of Selected Leading Writers of Today with Critical and Personal Sidelights, ed. Barbara Harte and Carolyn Riley (Detroit: Gale Research Co., 1969), pp. 31-32.

Gives some basic biographical facts about Barth, excerpts from several of his reviewers and critics, excerpts from interviews, and sketchy primary and secondary bibliographies.

G22 "Barth Resigning Aug. 31 From UB English Dept." Buffalo Evening News, 25 Jan. 1973, p. 43.

Announces Barth's decision to join the faculty at Johns Hopkins in Sept. 1973 and provides a brief biographical sketch.

G23 "Barth, Rodgers Nominated for Book Award." State College and Bellefonte, Pa., Centre Daily Times, 11 Feb. 1969, p. 10.

Announcement of Barth's nomination for the 1969 National Book Award for fiction for LF.

G24 "Barth Taking Leave To Teach at Boston." Buffalo Evening News, 3 Feb. 1972, p. 35.

Announces that Barth will take a leave of absence from SUNY-Buffalo in order to teach for a year at Boston University beginning in the fall of 1972.

G25 "Barth To Spend Terms in Spain." State College and Bellefonte, Pa., Centre Daily Times, 3 Oct. 1962, p. 23.

Announcement of Barth's sabbatical in Spain during the 1962-63 academic year.

G26 "Barth Wins National Book Award." Buffalo Evening News, 11 Apr. 1973, p. 21.

Barth named co-winner of the 1973 National Book Award for fiction for his book Chimera.

G27 "Barth's Work Goes to Library of Congress." Buffalo Evening News, 15 May 1969, p. 1.

Notes that the Library of Congress received the first installment of John Barth's papers (see G56 for a description of the deposit).

G28   The Best American Short Stories 1964 and the Yearbook of the American Short Story. Ed. Martha Foley and David Burnett. Cambridge, Mass.: The Riverside Press, 1964. [p. 351]

"Water-Message" is cited as one of the "distinctive" short stories published in an American magazine in 1963

G29   The Best American Short Stories 1967 & the Yearbook of th American Short Story. Ed. Martha Foley and David Burnett. Boston: Houghton Mifflin, 1967. [p. 347]

"Night-Sea Journey" is cited as one of the "distinctive short stories published in an American magazine in 1966

G30   The Best American Short Stories 1968 & the Yearbook of th American Short Story. Ed. Martha Foley and David Burnett. Boston: Houghton Mifflin, 1968. [p. 357]

"Lost in the Funhouse" is cited as one of the "distinctive" short stories published in an American magazine in 1967.

G31   "Books About to Be." The New York Times Book Review, 3 Sept. 1972, pp. 4-5. [p. 5]

Announces the pending publication of Chimera.

G32   "Brandeis Awards 10th Arts Prizes." The New York Times, 25 Apr. 1966, p. 13.

Tells that Barth received a citation from the Brandeis arts committee, although Eudora Welty won the University's 1966 award for literature.

G33   "Christine Barth Engaged." State College and Bellefonte, Pa., Centre Daily Times, 6 Sept. 1974, p. 9.

Announcement of the betrothal of Barth's daughter.

G34   "Events in the Offing." Library of Congress Information Bulletin, 26 (1967), 253-54.

Gives a brief biographical sketch of Barth and announce that he will read selections from his works in the Coolidge Auditorium of the Library of Congress on 1 May 1967.

G35   "Existentialist Comedian." Time, 89 (17 Mar. 1967), 109.

Barth's biography is sketched; his four novels are summarized; and several of his comments are recorded.

G36   "Foss to Participate in UB Project." Buffalo Courier-Express, 17 Apr. 1970, p. 22.

Barth to read from "Perseid" on 11 May 1970 in the Mary Seaton Room of Buffalo's Kleinhan's Music Hall in "An Evening of Words and Music," a benefit designed to rais

-74-

funds to pay the legal fees incurred by forty-five SUNY-
Buffalo faculty members arrested during a 15 Mar. 1970
sit-in on the SUNYAB campus.

G37 "Homebound John Barth." Buffalo Evening News, 26 Jan.
1973, p. 30.

Laments SUNY-Buffalo's loss of Barth to Johns Hopkins.

G38 John Barth. New York: The Poetry Center, 1967.

A broadside, presented at a 20 Nov. 1967 Barth reading
at New York's YM-YWHA, which contains several paragraphs
of biography.

G39 "John Barth." In Black and White: Stories of American
Life. Ed. Donald B. Gibson and Carol Anselment. New
York: Washington Square Press, 1971. P. 249.

One-paragraph biographical sketch.

G40 "John Barth." In The Esquire Reader. Ed. Arnold Gingrich, L. Rust Hills, and Gene Lichtenstein. New York:
Dial Press, 1960. P. 317.

Summarizes Barth's literary career through 1959.

G41 "John Barth." In "John Barth". State College, Pa.:
The Pennsylvania State University, 1968. P. 1. Rpt.
in "John Barth (Parkside, Wisc.: The University of
Wisconsin-Parkside, 1970), p. 1.

Three-paragraph biographical sketch included in a program for a Barth reading.

G42 "John Barth." In The Naked I: Fiction for the Seventies.
Ed. Frederick R. Karl and Leo Hamalian. Greenwich,
Conn.: Fawcett (Fawcett Premier Books), 1971. P. 122.

Three-sentence biographical sketch.

G43 "John Barth Among 11 Named to Arts and Letters Body." The
New York Times, 7 Feb. 1974, p. 45.

Tells of Barth's election to the National Institute of
Arts and Letters' honor society.

G44 "John Barth (b. 1930)." In Short Stories: Classic, Modern, Contemporary. Ed. Marcus Klein and Robert Pack.
Boston: Little, Brown and Company, 1967. P. 597.

Two-paragraph biographical sketch.

G45 "John Barth 1st Speaker on University Lecture Series."
State College and Bellefonte, Pa., Centre Daily Times,
23 Sept. 1968, p. 12.

Announces the program for the 1968-69 Pennsylvania State
University Lecture Series, in which Barth was the first

speaker.

G46 "John Barth Gets Award For Fiction." State College and Bellefonte, Pa., Centre Daily Times, 11 Apr. 1973, p. 24.

Announcement of Barth's 1973 National Book Award for fiction for Chimera.

G47 "John Barth: Goat-Boy's Father." Playboy, 14 (Mar. 1967), 142.

A sprinkling of quotes from interviews highlight this one-paragraph blurb, which appears in Playboy's "On the Scene" series of profiles of important personages.

G48 "John Barth (1930—)." In American Literature: The Makers and the Making. Ed. Cleanth Brooks, R. W. B. Lewis, and Robert Penn Warren. New York: St. Martin's Press, 1973. II, 2907.

Lists a few biographical facts and the dates of Barth's books.

G49 "John Barth [1930—]." In American Poetry and Prose. 5th ed. Ed. Norman Foerster, Norman S. Grabo, Russel B. Nye E. Fred Carlisle, and Robert Falk. Boston: Houghton Mifflin, 1970. Pp. 1553-54.

Five paragraphs which attempt to sketch Barth's teaching and writing careers as well as discuss his contemporaneity.

G50 "John Barth (1930—)." In The American Tradition in Literature. 4th ed. Ed. Sculley Bradley, Richard Croom Beatty, E. Hudson Long, and George Perkins. New York: Grosset & Dunlap, 1974. II, 1781.

Gives important dates in Barth's life, a brief description of his four novels and Chimera, and a rudimentary bibliography.

G51 "John Barth 1930—." In The Art of Fiction: A Handbook and Anthology. 2nd ed. Ed. R. F. Dietrich and Roger H. Sundell. New York: Holt, Rinehart and Winston, 1974. Pp. 508-09.

Brief biographical sketch, accompanied by an explanation of Barth's thematic concerns and a description of his fictional techniques.

G52 "John Barth 1930—." In Introduction to Fiction. Ed. Paul J. Dolan and Joseph T. Bennett. New York: John Wiley and Sons, 1974. P. 510.

A one-paragraph description of Barth's fictional aims.

G53 "John Barth: 'Poet in Prose.'" In The International Poetry

Forum. Pittsburgh: Carnegie Library, 1968. P. 14.

A five-sentence biographical sketch, which accompanies an announcement that Barth will give a reading at the Carnegie Lecture Hall on 24 Apr. 1969.

G54 "Kennan Announces 9 Literary Awards." The New York Times, 20 Apr. 1966, p. 43.

Reports that The National Institute of Arts and Letters awarded Barth a $2,500 grant.

G55 "Lecturing Novelist Acclaimed as One Of Decade's Best." State College and Bellefonte, Pa., Centre Daily Times, 25 Sept. 1968, p. 6.

A panageric which accompanies an announcement of a 28 Sept. 1968 Barth reading of "Menelaiad" at Penn State University.

G56 "Literary and Cultural History." The Quarterly Journal of the Library of Congress, 26 (1969), 243-49.

A catalogue of the first installment of Barth's papers given to the Library of Congress: at least two manuscript versions of each of the four novels; notecards for SWF; manuscripts of "Ambrose His Mark," "Water-Message," "Muse, Spare Me," and "The Literature of Exhaustion"; and several introductions written to precede the public appearances of Borges, Updike, Heller, and Barth himself.

G57 "Manuscript Division Acquisitions, 1968." The Quarterly Journal of the Library of Congress, 26 (1969), 256-69. [p. 262]

Tells that Barth gave thirty-five manuscript items to the Library of Congress in 1968.

G58 "Manuscript Division Acquisitions, 1970." The Quarterly Journal of the Library of Congress, 28 (1971), 307-25. [p. 317]

Tells that Barth donated ten manuscript items to the Library of Congress in 1970.

G59 "Mother Charges Son With Harrassment." Buffalo Courier-Express, 12 May 1970, p. 30.

An account of a domestic incident in which Barth's first wife, Anne, filed charges against the Barths' son John who, she alleged, shoved and pushed her, threw furniture at her, and threatened her.

G60 "New Barth Novel Wins Wide Critical Acclaim." State College and Bellefonte, Pa., Centre Daily Times, 9 Aug. 1966, p. 2.

A condensation of the early critical opinion on GGB.

G61 "Novelist John Barth To Join Johns Hopkins Faculty." The Johns Hopkins Gazette, 25 Jan. 1973, pp. 1-2. Rpt. in Johns Hopkins Journal, 7, No. 1 (1973), 2.

A recapitulation of Barth's literary career and a retrospective of his undergraduate days at Johns Hopkins.

G62 "Novelist To Give Opening Lecture." State College and Bellefonte, Pa., Centre Daily Times, 24 Sept. 1968, p. 5.

An announcement of Barth's 28 Sept. 1968 reading of "Menelaiad" at Penn State University.

G63 "Novelist to Present Work In Concert-Like Reading." Buffalo Evening News, 21 Feb. 1968, p. 31.

Barth scheduled to read "Menelaiad" at Buffalo's Albright-Knox Art Gallery on 9 Mar. 1968.

G64 "Of Making Many Books." Buffalo Evening News, 23 Sept. 1971, p. 44.

Barth is mentioned as being one of the most prolific authors on the SUNY-Buffalo faculty.

G65 "Old Office Mates Share 2nd Honor." State College and Bellefonte, Pa., Centre Daily Times, 31 Mar. 1973, p. 7.

Barth nominated for the 1973 National Book Award for fiction for Chimera.

G66 "Personal Matters." The Pennsylvania State University Faculty Bulletin, 50 (19 Oct. 1962), 2.

Announcement of Barth's sabbatical in Spain during the 1962-63 academic year.

G67 "Philharmonic to Play Today, Tuesday." Buffalo Courier-Express Focus, 10 May 1970, p. 28.

Barth to read in "An Evening of Words and Music" (see G36).

G68 "Profs Given Book Award." The (Pennsylvania State University) Daily Collegian, 14 Feb. 1969, p. 8.

Observes that Barth has been nominated for the 1969 National Book Award for fiction for LF.

G69 "Time Gives Key Spot to Barth Novel." State College and Bellefonte, Pa., Centre Daily Times, 22 July 1958, p. 11.

Praises Barth and his then new novel ER, includes excerpts from I31.

G70 "UB Chairs Go to Barth and Fiedler." Buffalo Courier-Express, 13 Oct. 1972, p. 28.

Announces that Barth has been awarded the Edward H. Butler Professorship of English Literature at SUNY-Buffalo and provides some background on the award, which features research and travel monies as well as graduate assistants.

G71 "UB's Barth Is Cited For Fiction." Buffalo Courier-Express, 11 Apr. 1973, p. 1.

Barth named co-winner of the 1973 National Book Award for fiction for Chimera.

G72 "Will Take Part in Benefit Show." Buffalo Evening News, 6 May 1970, p. 83.

Barth to read in "An Evening of Words and Music" (see G36).

SIGNED CONTRIBUTIONS

G73 Baldwin, Neil. "Our Literati in Residence." Buffalo Courier-Express Sunday Magazine, 16 Sept. 1973, pp. 4-5, 7, 9. [pp. 7, 9]

Baldwin mentions Barth while discussing the finest writers ever to have lived in Buffalo.

G74 Bannon, Anthony. "Barth Makes Literature of Tapes." Buffalo Evening News, 29 Nov. 1967, p. 15.

Report of a reading at SUNY-Buffalo's Norton Union in which Barth presented "Autobiography," "Echo," and "Title."

G75 B[radbury], M[alcolm]. "Barth, John (1930—)." In The Penguin Companion to American Literature. Ed. Malcolm Bradbury, Eric Mottram, and Jean Franco. New York: McGraw-Hill, 1971. P. 26.

Describes Barth's first five books.

G76 Brady, Karen. "Buffalo Area Alive With Authors; Many Well Known, All Are Busy." Buffalo Evening News Magazine, 23 July 1966, p. B-1.

Brady hails Barth as Buffalo's "most important writing newcomer." Barth remarks that, since coming to Buffalo in the summer of 1965, he completed work on GGB and engaged in the revision of his earlier novels.

G77 ----------. "Master Chef Barth Spices Homer's Myth for a 7-Layer Treat." Buffalo Evening News, 11 Mar. 1968, p. 32.

Report of Barth's "Menelaiad" reading at Buffalo's
Albright-Knox Art Gallery.

G78   C[ollins], E[lizabeth] T[unstall]. "John Barth." The
Hollins Critic, 3 (Dec. 1966), 5.

Very brief biographical sketch.

G79   Federman, Raymond. "Contributors." In Surfiction:
Fiction Now . . . and Tomorrow. Ed. Raymond Federman.
Chicago: Swallow Press, 1975. Pp. 291-94. [p. 291]

Two-sentence biographical sketch.

G80   Golwyn, Judith. "New Creative Writers: 35 Novelists
Whose First Work Appears This Season." Library Journal, 81 (1 June 1956), 1496-1503, 1513. [pp. 1496-97]

Describes Barth's then forthcoming book FO; gives a
brief biographical sketch of Barth; and prints some
of a letter from Barth which discusses the rationale
for his Maryland novels, his marriage, and his Dorchester Tales.

G81   Gulassa, Cyril M. "Biographical Notes." In The Fact of
Fiction: Social Relevance in the Short Story. Ed.
Cyril M. Gulassa. San Francisco: Canfield Press,
1972. Pp. 390-95. [p. 390]

Three-sentence biographical sketch.

G82   Hart, James D. "Barth, John (1930—)." In The Oxford
Companion to American Literature. 4th ed. New York:
Oxford Univ. Press, 1965. P. 60.

Gives brief descriptive statements about each of
Barth's Maryland novels.

G83   Homan, Richard. "Barth Blasts 'Perversion of Authority'
in Cambridge." The Washington Post and Times Herald,
22 Aug. 1967, p. Cl.

Homan puts Barth's letter to the Cambridge papers
chastizing the city's police chief and fire department
for their mishandling of a fire during a 24 July 1967
racial disturbance (see C20) in context and quotes
liberally from the letter.

G84   Howard, Daniel F. "John Barth b. 1930." In The Modern
Tradition: An Anthology of Short Stories. 2nd ed. Ed
Daniel F. Howard. Boston: Little, Brown, 1972. P. 53

This brief introduction to Barth's fictional world is
sprinkled with some basic biographical data.

G85   Hughes, Douglas A. "John Barth (1930)." In Studies in
Short Fiction: Five Short Novels & Thirty Stories. 2r
ed. Ed. Douglas A. Hughes. New York: Holt, Rinehart

and Winston, 1974. P. 487.

Hughes recounts a few biographical details and contends that Barth is a writer of "ironic fables . . . interlaced with philosophical meaning."

G86 Kaplan, Charles. "John Barth (1930—)." In *Literature in America: The Modern Age*. Ed. Charles Kaplan. New York: The Free Press, 1971. P. 601.

Three-sentence biographical sketch.

G87 Kennedy, Mopsy Strange. "Roots of An Author." *The Washington Post Potomac*, 3 Sept. 1967, pp. 17-19.

Barth's father "Whitey," his mother, his brother Bill, his twin sister Jill, and his former high school English teacher Mrs. Wright discuss Barth as a person and as a writer.

G88 Knoll, Elizabeth. "Barth Helps Orient Audience." *Washington University Student Life*, 5 Sept. 1975, pp. 1, 3.

An account of a 4 Sept. 1975 lecture given by Barth at Washington University in St. Louis, in which he discussed *FO*, *ER*, *SWF*, *GGB*, and *Chimera*.

G89 Lask, Thomas. "Art Is Artifice in Barth Reading." *The New York Times*, 21 Nov. 1967, p. 52.

A generally favorable report of Barth's 20 Nov. 1967 performance of "Autobiography," "Echo," and "Title" at the 92nd Street YM-YWHA in New York.

G90 Litz, A. Walton. "John Barth (1930—)." In *Major American Short Stories*. Ed. A. Walton Litz. New York: Oxford Univ. Press, 1975. P. 798.

A scanty paragraph of background materials as well as a brief list of critical articles on Barth's work.

G91 Mason, Julian D. "Acquisition Notes." *Library of Congress Information Bulletin*, 28 (1969), 237.

A brief version of an announcement made a few months later in *The Quarterly Journal of the Library of Congress* regarding Barth's donation of his manuscripts (see G56).

G92 McKenzie, Barbara. "John Barth." In *The Process of Fiction: Contemporary Stories and Criticism*. 2nd ed. Ed. Barbara McKenzie. New York: Harcourt Brace Jovanovich, 1974. Pp. 559-60.

A four-paragraph biographical sketch which includes several excerpts from Barth's interviews.

G93 McMichael, George. "John Barth 1930—." In *Anthology of American Literature*. Ed. George McMichael. New

York: Macmillan, 1974. II, 1885-86.

Three-paragraph biographical sketch, most of which is devoted to summarizing the contents of Barth's works.

G94 Meyer, Dorothy C. "John S. Barth, English Teacher, Author Featured." State College and Bellefonte, Pa., Centre Daily Times, 16 Jan. 1963, p. 9.

A tribute to John Barth, then a local talent, laced with excerpts from G97.

G95 Miller, James E., Jr. "1930— John Barth." In The Literature of the United States. 3rd ed. Ed. Walter Blair Theodore Hornberger, Randall Stewart, and James E. Miller, Jr. Glenview, Ill.: Scott, Foresman, 1969. III, 643.

A three-paragraph survey of Barth's life and literary career.

G96 Morrell, David Bernard. "John Barth in Chiaroscuro, 1969. In "John Barth: An Introduction." Diss. The Pennsylvani State University, 1970. Pp. 177-222.

The fullest extant account of Barth's life and literary career.

G97 Murphy, Richard W. "In Print: John Barth." Horizon, 5, No. 3 (1963), 36-37.

Contains a description of Barth's Maryland trilogy as well as brief excerpts from the novels. Also included are remarks by Barth concerning his anti-realistic fictional impulses and the theme of innocence in his novels

G98 Nabokov, Vladimir. "J. Barth." In Anniversary Notes (A Supplement to Tri-Quarterly 17). Evanston: Northwestern Univ. Press, 1970. P. 13.

Nabokov thanks Barth for his birthday greetings (see C21) and adds that he, like Barth, appreciates Max Planck, but not Cervantes.

G99 Pace, Eric. "The National Book Award in Fiction: A Curious Case." The New York Times Book Review, 6 May 1973, pp. 16-17.

A blow-by-blow description of how the 1973 National Book Award for fiction came to be split between Barth (for Chimera) and John Williams.

G100 ----------. "2 Book Awards Split for First Time." The New York Times, 11 Apr. 1973, p. 38.

An account of how the 1973 National Book Award for fiction came to be split between Barth (for Chimera) and John Williams.

G101 Pickering, James H. "Barth." In Fiction 100: An Anthology of Short Stories. Ed. James H. Pickering. New York: Macmillan, 1974. Pp. 1028-29.

Five-sentence summary of Barth's literary and professional career.

G102 Putman, Thomas. "900 Hear Barth, Foss In 'Words and Music.'" Buffalo Courier-Express, 12 May 1970, p. 6.

A favorable report of Barth's "Perseid" reading in "An Evening of Words and Music" (see G36).

G103 Rahv, Philip. "Notes on Contributors." In Modern Occasions. Ed. Philip Rahv. New York: Farrar, Straus and Giroux, 1966. Pp. 367-69. [p. 367]

Two-sentence biographical blurb.

G104 Rogers, Thomas. "John Barth: A Profile." Book Week, 7 Aug. 1966, p. 6.

Rogers, a colleague of Barth's at Penn State, writes of "the strange mixture of knowledge and innocence in Barth" which he discovered upon meeting the author.

G105 Schorer, Mark. "John [Simmons] Barth (1930—)." In The Literature of America: Twentieth Century. Ed. Mark Schorer. New York: McGraw-Hill, 1970. Pp. 1029-30.

A full-page synopsis of Barth's life and four novels, plus some excerpts from his interviews.

G106 Shafer, Ronald G. "A Group of Scholars Gathers by Eggplant For . . . Yes. Well, Wow." The Wall Street Journal, 24 Jan. 1973, p. 1. Rpt. in State College and Bellefonte, Pa., Centre Daily Times, 27 Jan. 1973, p. 5.

An account of the goings-on of the Society for the Celebration of Barthomania.

G107 S[herman], W. D. "Barth, John (1930—)." In Webster's New World Companion to English and American Literature. Ed. Arthur Pollard and Ralph Willett. New York: World Publishing, 1973. Pp. 38-39.

Brief biographical sketch, augmented by a one-paragraph examination of FO, ER, SWF, and GGB.

G108 Simon, Jeff. "At Home When Writing Here." Buffalo Evening News Magazine, 8 Sept. 1973, p. B-1.

Picture of Barth, with a three-sentence caption explaining that he continues to spend his summers on Lake Chautaqua (near Buffalo) despite having moved from SUNY-Buffalo to Johns Hopkins.

G109   ----------. "A Barth Valedictory: 'Chimera' Readings."
        Buffalo Evening News, 28 Mar. 1972, p. 19.

        Tells of Barth's moving reading of "Dunyazadiad" at
        Buffalo's Albright-Knox Art Gallery.

G110   Stevick, Philip. "About the Authors." In Anti-Story: An
        Anthology of Experimental Fiction. Ed. Philip Stevick.
        New York: The Free Press, 1971. Pp. 315-19. [p. 315]

        Two-sentence biographical blurb.

G111   Wager, Willis. American Literature: A World View. New
        York: New York Univ. Press, 1968. [pp. 267-68]

        Brief descriptions of FO, ER, SWF, and GGB.

G112   Warren, Lucian C. "Novelist Barth Scolds Cambridge."
        Buffalo Courier-Express, 23 Aug. 1967, p. 7.

        Elaborates on the Washington Post account of Barth's
        letter to the Cambridge, Md., papers denouncing the
        city officials' mishandling of a fire during a racial
        disturbance (see G83).

H. CRITICAL COMMENTARY ON BARTH'S WORKS

<1959>

H1   Barnes, Hazel E. The Literature of Possibility: A Study in Humanistic Existentialism. Lincoln: Univ. of Nebraska Press, 1959. [p. 380]

Barnes sees ER as "a deliberate, careful satire of Sartre's thought, a reductio ad absurdum which is designed to show that if the theory [of humanistic existentialism] is put into practice, it is utterly nihilistic." Barnes finds Barth's attack "thought provoking," although it seems to her a "distorted application" of humanistic existentialism rather than a convincing refutation of the theory.

<1960>

H2   Fiedler, Leslie A. "Introduction: No! in Thunder." In No! in Thunder: Essays on Literature and Myth. Boston: Beacon Press, 1960. Pp. 1-18. [p. 17] Rpt. in The Collected Essays of Leslie Fiedler (New York: Stein and Day, 1971), I, 221-38. [p. 237]

Fiedler mentions Barth as a "strangely ignored" young novelist.

H3   ----------. Love and Death in the American Novel. New York: Criterion Books, 1960. [p. 471]

Fiedler alludes to the comic experimentation in FO.

<1962>

H4   Hassan, Ihab. "The Existential Novel." The Massachusetts Review, 3 (1962), 795-97. [p. 796]

Hassan refers to Jacob Horner of ER as one of the many anti-heroes in the post-World-War-II American novel. Such characters try to create "meaning out of meaninglessness, being out of nothingness, dignity out of humiliation," and all are faced with the problem of establishing their own identities.

-85-

H5 Young, Philip. "The Mother of Us All: Pocahontas Reconsidered." The Kenyon Review, 24 (1962), 391-415. [p. 406]

Young praises Barth's handling of the Pocahontas myth in SWF.

<1963>

H6 Hassan, Ihab. "Since 1945." In Literary History of the United States: History. 3rd ed., rev. Ed. Robert E. Spiller, et al. New York: Macmillan, 1963. Pp. 1412-41. [p. 1420n]

Hassan, in expounding on the scope of the post-War American novel, mentions ER as one of several "ironic comedies of a . . . vaguely existential character."

H7 Rovit, Earl. "The Novel as Parody: John Barth." Critique, 6, No. 2 (1963), 77-85.

Rovit discusses the digressive form of FO by way of introducing his main topic, the form of SWF. SWF, like Durrell's Alexandria Quartet, Nabokov's Pale Fire, and Borges' Labyrinths, is a "parody-novel." Barth's emphasis in SWF is control; the book exhibits a sort of jigsaw-puzzle construction which leads it, in the long run, to become little more than "a bewildering plaything." Unlike earlier users of parody (Cervantes, Defoe, Fielding, Flaubert, Twain, Joyce, and Mann), for whom parody is a device, contemporary parodists have allowed parody to become an end in itself and, in so doing, have headed themselves down a literary cul de sac. The history of Colonial Maryland and the literary conventions of the eighteenth-century novel (picaresque form and the themes of uncertain parentage, incest, the blurring of appearance and reality, disguise, and coincidence) are the vehicles through which Barth carries out his parody. Unfortunately, Rovit concludes, the book is divorced from human experience; it seems to be a failed attempt at satire, although the protean character of Henry Burlingame and the novel's "sexual athletics" have some limited satiric successfulness.

H8 Schickel, Richard. "The Floating Opera." Critique, 6, No. 2 (1963), 53-67.

Most of Schickel's essay is devoted to summarizing the plot of what was, at the time of this article's publication, an all-but-unknown novel. Shickel does, however, discuss the symbolic aspect of Todd Andrews' character, Barth's existentialism, his manipulation of language in FO, and the novel's flawed ending.

H9 Smith, Herbert F. "Barth's Endless Road." *Critique*, 6, No. 2 (1963), 68-76.

After examining the way in which Barth, in ER, challenges our fundamental concepts of existence, Smith sketches the similarities between Todd Andrews of FO and ER's Jacob Horner, discusses the ways in which ER parodies the love-triangle novel, and explains how Barth establishes conflicting ethical positions in ER through the use of allegorical tableaux. ER dramatizes Jacob Horner's "'road' from paralysis to responsibility," and much of the novel involves a "satiric criticism of the limited goals of existentialism."

H10 Trachtenberg, Alan. "Barth and Hawkes: Two Fabulists." *Critique*, 6, No. 2 (1963), 4-18.

Barth, according to Trachtenberg, is not a realist but a fabulist: he is more concerned with man's mind than with society. At the heart of Barth's fiction resides the problem of existence and identity. Each of the protagonists of Barth's Maryland trilogy experiences cosmopsis (cosmic paralysis) when confronted with the randomness of existence. This is due to the fact that all are sensitive, innocent, and somewhat passive. FO introduces the theme of cosmopsis; ER "sharpens and clarifies it"; and SWF "develops its implications floridly." In ER and SWF, Barth counterpoints his paralyzed characters with "free" characters, the Doctor and Henry Burlingame: both are Barthian versions of the American Dream of freedom from responsibility and from the pains and perils of selfhood, who teach us "the limits of our own solemn pretensions to responsible behavior."

H11 West, Paul. *The Modern Novel*. London: Hutchinson & Co., 1963. [pp. 310-11, 314]

Citing FO, ER, and SWF as examples, West observes that Barth's work is typical of most post-World-War-II American fiction.

<1964>

†H12 Ciancio, Ralph Armando. "The Grotesque in Modern American Fiction: An Existential Theory." Diss. University of Pittsburg, 1964. [*DA*, 26:365-66]

Ciancio argues that the structure of modern grotesque is founded on the paradox that "man is at once Being Nothingness." Modern grotesque involves "a revolt against rationalism and the modern age insofar as the age is dominated by rationalism" and "a revolt against the absurd" (i.e., against the grotesque). Modern

H13 Fiedler, Leslie A. Waiting for the End. New York: Stein and Day, 1964. [pp. 131, 138, 146, 153-54, 164, 170]

Fiedler touches on the mythic aspect of SWF, the antiacademic thrust of ER, Barth's eccentric genius for fiction, and Barth's unwritten declaration of the death of the novel.

H14 ----------. "The War Against the Academy." Wisconsin Studies in Contemporary Literature, 5 (1964), 5-17. [pp. 5, 11] Rpt., in a slightly revised form, in Waiting for the End (New York: Stein and Day, 1964), pp. 138-54. [pp. 138, 146, 153-54]

Fiedler argues that, in ER, Barth camouflages the "naked horror" of the academic writer behind a screen of superficial humor.

H15 Knickbocker, Conrad. "Humor With a Mortal Sting." The New York Times Book Review, 27 Sept. 1964, pp. 3, 60-61. Rpt. in The World of Black Humor: An Introductory Anthology of Selections and Criticism, ed. with intros. by Douglas M. Davis (New York: E. P. Dutton, 1967), pp. 299-305.

Fictions such as SWF are, Knickerbocker asserts, characteristic of a new brand of humor, Black Humor. Barth and his fellow Black Humorists square off with the American Dream and demolish it while their audience laughs—hollowly. Knickerbocker feels that the Black Humorists have, by default, become the keepers of America's conscience.

<1965>

H16 Anon. "American Fiction: The Postwar Years, 1945-65." Book Week, 26 Sept. 1965, pp. 1-3, 5-7, 18, 20, 22, 24-25.

Barth is mentioned as one of the twenty most distinguished post-World-War-II American fiction writers, and SWF is ranked as the eighteenth best post-War novel. Katherine Anne Porter expresses her fondness for SWF; Albert Guerard suggests that Barth may become a "major" writer; and Theodore Solotaroff observes that reading Barth helps to keep one in touch with what it means to be a post-War American.

H17   Anon. "The Black Humorists." Time, 85 (12 Feb. 1965), 94-96.

Praises the "freewheeling" aspect of SWF.

H18   Crews, Frederick C. "They're Mannerists, Not Moralists." Book Week, 10 Jan. 1965, pp. 5, 27.

According to Crews, SWF typifies the "new" novel of the 1960's, a genre characterized by whimsy, artifice, and "an aloof and perfunctory handling of sex."

H19   Davis, Douglas M. "'The New Mood': An Obsession With the Absurd." The National Observer, 15 Feb. 1965, p. 22.

Davis attempts to characterize Black Humor and goes on to discuss the "pale affirmation" which keeps Barth, in FO and SWF, from plunging into utter nihilism.

H20   Fiedler, Leslie A. "The New Mutants." Partisan Review, 32 (1965), 505-25. [pp. 507-08] Rpt. in The Collected Essays of Leslie Fiedler (New York: Stein and Day, 1971), II, 379-400. [pp. 381-82]

Fiedler states that Barth is the sort of science-fiction writer young readers can respond to sympathetically.

H21   Friedman, Bruce Jay. "Foreword." In Black Humor. Ed. with an intro. by Bruce Jay Friedman. New York: Bantam Books, 1965. Pp. vii-xi. Rpt. in The Sense of the Sixties, ed. Edward Quinn and Paul J. Dolan (New York: The Free Press, 1968), pp. 435-39; a slightly altered version of this essay appears in Book Week, 18 July 1965, pp. 2, 7, under the title "Those Clowns of Conscience."

Friedman classifies Barth as a Black Humorist, a term which he defines sociologically. For Friedman, the essence of Black Humor lies in the writer's more-than-satirical protest against a world gone mad.

H22   Hawkes, John. "The Revolving Bookstand." The American Scholar, 34 (1965), 474, 476, 478, 480, 482, 484, 486, 488, 490, 492, 494, 496. [p. 482]

In recalling some of the best writing of the decade 1955-1965, Hawkes includes "the brilliant fictional discoveries . . . of John Barth."

H23   Kostelanetz, Richard. "The New American Fiction." In The New American Arts. Ed. Richard Kostelanetz. New York: Horizon Press, 1965. Pp. 194-236. [pp. 202-12, 214-36 passim] Part rpt. in Ramparts, 3, No. 5 (1965), 57-60, 62; *part rpt. in The Scotsman, 10 Apr. 1965; the Scotsman piece rpt. in On Contemporary Literature, expanded ed., ed. with an intro. by Richard Kostelanetz (New York: Avon [Discus Books], 1969), pp. 634-43

[pp. 635-40] and in a French translation by Josette
Hesse in Les Temps Modernes, 21 (1966), 1856-66 [pp.
1857-62].

Kostelanetz feels that FO is "not very interesting" and
that ER is uneven and disorganized, but he praises SWF
as "one of the greatest works of fiction of our time."
SWF, according to Kostelanetz, burlesques written history, ridicules a variety of literary conventions, and
argues that life is absurd. Moreover, it displays
Barth's verbal brilliance, evidences his superior,
sophisticated comedy, and demonstrates an awesome eru-
dition. Kostelanetz's essay also contains part of a
letter Barth wrote to Kostelanetz concerning GGB.

H24 ----------. "Notes on the American Short Story Today."
The Minnesota Review, 5 (1965), 214-21. [p. 219]
Rpt. in 12 from the Sixties, ed. with an intro. by
Richard Kostelanetz (New York: Dell [Laurel Books],
1967), pp. 9 - 21. [p. 17]

Kostelanetz observes that Barth, like Pynchon and Heller, is involved (presumably in SWF) in showing "in a
sprawling, diffuse narrative that history—both in its
single events and on the whole—is absurd."

H25 ----------. "The Point Is That Life Doesn't Have Any
Point." The New York Times Book Review, 6 June 1965,
pp. 3, 28, 30. Rpt. as "The American Absurd Novel
(1965)," in The World of Black Humor: An Introductory
Anthology of Selections and Criticism, ed. Douglas M.
Davis (New York: E. P. Dutton, 1967), pp. 306-13.

According to Kostelanetz, Barth, in SWF, is not satis-
fied with presenting certain of life's events as pre-
posterous, but, through his use of burlesque, he shows
life as a whole to be absurd.

H26 Lewis, R. W. B. Trials of the Word: Essays in American
Literature and the Humanistic Tradition. New Haven and
London: Yale Univ. Press, 1965. [pp. 63, 185, 220-26]

Lewis argues that there is a tradition of comic-apocalyptic fiction in American literature which begins with
Melville's The Confidence-Man and runs through Twain
and Nathanael West to post-Modernists such as Ellison,
Barth, and Pynchon. In SWF, as in The Confidence-Man,
there is depicted the pending self-extinction of a
world characterized by deceit and teeming with imposters
and masqueraders (especially the protean Henry Burlingame
III). ER is also in the comic-apocalyptic tradition,
though its tone is clearly more serious than that of SWF
Barth's second novel relates to SWF as West's Miss
Lonelyhearts does to The Day of the Locust.

H27 Rubin, Louis D., Jr. "Notes on the Literary Scene: Their

Own Language." Harper's Magazine, 230 (Apr. 1965), 173-75.

Rubin discusses the ways in which Barth's Maryland trilogy differs from the traditional modes of Southern fiction.

†H28   Shapiro, Stephen Alan. "The Ambivalent Animal: Man in the Contemporary British and American Novel." Diss. University of Washington, 1965. [DA 26: 2760-61]

H91 is a distillation of this dissertation.

H29   Widmer, Kingsley. The Literary Rebel. With a preface by Harry T. Moore. Carbondale and Edwardsville: Southern Illinois Univ. Press, 1965. [p. 235]

Widmer, thinking of ER and SWF, remarks: "Barth seems to be an abstruse diabolist counterfeiting as an allegorical moralist."

<1966>

H30   Aldrich, Terence O. "Dialectic and Demonstration in Black Humor: The Novels of John Barth and Terry Southern." Thesis, University of Iowa, 1966.

Aldrich argues that Black Humor arises from the incongruity involved in rational man's confrontation with a completely chaotic environment, whereas the protagonists in the works of most "traditional satirists" foster humor by attempting to carry out irrational or eccentric plans in a relatively crdered environment. And the Black Humorist, unlike the traditional satirist, does not believe in the possibility of social reform. The protagonists of Black Humor novels can only be saved "at the moment when they realize the futility of attempting to impose order on their respective environments." There are two veins of Black Humor: one which relies heavily on dialogue and introspection to produce comedy and a second which relies primarily on plot and action to depict the world's absurdity. Barth's fiction, as his first three novels attest, "moves forward on the impetus of his elaborate dialectic."

H31   Alter, Robert. "The Apocalyptic Temper." Commentary, 41 (June 1966), 61-66. Rpt. in After the Tradition: Essays on Modern Jewish Writing (New York: E. P. Dutton, 1969), pp. 46-60.

Alter argues that the comic-apocalyptic novel, a subgenre in which SWF belongs, is not as praiseworthy as R. W. B. Lewis (see H26) has suggested. Christianity was born out of the decadent, apocalyptic side of Judaism, and the apocalyptic authors, from Melville to Twain to West (himself a Jew) to Barth, are products of that tradition. What these writers do (at least when they write apocalyptically) is "to absolutize a lack of faith in man and history and project it into literature." To do so is to cop out.

H32   Beagle, Peter S. "John Barth: Long Reach, Near Miss." Holiday, 40 (Sept. 1966), 131-32, 134-35.

In this beautifully written appreciation of Barth, Beagle traces the theme of cosmopsis (cosmic paralysis) through the Maryland novels and praises, in particular, SWF. GGB, he feels, is "a brave failure" which, after a while, becomes boring because of flawed characters that are unable to transcend their symbolic dimensions.

H33   Binni, Francesco. "John Barth e il romanzo di società." Studi Americani, 12 (1966), 277-300.

Binni investigates the theme of "the negation of identity" and Barth's use of "role playing" in FO, ER, SWF, and GGB. Todd Andrews and Jacob Horner are unable to make authentic choices or even to react emotionally, whereas Ebenezer Cooke and Giles Goat-Boy possess some ability to feel and to assert themselves.

H34   Burgess, Anthony. "The Postwar American Novel: A View from the Periphery." The American Scholar, 35 (1966), 150, 152, 154, 156. [p. 152]

Burgess wants to know what Barth has been up to since the publication of SWF. The British feel that too many young American writers are one-book men.

H35   Davis, Douglas M. "And Up Pops the 'Pop Novel,' or Black Humor Without a Sting." The National Observer, 4 Apr. 1966, p. 19.

Davis endeavors to contrast the Black Humor novel with the Pop novel. It all boils down to mood, argues Davis: the Black Humorist laughs out of despair; the traditional satirist is somewhat more optimistic about man's ability to change; and the Pop novelist laughs out of indifference. The Pop novel superficially resembles the Black Humor novel, though it is essentially happy rather than gloomy. The works of Heller, Barth, Burroughs, and Donleavy exemplify the Black Humor genre, whereas David Markson's The Ballad of Dingus Magee is a Pop novel.

H36   Elliott, George P. "The Nothing Game." Book Week, 2 Oct. 1966, pp. 6, 19.

Elliott feels that, whereas SWF is "a perfection of parody for the sake of bawdy fun," GGB indulges in such

-92-

"total parody" that it ends up as an exhausted and exhausting exercise in "esthetic nihilism."

H37   Fiedler, Leslie A. Love and Death in the American Novel. Rev. ed. New York: Stein and Day, 1966. [pp. 80, 494]

Fiedler mentions SWF as a "debunking male travesty" of the Pocahontas myth and alludes to the comic experimentation in FO.

H38   Galloway, David D. The Absurd Hero in American Fiction: Updike, Styron, Bellow, Salinger. Austin and London: Univ. of Texas Press, 1966. [p. ix]

Galloway mentions Barth as a writer whose work promises "to usher in a vital new phase in American fiction."

H39   Garis, Robert. "What Happened to John Barth?" Commentary, 42 (Oct. 1966), 89-90, 92, 94-95.

Garis feels that SWF and GGB are tedious and self-indulgent. Barth, in these novels, fails to dramatize his philosophical concerns, whereas, in ER, he grapples successfully with basic moral and ethical issues.

H40   Hassan, Ihab. "The Dial and Recent American Fiction." The CEA Critic, 29, No. 1 (1966), 1, 3.

Hassan divides post-World-War-II fiction into five subgenres. ER and SWF are examples of what he calls the Ironic Novel. Nabokov's Lolita and Pale Fire also exemplify the type. All of these works involve a negative transcendence since they transcend satire, sophistication, and even parody.

H41   Kiely, Benedict. "Ripeness Was Not All: John Barth's Giles Goat-Boy." The Hollins Critic, 3 (Dec. 1966), 1-12. Rpt. in The Sounder Few: Essays from the Hollins Critic, ed. R. H. W. Dillard, George Garrett, and John Rees Moore (Athens: Univ. of Georgia Press, 1971), pp. 194-206.

Kiely's piece is a sort of poetic prose extravaganza-panegyric which briefly discusses FO and ER, focuses on SWF and GGB, and lauds Barth's fiction for its wealth of encyclopedic knowledge, prose lyricism, and exuberant sexuality. The essay tends too strongly toward plot summary to be of much use to the critic and is written too eccentrically to be of much use to the uninitiated, but it is fun to read—and this, Kiely tells us, is the essential virtue of Barth's fiction.

H42   Leighton, Wallace Ralph. "Black Humor: A Comic Vision of the World." Thesis, Kansas State Teachers College, 1966. [pp. 1, 9-10, 12, 23-24, 27-28, 56-62, 74, 79-87, 101]

Leighton discusses the parodic form of SWF and the

bitter comedy which informs Barth's portraits of Renni Morgan, Peggy Rankin, Jacob Horner, Joan Toast, and Anna and Ebenezer Cooke.

H43 Miller, Russell H. "The Sot-Weed Factor: A Contemporary Mock-Epic." Critique, 8, No. 2 (1966), 88-100.

Miller argues that SWF, the structure of which closely parallels that of the Odyssey, is clearly mock-epic in form and that, like Pope's "Rape of the Lock," it is "an essentially comic work which makes an essentially serious statement about man and society." What that serious statement is, Russell does not tell us, although he more than amply demonstrates Barth's mock-epicizing tendencies.

H44 Noland, Richard W. "John Barth and the Novel of Comic Nihilism." Wisconsin Studies in Contemporary Literature, 7 (1966), 239-57.

Noland examines Barth's Maryland trilogy and concludes that the novelist's "most interesting and important achievement to date is the embodiment of philosophical ideas in a form both tragic and comic." Although Barth's characters are thin (the novelist's chief flaw), the books do depict "each of the ways in which Western man has attempted to fill his life with value after the death of the old gods." Barth's ability or inability to express, in his future work, a personal belief that will provide moral meaning will determine his position in American letters: "Barth may use parody as a way of clearing his vision, but he can hardly res in it if he is to develop at all."

H45 Rubin, Louis D., Jr. "The Curious Death of the Novel; or, What to Do about Tired Literary Critics." The Kenyon Review, 28 (1966), 305-25. [pp. 305-06, 312-14, 322, 324-25] Rpt., in revised form, in The Curious Death of the Novel: Essays in American Literature (Bat Rouge: Louisiana State Univ. Press, 1967), pp. 3-23. [pp. 3-4, 9-11, 19-20, 22-23]

Rubin feels that novels such as those by Barth argue that the novel is not dead. Such books may be based o post-Modernist rather than Modernist aesthetics, but that does not make them any less worthwhile.

H46 Scholes, Robert. "Disciple of Scheherazade." The New York Times Book Review, 8 May 1966, pp. 5, 22.

Scholes labels Barth a "bawdy allegorist" and examines FO, ER, and SWF as philosophical novels. He concludes that the books give us thought, laughter, and movement at the expense of emotional depth.

H47 ----------. "'Mithridates, he died old': Black Humor an

-94-

Kurt Vonnegut, Jr." The Hollins Critic, 3 (Oct. 1966), 1-12. [pp. 1-6] Rpt. in The Sounder Few: Essays from the Hollins Critic, ed. R. H. W. Dillard, George Garrett, and John Rees Moore (Athens: Univ. of Georgia Press, 1971), pp. 172-85 [pp. 173-79]; also rpt., in revised form, in Ch. 3 of The Fabulators (New York: Oxford Univ. Press, 1967) [pp. 35-41].

Scholes traces the ancestry of Black Humor and suggests that contemporary examples of the genre are "more certain aesthetically and less certain ethically" than their predecessors (the works of Aristophanes, the Roman satirists, Cervantes, Rabelais, Swift, Voltaire, etc.). The Black Humorist, argues Scholes, "is not concerned with what to do about life but with how to take it."

H48   Stubbs, John C. "John Barth As a Novelist of Ideas: The Themes of Value and Identity." Critique, 8, No. 2 (1966), 101-16.

Stubbs argues that two themes are central to Barth's fiction: the individual's quest for value and his search for identity in a world of gratuitous events. These twin themes are introduced and developed in FO and ER, brought to fruition in SWF, and redefined in "Ambrose His Mark."

*H49   Young, Raymond C. "The Unanswered Man: A Comparative Study of John Barth, The End of the Road; Samuel Beckett, Molloy; Albert Camus, The Stranger; Hermann Hesse, Steppenwolf; and Eugene O'Neill, The Iceman Cometh." Thesis, Fairleigh Dickinson University, 1966.

<1967>

*H50   Anon. Blueprint for a Bestseller. London: Secker & Warburg, 1967.

Leaflets advertising GGB.

H51   Burgess, Anthony. The Novel Now: A Student's Guide to Contemporary Fiction. London: Faber & Faber, 1967. [p. 136]

Burgess praises SWF as a successful parody of the historical novel.

*H52   Clark, Mary L. "John Barth: From Anti-Hero to Hero." Thesis, Temple University, 1967.

H53   Davis, Douglas M., ed. with intros. The World of Black

-95-

Humor: An Introductory Anthology of Selections and Criticism. New York: E. P. Dutton, 1967. [pp. 14, 19, 22, 25, 249, 250, 297]

Davis makes a number of points: that cosmopsis (cosmic paralysis) is "the continuing subject" of all of Barth's novels, that Black Humorists such as Barth have managed to reaffirm the importance of story, that "Black Humor fares very badly at novel length" but "manifests itself best in random bursts of unhampered freedom," and that Todd Andrews is a "viewpoint character" who functions as the unifying agent of FO.

H54   Hicks, Walter Jackson. "John Barth's Early Novels." Thesis, The University of North Carolina at Chapel Hill, 1967.

After surveying Barth's literary productions from "Lilith and Lion" through GGB, Hicks examines FO, ER, and, to some lesser degree, SWF as a "nihilistic trilogy" in which Barth treats the problems of value, identity, and causality. Hicks clearly prefers the control which Barth exercises in his early novels to the extravagance of SWF and GGB.

H55   Kostelanetz, Richard. "'New American Fiction' Reconsidered." Tri-Quarterly, No. 8 (1967), pp. 279-86. [pp. 279, 281-83] Part rpt. in On Contemporary Literature, expanded ed., ed. with an intro. by Richard Kostelanetz (New York: Avon [Discus Books], 1969), pp. 643-52. [pp. 646-50]

Kostelanetz asserts that, although GGB is "surely among the dozen or so best novels of the passing sixties," it is inferior to Barth's masterpiece SWF. Barth's handling of point of view, style, and parody in Giles, as well as his talent for caricature, are praiseworthy, but the book is ultimately a failed parable which suffers from various excesses.

H56   Levine, Paul. "The Intemperate Zone: The Climate of Contemporary American Fiction." The Massachusetts Review, 8 (1967), 505-23. [pp. 514, 522-23]

Levine briefly refers to the ironic and fantastic elements in FO, SWF, and GGB.

H57   Miller, James E., Jr. Quests Surd and Absurd: Essays in American Literature. Chicago and London: Univ. of Chicago Press, 1967. [pp. 13, 24-25]

Miller briefly discusses FO, ER, SWF, and GGB as Black Humor novels. He is bothered by the fact that Barth's characters have a tendency to become philosophical abstractions manipulated by an ingenious author.

H58   Rice, Joseph Allen. "Flash of Darkness: Black Humor in

the Contemporary American Novel." Diss. Florida State
University, 1967. [pp. 1-3, 9, 13-14, 23, 25-26, 33,
35, 40, 44, 47, 52-54, 66-67, 74-75, 84, 95, 96-97, 101,
110-11, 114-15, 117, 123, 130-33, 137-38, 142, 150-51,
155-58, 167, 171] [DA, 28: 5067A-68A]

Rice begins his typological examination of American Black Humor fiction by characterizing the male and female protagonists. Ebenezer Cooke is a schlemihl or Loman type; Todd Andrews and Jacob Horner are Chameleons; and Giles Goat-Boy is "an authorial attitude, Loman, Chameleon and Bull Prodder . . . diffusely portrayed." Rice labels Joan Toast a Steel Wooler (the type of woman one runs from), Rennie Morgan a Pressed Flower (i.e., a tragic, nineteenth-century-variety romantic), and GGB's Anastasia a Two-Backed Beast, who is interested solely in raw sex. Harold Bray and Henry Burlingame III are described as Bloody Chiclitz-type antagonists (i.e., Satanic male opponents). And Rice goes on to describe Captain Osborn Jones of FO as a Rectal TV type (i.e., a functionless old person) and to discuss Ebenezer Cooke as an Eye Maker or artist. These characters act out their parts in a hostile environment: the American Dream has been shattered, traditional religious values no longer apply, men have become machines, a debilitating force seems to pervade the cosmos, and the day of apocalypse is not far off. Content then gives way to technique, as Rice examines the bawdiness and excrementality, the nonsense names and jargon, the parody, and the inventiveness which characterize Barth's four novels.

H59 Scholes, Robert. The Fabulators. New York: Oxford Univ. Press, 1967. [pp. 11-14, 35-41, 73-74, 80, 133-73]

Scholes takes note of the rococo plot and "excremental gaiety" of SWF, but his focus is GGB. He examines Barth's "sacred book" as a psychological, historical, sociological, philosophical, mythic, and literary allegory. Scholes' chapter on GGB has been cited by virtually every critic of that novel.

H60 Skerrett, Joseph Taylor, Jr. "Dostoievsky, Nathanael West, and Some Contemporary American Fiction." The University of Dayton Review, 4, No. 1 (1967), 23-36.

Skerrett argues that the contemporary Black Humor movement can be traced back to West and, to some lesser degree, Dostoievsky. The naïve Ebenezer Cooke falls prey to a "shoddy" world in SWF just as Lemuel Pitkin does in West's A Cool Million. West's Miss Lonelyhearts, Dostoievsky's Prince Myshkin (in The Idiot), and Barth's Jacob Horner are all tormented by their self-consciousness. The "new man" depicted by the Black Humorists, a character such as Todd Andrews of FO, is not concerned with the nobility of enduring in the face of the terrors of living as are the characters of Hemingway and Faulkner; he is simply caught up in an absurd existence.

H61　Solow, Martin, Allan J. Tobin, Howard Goldberg, Harry Lawton, and Robert Garis. "Barth Defended." Commentary, 43 (Jan. 1967), 16, 20.

Controversy evoked by Garis' article in the Oct. 1966 issue of Commentary (see H39). Solow catches Garis in some factual errors and praises SWF. Tobin feels that Garis' essay is pedantic. Goldberg praises the allegorical dimension of GGB and interprets the book as a statement of man's "spiritual and moral impotence." Lawton attacks the superficiality of Garis' reading of GGB and comments on the book's Christian and pagan substructures. Garis acknowledges that Solow has caught him "fairly and embarrassingly" but feels that his central contentions have not been refuted by these four critics.

H62　Tanner, Tony. "The Hoax That Joke Bilked." Partisan Review, 34 (1967), 102-09.

Tanner discusses the related concepts of freedom, masking, and metamorphosis in Barth's four novels and observes that one can always feel Barth's prominence in his books. FO and ER seem to Tanner to be considerably less successful than SWF, "a hugely entertaining demonstration of the independence, ingenuity and power of John Barth, his mind, his words, his tune." Although composed of many of the same ingredients as its predecessor, GGB is less forceful than SWF. In Giles, Barth has allowed his mental powers to take precedence over the story; as a result, the book is damaged rather than nourished.

H63　Thomas, Jesse James. "John Barth." In "The Image of Man in the Literary Heroes of Jean-Paul Sartre and Three American Novelists: Saul Bellow, John Barth, and Ken Kesey—A Theological Evaluation." Diss. Northwester University, 1967. Pp. 114-34. [DA, 28: 2333A]

According to Thomas, the problems of right action and responsibility in a world of chaos are central to Barth' fiction, since the protagonists in each of his novels struggle with these very issues. Ebenezer Cooke "eventually arrives at a genuine sense of involvement and responsibility," and the conclusion of GGB "seems to be moving in a soteriological direction." Todd Andrews' acceptance of responsibility, however, is far more limited, and Jacob Horner makes only one attempt to be responsible—it proves futile.

H64　Wells, Daniel Arthur. "John Barth and Attitudes toward Reality." Thesis, Duke University, 1967.

Wells examines the themes of value and identity in Barth's fiction and argues that the lessons learned by Barth's protagonists, from Todd Andrews to Giles Goat-Boy, become progressively more nihilistic. Barth moves from affirming relative values and human dependency "to a point where he has nothing at all to recommend about life except in a negative sense."

<1968>

H65   Aldridge, John. "Contemporary Fiction and Mass Culture." The New Orleans Review, 1 (1968), 4-9. [pp. 5-6, 9]

Aldridge, in discussing "the decay of the old social novel and the growth of the new novel of Dark Comedy and self-parody," mentions that Barth's SWF burlesques the traditional English picaresque novel form and that the book devastates some of America's most cherished myths. Aldridge hopes that the two streams of the novel will soon become confluent—that the Black Humorists will begin to aim their satirical weaponry at the New Bohemia, which "is devoloping into a conformist establishment and a veritable Babbittry of the educated classes."

H66   Bier, Jesse. The Rise and Fall of American Humor. New York: Holt, Rinehart and Winston, 1968. [pp. 339-40, 353-55, 358, 419n, 421]

Bier commends Barth for his comic energy, especially as it is evidenced in SWF, but he feels that SWF, like FO and GGB, suffers from Barth's "intellectual fancifulness" and his "resistless expression" as well as too high a degree of derivativeness.

H67   Boyers, Robert. "Attitudes toward Sex in American 'High Culture.'" The Annals of the American Academy of Political and Social Science, 376 (1968), 36-52. [pp. 47-49]

ER, according to Boyers, creates an image of man as a masturbator, unwilling to commit himself to anything beyond his own pleasure. Boyers sees Jacob Horner as the villain of the novel: "He is an inveterate son of a bitch, though he says some brilliantly witty things, and does manage even to suffer a bit."

H68   Byrd, Scott. "A Separate War: Camp and Black Humor in Recent American Fiction." Language Quarterly, 7, Nos. 1-2 (1968), 7-10. [p. 10]

Byrd mentions GGB while making the point that many of the works of the Black Humorists "contain heroes as well as deserving victims."

H69 Diser, Philip. "The Historical Ebenezer Cooke." Critiq 10, No. 3 (1968), 48-59.

Diser demonstrates that Barth thoroughly researched th historical Ebenezer Cooke before drawing his fictional ized portrait in SWF. Most of Diser's essay is devote to delineating those details which Barth borrowed and those which he knowingly altered.

H70 Elliott, George P. "Destroyers, Defilers, and Confusers of Men." The Atlantic Monthly, 222 (Dec. 1968), 74-80. [p. 78]

Elliott feels that contemporary fiction is headed down a blind alley. He classifies FO and ER as novels of destruction (i.e., nihilism), SWF as a novel of defile ment (i.e., everything from mimicry and parody to blasphemy and pornography), and GGB as a novel of confusion ("the last stretch on the literary way to Nothing").

H71 Feldman, Burton. "Anatomy of Black Humor." Dissent, 15 (1968), 158-60. Rpt. in The American Novel Since Wor War II, ed. with an intro. by Marcus Klein (Greenwich, Conn.: Fawcett, 1969), pp. 224-28.

Feldman faults the Black Humorists for being detached, when they wish—or so Feldman tells us—to be scathing social critics. "Black Humor would like to be pitiles comedy," but it settles for mimicing the violence of life.

H72 Fiedler, Leslie. The Return of the Vanishing American. New York: Stein and Day, 1968. [pp. 14, 15, 81, 150-5 159, 161, 174-75]

Fiedler discusses SWF as an example of the New Western a form which exploits the Pop Western "with irreverenc and pleasure." He argues that Barth's handling of the Pocahontas myth creates a "counter-parable" of our be-ginnings in Virginia and "a truer metaphor of our actu relations with the Indians than the pretty story so lc celebrated in sentimental verse."

H73 ----------. "Some Notes on the Jewish Novel in English or Looking Backward from Exile." The Running Man, 1, No. 2 (1968), 18-21. [p. 19] Rpt. in The Collected Essays of Leslie Fiedler (New York: Stein and Day, 1971), II, 156-63. [p. 159]

Fiedler notes that Barth is firmly entrenched in Ameri can life; it is impossible to imagine him exiling him-self to England as did Mordecai Richler.

H74 French, Michael R. "The American Novel in the Sixties."

-100-

The Midwest Quarterly, 9 (1968), 365-79. [pp. 368-69, 371-72]

French feels that Barth's early work (presumably FO and ER) belongs to the school of "psychological realism," and he labels Jacob Horner an "anti-hero."

H75 Graff, Gerald E. "Mythotherapy and Modern Poetics." Tri-Quarterly, No. 11 (1968), pp. 76-90.

Graff contends that the problem Jacob Horner faces in ER, endeavoring to escape from the debilitating confines of one's own self-consciousness, is the same predicament faced by many modern poetic theorists and poetry critics. I. A. Richards felt that one could avoid the dilemma through the creation of a mythos, a sentiment echoed by other New Critics. But the difficulty then becomes man's inability to attach objective meaning to the newly created myth in a relativistic world without writing poetry which is as arbitrary and trivial as the Mythotherapy proposed by Jacob Horner's Doctor.

H76 Greene, Michael Thomas. "Agony in the Essence Chamber: John Barth's First Three Novels." Thesis, Boston College, 1968.

"The purpose of this paper is to demonstrate the close relationships which exist between Barth's first three novels and the way in which these works attempt to make clear a particular body of ideas." Greene does so by examining the themes of value and identity which are "introduced and developed" in FO and ER and "developed more fully and complexly" in SWF. The protagonists in all three novels are "forced to accept the world as Hericlitean flux and to accept some measure of responsibility in it"; each makes a "'muted affirmation of the human condition.'" Greene concludes his study by attempting to demonstrate that Barth's formal experimentation is consistent with his moral relativism.

H77 Gross, Beverly. "The Anti-Novels of John Barth." Chicago Review, 20, No. 3 (1968), 95-109.

Gross examines FO, ER, SWF, and GGB and contends that the books, when read in sequence, show Barth's movement toward the repudiation of narrative art. Each novel begins affirmatively but ends paradoxically. Todd Andrews finds living and dying to be equally meaningful; Jacob Horner is paralyzed by his relativism; Ebenezer Cooke resolves none of his problems; and Giles Goat-Boy accepts a dialectic that has no synthesis. The novels ultimately wind up attacking themselves, the novel genre, the narrative impulse, and their author—yet somehow they were written. Gross finds the answer to this paradox in Barth's short story "Title": Barth may not be able to wholly affirm art, but he is committed to negating silence.

H78   Hill, Hamlin. "Black Humor: Its Cause and Cure." The
       Colorado Quarterly, 17 (1968), 57-64.

       Hill defines Black Humor as "a technique, not a form";
       it is "deadly serious in its intent" and tends to be
       emetic as well as mimetic; its irreverence is in op-
       position to commonly accepted societal mores, and it
       involves "the realistic comic exploitation of the in-
       congruities between overt social values (chiefly sex-
       ual) and its audience's overt impulses."

H79   Hills, Penney Chapin and L. Rust Hills, ed. with intros.
       How We Live: Contemporary Life in Contemporary Fiction.
       New York: Macmillan, 1968. [pp. 36-37, 981-82, 999-
       1000]

       The Hillses feel that Jacob Horner of ER is "the ad
       absurdum ultimate of the kind of directionless, adrift
       'hero' one finds increasingly in contemporary fiction,"
       and they discuss "Night-Sea Journey" as a blackly comic
       description of the ludicrous circumstances of the human
       condition. They then go on to list Barth with Bellow,
       Nabokov, Cheever, and Mailer as America's greatest
       living authors.

H80   Holder, Alan. "'What Marvelous Plot . . . Was Afoot?'
       History in Barth's The Sot-Weed Factor." American
       Quarterly, 20 (1968), 596-604.

       Holder laments the fact that, although SWF contains
       what is basically a comic, reductive view of Colonial
       American history, Barth refuses to commit himself to
       any one particular conception of historical truth. In-
       stead, he wants the freedom to embrace a variety of
       possibilities: that the orthodox conception of Colonial
       Maryland's heroes and villains is accurate, that the
       application of these terms should be reversed, and that
       the men never existed at all. It bothers Holder that
       Barth seems to stand outside history. As a result,
       history, in SWF, "exists primarily as a repository of
       details and plots that Barth wants to master and outdo."

H81   Kennard, Jean Elizabeth. "Towards a Novel of the Absurd:
       A Study of the Relationship Between the Concept of the
       Absurd as Defined in the Works of Sartre and Camus and
       Ideas and Form in the Fiction of John Barth, Samuel
       Beckett, Nigel Dennis, Joseph Heller, and James Purdy."
       Diss. University of California, Berkeley, 1968. [pp.
       102-30, 157-66]   [DA, 29: 3144A]

       This dissertation served as the basis for H148.

H82   Klein, Marcus. "'Menelaiad.'" In "John Barth". State
       College, Pa.: The Pennsylvania State University, 1968.
       P. 2. Rpt. in "John Barth (Parkside, Wisc.: The Uni-
       versity of Wisconsin-Parkside, 1970), p. 2.

A reprint of the liner notes prepared for Barth's 9 Mar. 1968 reading of "Menelaiad" in Buffalo (see G63 and G77). I have been unable to locate a copy of the program in which Klein's essay first appeared.

H83 Kostelanetz, Richard. "Dada and the Future of Fiction." Works, 1, No. 3 (1968), 58-66. [pp. 62-63, 64]

According to Kostelanetz, Barth, in SWF, conveys "the Dadaist theme that history itself is as ridiculous as most attempts to definitively understand it." In the short story "Title," Barth "adapts the Dadaist invention of poème simultané to invigorate the decadent art of a literary recital."

H84 Lee, L. L. "Some Uses of Finnegans Wake in John Barth's the Sot-Weed." James Joyce Quarterly, 5 (1968), 177-78.

Lee finds that there are some verbal echoes of Finnegan's Wake in SWF, and he concludes that, in a witty way, Barth is evoking the character of H. C. E[arwicker] in Henry Burlingame III and that of Earwicker's wife A[nna] L[ivia] P[lurabelle] in Anna Cooke. The borrowing also underscores certain Joycean themes used by Barth: innocence, original sin, and the multifariousness of the world.

H85 Leonard, Lionel R., Jr. "A Study of John Barth's Giles Goat-Boy as an 'Anatomy.'" Thesis, Chico State College, 1968.

According to Leonard, GGB is similar to and compares favorably with such anatomies as Burton's Anatomy of Melancholy, Rabelais' Gargantua and Pantagruel, Swift's Gulliver's Travels and A Tale of the Tub, and Sterne's Tristram Shandy. All employ intellectualized or stereotyped characters, philosophi gloriosi (or pedantic fools) who are ridiculed, a wealth of erudite material, and expansive and digressive structures which evidence the free play of their creators' intellectual fancy. Leonard feels that Giles, like the other aforementioned anatomies, is implicitly moralistic.

H86 Numasawa, Koji. "Black Humor: An American Aspect." Studies in English Literature (The English Literary Society of Japan), 44 (1968), 177-93. [pp. 177-80]

Barth's name is dropped several times as Numasawa attempts to classify the representative veins of Black Humor.

H87 Poirier, Richard. "The Politics of Self-Parody." Partisan Review, 35 (1968), 339-53. [pp. 342-48, 351] Rpt., in revised form, in The Performing Self: Compositions and Decompositions in the Languages of Contemporary Life

(New York: Oxford Univ. Press, 1971), pp. 27-44. [pp. 31-38, 42]

Poirier complains that, although Barth is "intellectually attuned" and "philosophically adroit," his work (GGB is foremost in Poirier's mind) evidences Barth's lack of faith in the essential worth of humanity. Barth is too concerned with systems and literary modes and has therefore created fiction which is less satisfactory and of less importance than that of Joyce, the master self-parodist.

H88   Raban, Jonathan. The Technique of Modern Fiction: Essays in Practical Criticism. London: Edward Arnold, 1968. [pp. 24, 70-78, 142]

Raban quotes at length from the first chapter of ER and then analyzes the novel's narrative technique. He finds it interesting that contingency keeps reasserting itself throughout Jacob Horner's narration: "All the time we are involved in the interview [between Jacob and the Doctor] in which logic and cause win outright, we are simultaneously confronted with a world of random sensations and irrelevant speculations." The pattern of contingency continues in various forms throughout the novel. Raban, later in his book, adds that "Barth's brilliant linguistic caricature [in SWF] conjures up a world and form so remote from us that it casts an ironic light on the contemporary issues which lie, thinly disguised, just below the surface of the narrative." Barth, in SWF, links together the eighteenth-century bourgeois sensibility and the twentieth-century existentialist sensibility to produce "an incendiary contrast between language on the one hand and topic on the other."

H89   Scholes, Robert. Elements of Fiction. New York: Oxford Univ. Press, 1968. [pp. 18-19]

Scholes refers to Barth as an allegorist, one who fills out the thinness of his characters with philosophical ideas and attitudes rather than with psychological details, as would a realist.

H90   Schulz, Max F. "Pop, Op, and Black Humor: The Aesthetics of Anxiety." College English, 30 (1968), 230-41. [p. 238]

Schulz mentions that Barth's concept of time in SWF and GGB is one of endless circularity.

H91   Shapiro, Stephen A. "The Ambivalent Animal: Man in the Contemporary British and American Novel." The Centennial Review, 12 (1968), 1-22. [pp. 3, 13]

Shapiro briefly comments on the dipolarity which informs ER and SWF.

-104-

†H92   Sherman, William David. "The Contemporary American Novel: Beyond Comic Anarchy." Diss. State University of New York at Buffalo, 1968. [DA, 29: 614A]

Sherman feels that there is a common theme, which he calls "comic anarchy," that runs through the American novel of the 1960's. The heroes of the comic-anarchic novel have been cut off from society and now devote their energies toward attaining satisfaction as isolated individuals. Ironically, Sherman contends that, although the books' comedy is undoubtedly their most appealing attribute, the novels are "most artistically satisfying at those moments in the work when the writer refuses to allow the reader to laugh and forces the hero to be stripped of his ironic poses."

H93   Smith, [Harry]. "Bestsellers Nobody Reads." The Smith, No. 10 (1968), pp. 182-84.

Of 229 respondents to a Smith questionnaire which was mailed to 1,000 persons, eighty-one had purchased a copy of GGB—more than any other book asked about except Styron's The Confessions of Nat Turner. But of these eighty-one, only seven had finished the novel; twenty-one others had read an average of twenty pages (seven of those found it "dull, incomprehensible, or incomprehensibly dull"); and fifty-three hadn't cracked the book's spine. None of the readers offered any positive comments about the novel.

H94   Spackey, James A. "Inhuman Comedy: The Nihilism of John Barth." Thesis, Kent State University, 1968.

Spackey studies the evolution of Barth's nihilism from its existential beginnings in FO and ER, books mainly concerned with the repudiation of conventional sexual morality, to its cosmic applications in SWF and GGB. Spackey sees Giles as a tragic book in which Barth "reveals a complete repudiation of any categorical imperative."

*H95   Sugiura, Ginsaku. "John Barth and The End of the Road: An Aspect of American Literature in the '50's." Amerika Bungaku, Autumn 1968, pp. 1-7.

H96   Sutton, Henry. "Notes toward the Destitution of Culture." The Kenyon Review, 30 (1968), 108-15. [p. 111]

The author of The Exhibitionist labels GGB a "paranoid simplification of the world," which attempts to provide some suggestion about the way in which reality functions.

H97   Tatham, Campbell. "The Novels of John Barth: An Introduction." Diss. The University of Wisconsin, Madison, 1968. [DA, 29: 4471A]

This is the first truly important study of Barth's fi‹
tion, and it remains one of the best. Tatham explain
the way in which Barth's formal concerns "force upon
the reader a new perspective," the way in which his
aesthetic principles "become principles of life."
Barth, Tatham contends, is primarily an aesthetician,
but he is not a performer of "mere circus tricks." H
books display what Barth himself has referred to as
"passionate virtuosity." Barth, through his experime
tation with narrative point of view in FO and ER, wit
history and the Double in SWF, and with all of these
plus "counter-allegory" in GGB, has created a fiction
for our time. His works express "the difficulty of
defining categorically any single aspect of existence
and meet "the aesthetic challenge of incorporating
fully that difficulty into a work of art." This com-
bination makes Barth's achievement a most impressive
one.

H98 Valencia, Willa Ferree. "The Picaresque Tradition in t‹
Contemporary English and American Novel." Diss. University of Illinois, 1968. [pp. 6, 128-31, 145-46,
162, 170-71, 173] [DA, 29: 618A]

According to Valencia, SWF "is not precisely a picaresque novel but a work of fiction in which many mode‹
are combined." The book's protagonist Ebenezer Cooke
is "a crusading Quixote," not a picaro. "The real
rogue of the story is Henry Burlingame, . . . a bona
fide scamp, even a parody of the picaro." Valencia
adds that neither the matter-of-fact prose nor the
loosely-knit plot of the traditional picaresque is
present in SWF.

†H99 Wilson, George Robert, Jr. "The Quest Romance in Contemporary Fiction." Diss. The Florida State University, 1968. [DAI, 30: 741A]

Wilson briefly discusses GGB in trying to make a distinction between the terms novel and romance as they
apply to contemporary fiction.

<1969>

H100 Abrahams, William. "Introduction: Prize Stories 1969."
In Prize Stories 1969: The O. Henry Awards. Ed. with
an intro. by William Abrahams. New York: Doubleday,
1969. Pp. ix-xiii.

Abrahams discusses the "artfulness" of Barth's "Lost
the Funhouse," the third prize winner in the 1969 O.
Henry Awards competition.

H101 "Barth, John (1930—)." In A Library of Literary Criticism: Modern American Literature. 4th ed., enlarged. Ed. Dorothy Nyren Curley, Maurice Kramer, and Elaine Fialka Kramer. New York: Frederick Ungar, 1969. I, 76-78.

Reprints critical excerpts from H48, I34, I57, I59, I88, I105, and I107.

H102 Bowker, Stanley A., Jr. "John Barth and the Literature of Exhaustion." Thesis, Boston College, 1969.

Bowker's avowed purpose is to discuss the philosophical implications of Barth's first five books. FO and ER, according to Bowker, deal with the problems of human identity and human values. The books' protagonists "isolate themselves from experience and from other people, and, ironically, end in a solipsism far more corrosive and destructive than any involvement in the human misery." SWF, he feels, affirms man's need to embrace life's contradictions and make "a flesh-and-blood commitment to the world" in order to escape the potentially crippling sense of futility which seems to accompany human endeavors. A similar affirmation is central to GGB, a book which Bowker examines primarily in terms of its technical innovations and its exploration of certain mythic themes, the most important being the journey to hell. Bowker, in discussing LF, focuses on Barth's "self-conscious attempts to investigate the process of fiction" and the reasons why this process is nearing its terminus, especially as both of these are evidenced in "the longest and most important story in the book, 'Menelaiad.'"

H103 Bradbury, John M. "Absurd Insurrection: The Barth-Percy Affair." The South Atlantic Quarterly, 68 (1969), 319-29.

Barth and Walker Percy are discussed as Southern novelists who have, for the most part, broken with their literary forebearers: gone are the sentimentally romantic and the properly tragic. Barth's and Percy's protagonists, regardless of chronological age, are all "quite modernly alienated young men." The protagonists of Barth's Maryland trilogy form the basis for Bradbury's remarks: he discusses their absence of family, their unstable environment, their alienation, cosmopsis (cosmic paralysis), their deplorable women, and their fondness for therapies and philosophical stances. The same themes run through Percy's The Moviegoer and The Last Gentleman. But whereas Percy's answer to man's cosmic dilemma "suggests the Catholic existentialism of . . . Gabriel Marcel," it is "patently futile, even impertinent," to seek answers in Barth's work.

H104 Chiasson, Sharon D. "A Survey of John Barth's Narrative Art, With Emphasis upon Giles Goat-Boy." Thesis, Lamar State College of Technology, 1969.

Chaisson begins by examining Barth's kinship with the school of Black Humor, describing Barth's aesthetic concerns, and analyzing the structure, narrative devices, and allegory of GGB. The allegorical implications of George Giles (Christ), Maurice Stoker (Satan), and Peter Greene ("the multi-faceted and often paradoxical American character") are Chiasson's primary concerns; twenty pages of the thesis are devoted solely to Greene. Chiasson then examines the protagonists of FO, ER, SWF, and GGB as existentialist heroes who carry on quests for universally applicable values only to learn, through the process of trial and error, that each individual has to find out for himself what will bring him (and him alone) happiness and contentment.

H105 Davis, Robert Murray. "The Shrinking Garden and New Exits: The Comic-Satiric Novel in the Twentieth Century." Kansas Quarterly, 1, No. 3 (1969), 5-16. [pp. 13-14, 15]

Davis cites ER as a novel which works on the reader's fears by presenting him with oppressive detail. We are lead to empathize with the cramped conditions experienced by Jacob Horner at the beginning of the novel and come to recognize his—and our—"Terminal" state by the book's end.

H106 Dippie, Brian W. "'His Visage Wild; His Form Exotick': Indian Themes and Cultural Guilt in John Barth's The Sot-Weed Factor." American Quarterly, 21 (1969), 113-21.

Dippie concludes that Barth, in SWF, is dealing with various mythic themes: the European dream of the New World Garden, the American dream of Indian-white reconciliation (as a purgation of guilt), and, most importantly, the American search for identity. Barth explodes each of these myths: Eben Cooke's optimistic "Marylandiad" becomes the disillusioned "Sot-Weed Factor"; the John Smith-Pocahontas legend is demolished in such a way that guilt is created rather than purged; and when one combines Eben's unsure self-knowledge with the figure of Henry Burlingame III, who utterly blurs the distinction between savage and civilized man, it becomes apparent that the American has no definable identity.

H107 Fiedler, Leslie A. "Cross the Border, Close the Gap." Playboy, 16 (Dec. 1969), 151, 230, 252-54, 256-58. [pp. 230, 254] Rpt. in The Collected Essays of Leslie Fiedler (New York: Stein and Day, 1971), II, 461-85. [pp. 462, 473, 474]

Fiedler points out the need for a post-Modernist criticism which can deal sensibly with writers such as Barth, and he makes mention of Barth's experiments in the Western (SWF) and science fiction (GGB) sub-genres.

H108 Hunt, Sandra Ann. "John Barth: The Novel of Fiction." Thesis, The University of North Carolina at Chapel Hill, 1969.

Hunt contends that Barth's four novels blend nihilism with eighteenth-century form in an exciting and original way. Through Barth's emphasis on persona in FO and ER and story in SWF and GGB, he has provided a way—perhaps the way—of revitalizing the modern novel. His books demonstrate a conscious return to the realm of fiction.

H109 Kalter, Marjorie Hope. "The Use of Metaphor in the Novels and Short Fiction of John Barth." Thesis, The University of Delaware, 1969.

The protagonists of FO and ER present us with extended metaphors which lend a basic structure to the books which they narrate. In GGB, the world-as-university metaphor assumes allegorical proportions, and in LF, tape is presented as "the ultimate metaphor for the fictional experience." But Barth's later works offer us technique at the expense of aesthetic achievement. Only in FO, ER, and an occasional story, such as "Night-Sea Journey," does Barth achieve aesthetic unity.

H110 Klein, Marcus. "Introduction." In The American Novel Since World War II. Ed. with an intro. by Marcus Klein. Greenwich, Conn.: Fawcett, 1969. Pp. 9-23. [pp. 9, 18, 20]

Klein, in discussing GGB, attempts to pin down some of the correspondences which underlie Barth's "elaborate allegory."

H111 Knapp, Edgar H. "Found in the Barthhouse: Novelist as Savior." Modern Fiction Studies, 14 (1969), 446-51. Rpt. in The Process of Fiction: Contemporary Stories and Criticism, 2nd ed., ed. Barbara McKenzie (New York: Harcourt Brace Jovanovich, 1974), pp. 582-89.

Knapp suggests that "Lost in the Funhouse" is a mixture of myth, masque, cinema, and symposium. Under myth, he discusses the story's Independence Day theme, Ambrose's initiation ceremonies, and Ambrose's "heroic suffering, death, and resurrection." The story's masque-like quality stems from the fact that "Lost in the Funhouse" dramatically works out the relationships between six characters: Ambrose and his father, Ambrose's brother Peter and the boys' Uncle Karl, and Ambrose's mother and Magda (respectively awareness and artistic intuition, the grosser passions, and the attractions of the flesh).

Scenic splicing, blocking to create a sort of symbolic ballet, and varied sensory appeals account for the story's cinematic dimension. Under symposium, Knapp examines Barth's complex handling of point of view, which results in "a running Platonic dialogue between the experimental Barth and the tradition out of which his work has grown."

H112 Lambert, Beverly Allen. "Rake, Saint, and Cynic: John Barth's Masks." Thesis, Georgia State University, 1969.

Lambert feels that, in each of Barth's four novels and in many of his Funhouse stories, the protagonists assume the masks of rake (in which emotion takes precedence over reason), saint (in which reason controls the emotions), and cynic (in which both reason and emotion are treated with suspicion). In seeking to derive meaning from the chaos of existence, Barth's protagonists come to synthesize their reason, emotions, and cynicism and, in so doing, achieve an intra- and interpersonal satisfaction, which is interconnected with their own as well as their author's artistic creativity.

H113 M[arsland], S[heila]. "Barth, John (1930—)." In Twentieth Century Writing: A Reader's Guide to Contemporary Literature. Ed. Kenneth Richardson. London and New York: Newnes Books, 1969. Pp. 49-50.

Marsland finds SWF to be "fragmented," but she praises ER for its "penetrating and disturbing insights into American college life" and GGB for its inventiveness and its depiction of one individual's search "for meaning in a technological, secularised society."

†H114 Olderman, Raymond Michael. "Beyond the Waste Land: A Study of the American Novel in the Nineteen-Sixties." Diss. Indiana University, 1969. [DAI, 30: 4998A]

This dissertation served as the basis for H230.

H115 Poirier, Richard. "A Literature of Law and Order." Partisan Review, 36 (1969), 189-204. [pp. 192, 194-95, 198-202] Rpt., in revised form, in The Performing Self: Compositions and Decompositions in the Languages of Contemporary Life (New York: Oxford Univ. Press, 1971), pp. 3-26. [pp. 10, 14, 18-23]

The value of "articulation," as it is described by Jacob Horner in ER and questioned by Barth in GGB and LF, is discussed by Poirier, who then goes on to argue that, in GGB, Barth's use of allegory and cant amounts to far more than a literary game. "He is really questioning the stability of what we take to be natural and obvious in the political, physical, and sexual organizations of life": he is implying that the human imagination "is impossibly entangled in its own creations, and that it would get even more entangled by any further effort on the part of interpretative critics to sort it all out." According to Poirier, Barth's "hip" aesthetics are really quite conservative and romantic, since they affirm the need for such basics as "nakedness and relinquishment." Barth would rather ensnare the reader in the web of his allegorical dream world than have us sort out the filaments only "to arrive at a clarified sense of life at once dreary and pointless."

H116 Rubin, Louis D., Jr. "Second Thoughts on the Old Gray Mare: The Continuing Relevance of Southern Literary Issues." In Southern Fiction Today: Renascence and Beyond. Ed. George Core. Athens: Univ. of Georgia Press, 1969. Pp. 33-50. [pp. 48-50]

Rubin views SWF as one piece of evidence which supports his contention that the Southern literary renascence, which began some decades ago, is far from finished. Barth's novel "give[s] promise of the continuation and even the intensification of what from Cabell to Faulkner to Wolfe to Welty has been an important comic inventiveness."

H117 Ryan, Marjorie. "Four Contemporary Satires and the Problem of Norms." Satire Newsletter, 6, No. 2 (1969), 40-46.

Ryan argues that FO is less satiric than Barth's other novels; "it is most definitely in [Northrop] Frye's fourth phase, where satire verges on irony, with both irony and comedy muted." Barth, by allowing us to see that Todd Andrews has an intellect which is divorced from his deepest impulses, mocks his protagonist. Barth satirizes Todd for his detached non-participation in life. Yet, ironically, Todd stays afloat. His account, unlike Tristram Shandy's, is perfectly coherent. Todd presents us with an ordered reality, whereas Tristram winds up immersing us in the chaos of experience.

H118 Schulz, Max F. Radical Sophistication: Studies in Contemporary Jewish-American Novelists. Athens: Ohio Univ. Press, 1969. [p. vii]

Schulz refers to Barth as a Black Humorist, one who holds an entropic view of the world and believes that things are without intrinsic value.

H119 Shore, William Alvin. "John Barth: A Contemporary Satirist." Thesis, Clemson University, 1969.

Shore attempts to demonstrate that, although SWF is allied to the Menippean satiric tradition by Barth's employment of traditional satiric themes and forms, it differs from traditional satire in its conclusions.

Whereas satirists such as Swift and Voltaire offer
philosophical bases for hope and reform, Barth offers
only a nihilistic resignation to man's folly and cor-
ruption.

H120 Sommavilla, Guido. "Il cinismo cosmico di John Barth."
Letture, 24 (1969), 98-110.

Sommavilla discusses Barth's cynicism and his use of
the love triangle in FO, ER, and SWF. Barth tempers
his nihilism somewhat in SWF, according to Sommavilla,
since the book ends on a quasi-Christian note.

H121 Sugiura, Ginsaku. "Imitations-of-Novels: John Barth no
Shosetsu." Eigo Seinen (The Rising Generation), 115
(1969), 612-13.

Sugiura uses Barth's "Literature of Exhaustion" essay
as a basis for a discussion of SWF and GGB; some attention is also given to FO, ER, and LF. Although Shimura
feels that SWF and GGB are somewhat extravagant, he
praises Barth for the way in which he turns exhaustion
against itself in those books by creating "imitations-
of-novels."

H122 Waldmeir, Joseph J. "Only an Occasional Rutabaga: American Fiction Since 1945." Modern Fiction Studies, 15
(1969), 467-81. [pp. 467-69, 473-75]

Waldmeir suggests that post-World-War-II American fiction can be broken down into five categories. Barth
is lumped together with Pynchon, Heller, Albee, Southern, and Purdy as well as Kerouac, Burroughs, and other
in the "beat-absurd-black humorist" school.

H123 Wasson, Richard. "Notes on a New Sensibility." Partisan
Review, 36 (1969), 460-77.

Wasson argues that post-Modernist literature involves
a rejection of the Modernist viewpoint, which insisted
that a writer had to possess the ability to order history by dramatizing it in mythic and metaphoric terms.
According to Wasson, Barth's second novel, through its
attacks on myth and Mythotherapy, marks "the end of th
road for myth and metaphor as the moderns understood
it." Barth does, however, hold out hope for a mytho-
plastic art which is "aware of its artificiality, its
incompleteness, its partial dumbness before reality."
Unlike the dramatic myths and unifying metaphors of
the Modernists, post-Modernist art affirms the separa-
tion of self and other, artifice and reality.

H124 Wylder, Delbert E. "Thomas Berger's Little Big Man as
Literature." Western American Literature, 3 (1969),
273-84. [pp. 274-75, 282, 284]

Wylder contends that Little Big Man is Barthian (i.e., absurd) in its approach, though it is dintinctly Western in terms of its attitude toward humanity and the human values it affirms.

H125   Zall, Paul, et al. "Modern Satire: A Mini-Symposium." Satire Newsletter, 6, No. 2 (1969), 1-18. [pp. 5-6]

Zall mentions SWF and GGB as two books which require an imaginative effort on the part of the reader if he is to understand the thrust of the novels.

<1970>

H126   Banks, Russell, Hayden Carruth, et al. "The Writer's Situation." New American Review, No. 9 (1970), pp. 61-99. [pp. 68, 80]

Banks feels that writers such as Barth and Fowles are "fooling away their talents in endless novelistic puzzles." Carruth notes that, although GGB is an allegory and, as such, is in a noble tradition of American literature, the tradition—as evidenced by Giles and other contemporary novels—is "a blood-line gone watery thin."

†H127   Bazzanella, Dominic John. "The Mad Narrator in Contemporary Fiction." Diss. Northwestern University, 1970. [DAI, 31: 5387A-88A]

Todd Andrews of FO and Jacob Horner of ER are representative of a group of narrators in the contemporary Anglo-American novel that Bazzanella terms "mad." Each is "acutely aware of existing in two worlds, an inner world of his own creation and a physical reality which surrounds him," and the need to reconcile these two worlds has become an obsession with them. The books, despite their surface bleakness, are implicitly optimistic insofar as they celebrate the possibility of human achievement—even if the full realization of that achievement may not be probable.

H128   Bergonzi, Bernard. The Situation of the Novel. Pittsburg: Univ. of Pittsburg Press, 1970. [pp. 20, 21, 33, 45, 71-72, 82, 83, 90-96, 97, 100, 101, 125, 127, 137, 170, 189, 197-98, 205, 210]

Bergonzi's comments are interesting, since he reacts to Barth from an avowedly English point of view. He endeavors to explain why Barth is less popular in England than he is in America: the English, Bergonzi feels, are loath to accept Barth's contention that the world of fiction provides a better version of reality than the world as it is traditionally conceived. Bergonzi admits

-113-

H129 Bryant, Jerry H. The Open Decision: The Contemporary American Novel and its Intellectual Background. New York: The Free Press, 1970. [pp. 9, 40, 100, 235, 239-40, 283-303]

According to Bryant, Barth is essentially a moralist, since his novels proceed from the tacit assumption that "it is in the nature of the human being to justify his life logically on premises of value." The fact that the world is paradoxical, of course, complicates the moral quests of Barth's protagonists: Todd Andrews of FO ends up as a relativist; Jacob Horner of ER learns that relative values—at least those formulated by Joe Morgan and the Doctor—cannot carry one through life, since they are detached from the true character of our existence; Ebenezer Cooke of SWF discovers that values do not reside "in the unthinking joy of innocence, but in the chastened, compassionate independence of human life"; and Giles Goat-Boy comes to understand, as does Eben Cooke, that only by embracing the human condition and living in the paradox of one's own subjectivity can one lay a solid foundation for moral action. It is through the "open decision" of man's heightened consciouness that value can be affirmed.

†H130 Clauss, Anne R. "Digression as Narrative Technique in Contemporary Fiction." Diss. The University of Wisconsin, 1970. [DAI, 31: 4758A-59A]

Clauss devotes a chapter of her dissertation to Barth's use of narrative digression in FO, ER, SWF, and GGB. She argues that digression allows the contemporary novelist to penetrate the recesses of time and space and to capture a hostile and fugative reality—thus allowing him to achieve unity and order in the midst of chaos.

H131 Dickstein, Morris. "City Life." The New York Times Book Review, 26 Apr. 1970, pp. 1, 38-43. [pp. 1, 38-39]

According to Dickstein, SWF exemplifies one major phase of rebellion in the fiction of the 1960's: the big, eclectic novel. LF exemplifies the other: short, multi layered fictions ("the Borgesian phase"). Dickstein feels that Barth, in LF, like Robert Coover in Pricksongs & Descants, becomes overwhelmed by "the writer's power to invent a scene, a character, a world, to choos which word and which sentence he will set down next." Donald Barthelme's City Life, on the other hand, is experimental yet avoids being either self-indulgent or imitative.

H132 Epstein, Leslie, Seymour Krim, et al. "The Writer's Situation: II." New American Review, No. 10 (1970), pp. 203-37. [pp. 204, 231]

Epstein says that SWF put him to sleep. Krim mentions Barth's warm critical reception.

H133 Fiedler, Leslie A. "The Dream of the New." In American Dreams, American Nightmares. Ed. David Madden, with a preface by Harry T. Moore. Carbondale and Edwardsville: Southern Illinois Univ. Press, 1970. Pp. 19-27. [pp. 23, 24, 26]

Fiedler mentions Barth's use of multi-media fiction and his penchant for parody and burlesque.

H134 Galloway, David D. The Absurd Hero in American Fiction: Updike, Styron, Bellow, Salinger. Rev. ed. Austin and London: Univ. of Texas Press, 1970. [pp. ix, xviii-xix]

Galloway feels that Barth is a promising novelist who is to be praised for his experimentation with both historical materials and form in SWF.

†H135 Gourevitch, Mary Turzillo. "The Writer as Double Agent: Essay on the Conspiratorial Mode in Contemporary Fiction." Diss. Case Western Reserve University, 1970. [DAI, 31: 3547A]

Gourevitch contends that the contemporary writer, caught between the necessity of accurately portraying a hostile cosmos and the desirability of explaining away that hostility in his fiction through imaginative lies, often becomes a sort of artistic double agent. In ER, for example, Barth discredits those existential ideas which, some feel, are capable of giving life meaning, but at the same time, he presents existentialism as a possible escape. As a result, the distinction between an unbearable reality and an impossible fantasy is blurred.

H136 Hall, James. "The New Pleasures of the Imagination." The Virginia Quarterly Review, 46 (1970), 596-612. [pp. 596-604]

Hall feels that the fantasy tradition in contemporary literature—Barth, Fowles, Hawkes, Pynchon, and Vonnegut being the leading practitioners—has provided some enjoyable fiction but that, due to its unreality, it fails to deal with the most loudly expressed interests of our culture. The fantasy writer no longer agonizes over existential choices as did the novelists of the 1950's; instead of attempting to deal with the problems of this world, even prophetically, the fantasist creates new worlds of his own imagining.

†H137 Harris, Charles B. "Contemporary American Novelists of

the Absurd." Diss. Southern Illinois University, 1970. [DAI, 31: 4162A]

This dissertation served as the basis for H175.

†H138   Harris, Eugenie. "The Novel as Critique of the Novel." Diss. New York University, 1970. [DAI, 32: 5228A-29A]

Harris devotes one chapter of her dissertation to arguing that LF is a novel, the locus of which can be found in the book's "three chapters of critical theory." Furthermore, she asserts that the quest for novelistic form in LF involves a progression from personal to mythological consciousness.

H139   Hassan, Ihab. "Frontiers of Criticism: Metaphors of Silence." The Virginia Quarterly Review, 46 (1970), 81-95. [p. 87] Rpt. in Paracriticisms: Seven Speculations of the Times (Urbana: Univ. of Illinois Press, 1975), pp. 17-28. [p. 22]

Hassan cites LF as an example of the literature of silence.

H140   Hauck, Richard B. "The Comic Christ and the Modern Reader." College English, 31 (1970), 498-506. [pp. 498, 504-06]

Hauck points out that Giles Goat-Boy is at once a true Christ, a figure of Christ, and an allegorical parody of literary Christ figures.

H141   Heilman, Robert B. "The Dream Metaphor: Some Ramifications." In American Dreams, American Nightmares. Ed. David Madden, with a preface by Harry T. Moore. Carbondale and Edwardsville: Southern Illinois Univ. Press, 1970. Pp. 1-18. [p. 7]

Heilman puts Ebenezer Cooke's dream of seventeenth-century America and his rude awakening into the broader context of literature written about visions of America.

H142   Henkle, Roger. "Symposium Highlights: Wrestling (American Style) with Proteus." Novel, 3 (1970), 197-207. [pp. 199, 201]

Barth's name comes up twice in this transcript of a panel discussion about contemporary fiction. Robert Scholes says that he understands Barth's handling of the Proteus myth in "Menelaiad" to mean that the writer must deal with his own inner reality, since extrinsic reality is not within his comprehension. And Kurt Vonnegut, Jr., suggests that he and Barth are the sort of writers who value and trust fictive "craziness" far more than fictive realism.

H143   Hicks, Granville. "Afterword." In Literary Horizons: A Quarter Century of American Fiction. With the assistance of Jack Alan Robbins. New York: New York Univ. Press, 1970. P. 272.

Hicks refers to GGB as a "philosophical allegory of the most ambitious sort" and mentions Barth's experimentation in LF.

†H144   Intrater, Roseline. "The Attrition of the Self in Some Contemporary Novels." Diss. Case Western Reserve University, 1970. [DAI, 31: 3550A-51A]

According to Intrater, Existentialism, Phenomenology, and Bergsonism provide the foundation for the four major concepts which comprise the nucleus of "the attrition of self" in contemporary fiction: Absurdity, Nothingness, Fragmentation, and Externality. Barth is one of three Anglo-American authors whose work is examined as evidencing literary self-attrition.

H145   Joseph, Gerhard. John Barth. Minneapolis: Univ. of Minnesota Press (Pamphlets on American Writers, No. 91), 1970.

A brief biography and a selected bibliography frame a discussion of Barth's first five books. Joseph begins by pointing out some of the things the books have in common: their debt to the Bildungsroman; Barth's fondness for philosophical debates, sexual encounters, doubles, and love triangles; the books' regional verisimilitude; their blend of realism and fable; and their protagonists' search for values. He then turns to the individual works. Joseph praises Barth for his handling of form in FO and ER but criticizes him for his limited psychological reach. SWF and GGB appeal more strongly to Joseph; he finds both books emotionally unsatisfactory but acknowledges that "a degree of emotional flatness is the price that the parodist agrees to pay for his knowledgeable artificiality and mannered thoroughness." Joseph concludes by defending LF against those reviewers who read the book as a literary dead end. Joseph's pamphlet might be useful to one unacquainted with Barth's work, but the Barth aficionado will find little here to capture his fancy.

Review:

   H146   Asselineau, Roger. Études Anglaises, 24 (July-Sept. 1971), 350.

H147   Katona, Anna. "Picaresque Satires in Modern American Fiction." Acta Litteraria Academiae Scientiarum Hungaricae, 12 (1970), 105-20. [pp. 116-20]

Katona argues that the black humor and irreverence in SWF help to make it picaresque, and she sees Barth as

a "conscience-ridden modern American intellectual who
tries to conceal by laughter the tormented American
conscience."

H148 Kennard, Jean E. "John Barth: Imitations of Imitations."
Mosaic, 3, No. 2 (1970), 116-31.

Kennard examines FO, ER, SWF, and GGB as existentialist
novels. There are a number of factual errors in the
essay that could have been rectified with a minimal
amount of research.

H149 Kilmer, Robert Christopher. "The Exemplary Narratives of
John Barth: The Floating Opera, The End of the Road,
The Sot-Weed Factor, and Giles Goat-Boy." Diss. The
University of Chicago, 1970.

Kilmer argues that Barth's novels are primarily didactic; all four concern the problem of finding happiness
and establishing one's identity in a world devoid of
absolute values. In FO and ER, Barth shows that excessive rationality and a lack of commitment lead to
the destruction of values and that, without values, man
can have no identity. SWF provides a response to
Barth's first two books: it dramatizes the way in which
man can overcome his rationality and weakness and
achieve some modicum of happiness—namely, by finding
meaning in human community and by accepting the responsibility not only for his values but also for the
consequences of acting on those values. In GGB, an
"intense and permanent sexual relationship" is shown
to be the key to happiness, but an individual can only
attain this state through personal experience and a
loss of innocence "combined with at least a temporary
willingness to relax the critical and deductive facul-
ties." Kilmer finds GGB to be a less satisfying novel
than SWF because the satiric element in GGB casts
doubt on the book's didactic element. Barth's fiction
evidences a "new" didacticism. Barth, aware of the
absurdity of attempting a rational attack on the evils
of rationalism, uses innovations in his narrative
structure, humor, and the device of the "sympathetic
character" to present his lessons to his reader's
heart. One of Kilmer's appendices contains the text
of a brief letter by Barth.

H150 Krupnick, Mark L. "Notes from the Funhouse." Modern
Occasions, 1 (1970), 108-12. [pp. 108-09]

Krupnick sees LF as exemplary of the fact that experimental fiction writing is a phase of retrenchment. He
views the title of the collection as a "perfectly
apt . . . metaphor for the situation of the artist
drowning in solipsism."

H151 Lehtonen, Reijo. Preface. In Matkan pää by John Barth. Helsinki: Werner Söderström, 1970. Pp. 5-13.

Lehtonen, in his preface to the Finnish edition of ER, observes that FO and ER are more realistic and less experimental than SWF, GGB, and LF, and he discusses the early books as parallel works which differ in tone more than they do in kind. FO is optimistic; ER is pessimistic. Todd Andrews can be likened to a Sisyphus who exercises; he is a thinker, a small Wittgenstein. Jacob Horner, on the other hand, is a Sisyphus who plods, a loyal striver, Wittgenstein's victim.

H152 Majdiak, Daniel. "Barth and the Representation of Life." Criticism, 12 (1970), 51-67.

Majdiak begins his examination of ER by focusing on Jacob Horner's search for identity, his role playing, his cosmopsis, and his—as well as Barth's—use of parody. Horner uses parody to undermine Joe Morgan's value system. Barth uses it to express the unreality of literature, but he only does so in order to render "a more credible picture of reality through a more viable fictional form." In the second part of the essay, Majdiak comments on Barth's use of names and settings and his handling of chronology, on Horner's method of summarizing lengthy arguments with the Morgans, and on Scriptotherapy.

H153 Morrell, David Bernard. "John Barth: An Introduction." Diss. The Pennsylvania State University, 1970. [DAI, 31: 4784A]

Morrell's dissertation is truly an "introduction" to Barth's fiction. Critical analyses of each of Barth's first five books are preceded by studies of each work's genesis and critical reception. To these sections are appended a forty-five-page biography (which includes analyses of "Lilith and the Lion," Shirt of Nessus, and some of Barth's Dorchester Tales) as well as a substantial bibliography.

H154 Powers, Dennis Allen. "The Themes of Identity through Value in John Barth's Novels." Thesis, University of Idaho, 1970.

Barth's first three novels, according to Powers, dramatize man's necessary acceptance of relative values as well as man's "attempt to interact sympathetically with other individuals." In FO, Barth depicts the establishment of a value system; Todd Andrews realizes that continuing to live is no more absurd than committing suicide, and he comes to accept a life of moral relativity. Both Jacob Horner and Eben Cooke are encouraged to assume a set of relative values in order to avoid the paralysis of indecision, but Jacob finds such role-playing to be impracticable and Eben's affirmation of an identity based on innocence turns out to be equally problematical. As Eben discovers, man is too complex, too emotional, and too sexually oriented to function under the guise of a simple, consistent mask. An annotated bibliography follows the text of Power's thesis.

H155 R[ambaud], M[aurice]. "Préface." In L'Enfant-Bouc ou Version revue et corrigée du Nouveau Syllabus by John Barth. 2 vols. Paris: Gallimard, 1970. I, i-xi.

Rambaud, in his preface to the French edition of GGB, contends that each of the characters in GGB, following George's lead, engages in an essentially moral and sometimes ruthless quest of himself. As quest, the novel takes place on two levels: it is an adventure story and a moral allegory. Additionally, the book satirizes America's educational and governmental systems as well as the foibles of the entire human race. Giles incorporates some of the traditional themes of American literature, a fact which Barth was obviously conscious of when writing the novel. Yet, even though the book is somewhat derivative, it evidences Barth's desire to explore and expand the limits of the novel form.

H156 Reich, Charles A. The Greening of America. New York: Random House, 1970. [p. 148]

Reich alludes to the shallow, reductive, mechanical marriage of Joe and Rennie Morgan in ER.

H157 Saporta, Marc. Histoire du roman américain. Paris: Seghers, 1970. [pp. 213, 282, 290]

Saporta notes that FO and GGB are highly intellectual novels which attracted considerable attention to Barth and adds that the latter is one of a proliferation of books concerned with university life. Saporta likens SWF to other post-World-War-II American novels such as Pynchon's V. and Heller's Catch-22 which are based on actual historical events and characters that have been transmogrified into fantastic and grotesque forms in order to project an apocalyptic vision. He feels that LF is an interesting work of experimental fiction.

H158 Scholes, Robert. "Metafiction." The Iowa Review, 1, No. 4 (1970), 100-15.

Scholes uses some of Barth's aesthetic comments in attempting to arrive at a definition of metafiction and examines LF in the context of his definition. He concludes that what energizes Barth's universe is the tension between reality and the world of the imagination.

H159 Scott, Nathan A., Jr. "The 'Conscience' of the New

Literature." In The Shaken Realist: Essays in Modern Literature in Honor of Frederick J. Hoffman. Ed. Melvin J. Friedman and John B. Vickery. Baton Rouge: Louisiana State Univ. Press, 1970. Pp. 251-83. [pp. 272-73]

Scott mentions FO and SWF as two significant post-Modernist novels which are representative of a new sensibility in the novel—one which is absurdist, ironic, larky, and joking and which produces fictions that are as formless as human existence.

H160 Solotaroff, Theodore. The Red Hot Vacuum and Other Pieces on the Writing of the Sixties. New York: Atheneum, 1970. [pp. 156-57]

Barth's works, writes Solotaroff, are "characteristic of a development in modern fiction that seems to grow directly out of the increasingly divided aspect of modern existence": the past is pitted against the present, the individual against society, and the natural against the actual.

H161 Tanner, Tony. "The American Novelist as Entropologist." London Magazine, NS 10 (Oct. 1970), 5-18. [pp. 5, 11-12] Rpt. as "Everything Running Down" in City of Words: American Fiction 1950-1970 (New York: Harper & Row, 1971), pp. 141-52. [pp. 141, 146-47]

Barth is one of more than half a dozen contemporary fiction writers to use the word entropy in his work, and he shares the entropologists' penchant for depicting people who are turning themselves into "isolated systems" or who are being turned into isolated systems by the world around them.

H162 Tatham, Campbell. "The Gilesian Monomyth: Some Remarks on The Structure of Giles Goat-Boy." Genre, 3 (1970), 364-75.

Tatham argues that Barth has relied more heavily on Joseph Campbell's monomyth in creating the character of Giles Goat-Boy than he has on Lord Raglan's concept of the hero. The way in which Barth parodies and otherwise manipulates certain aspects of the monomyth has a bearing on the novel's meaning. Giles' quest does not provide the reader with any enduring answers, but it does provide delight through Barth's "manipulation of aesthetic ultimacy."

H163 Tilton, John W. "Giles Goat-Boy: An Interpretation." Bucknell Review, 18, No. 1 (1970), 92-119.

GGB, according to Tilton, embodies "the full realization of a number of unrealized possibilities in The Sot-Weed Factor and, for that matter, in The Floating Opera and The End of the Road as well"; for Giles, unlike Barth's earlier novels, provides a consistent and comprehensive insight into the condition of man in an absurdly meaningless universe. This is accomplished through the book's precise fusion of form and content. Tilton supports these contentions by examining what he regards to be the novel's three basic mythological components: the Hero Myth, the Founder's Hill Myth, and the Boundary Dispute Myth. He feels that each myth explores a component of man's psyche and that the three, when taken together, dramatize Barth's central concern: "to illuminate mythopoetically the plight of man divided against himself and man divided against man."

H164 Weinberg, Helen. The New Novel in America: The Kafkan Mode in Contemporary Fiction. Ithaca and London: Cornell Univ. Press, 1970. [pp. 11-12]

Barth's ER, SWF, and GGB are mentioned by Weinberg as absurdist novels which, like Kafka's The Trial, use surreal means to present the victim-hero's situation.

<1971>

H165 Altieri, Charles. "Organic and Humanist Models in Some English Bildungsroman." The Journal of General Education, 23 (1971), 220-40. [pp. 220-21, 233-37]

Altieri examines Barth's complex treatment of the processes of self-development and the problems of acute self-consciousness in LF. He focuses on the protagonists of "Night-Sea Journey," "Water-Message," and "Anonymiad" and pays considerable attention to "Frame-Tale." According to Altieri, LF is itself an answer to the problem of subjectivity which plagues all of the book's characters, since the reader and writer together discover "that they are both readers of and participants in a broader text or all-inclusive fiction."

H166 Bean, John C. "John Barth and Festive Comedy: The Failure of Imagination in The Sot-Weed Factor." Xavier University Studies, 10, No. 1 (1971), 3-15.

Bean contends that the curative, regenerative spirit of festive comedy is missing from SWF, though the matter and style of festive comedy are very much present in Barth's novel. Barth's characters are not shielded from external contingencies and the demands of choice and responsibility as are those in Shakespeare's comedies, for example, and, as a result, Barth fails to recapture the essential comic spirit that pervades the writings of Shakespeare, Fielding, Cervantes, and the like—something which he claims to be attempting to do.

Barth's plot may be brilliant and surprising, concludes
Bean, but without the presence of a redemptive force,
SWF "is reduced to a series of gags which proceed one
after another until the energy finally wears out . . . .
The novel returns finally to the same dead end streets
that Barth longed to escape."

H167   Berthoff, Warner. Fictions and Events: Essays in Criticism and Literary History. New York: E. P. Dutton, 1971. [pp. 106-07, 110-11, 113-14]

Berthoff discusses how difficult it is for a serious
creative writer to find a readership in an American
society dominated by the news media. He conjectures
that this dilemma may explain why the contemporary
novelist has turned his back on social concerns in
favor of "the simple parody of the put-on" as Barth
has done in SWF and GGB.

H168   Bradbury, Malcolm. "The Art of Novel Writing, 1945-1970."
In Diverging Parallels: A Comparison of American and
European Thought and Action. Ed. A. N. J. denHollander.
Leiden: E. J. Brill, 1971. Pp. 108-27. [pp. 121, 124]

Bradbury argues that Barth is one of a number of contemporary American novelists whose work exhibits an
imaginative, freewheeling structure and a "practical"
absurdity which distinguishes the fictional productions of American contemporaries from those of most
of their European counterparts.

†H169   Bufithis, Philip Henry. "The Artist's Fight for Art: The
Psychiatrist Figure in the Fiction of Major Contemporary
American Novelists." Diss. University of Pennsylvania,
1971. [DAI, 32: 2083A]

Bufithis examines works by eight contemporary American
novelists, including Barth's ER, in which an artist is
pitted against his psychiatrist. Because psychiatrists
are more highly thought of by the American public than
are artists, the artists in these books tend, for a
time, to assume a psychiatric role. But they end up
as executants of the Pleasure Principle, leaving the
Reality Principle to their scientific counterparts and
doing what they best know how to do—building a house
of language which will reconstitute the world and create
value.

H170   Churchill, Thomas. "An Interview with Anthony Burgess."
Malahat Review, No. 17 (1971), pp. 103-27. [pp. 105, 125-26]

Burgess remarks that he gave Barth short shrift in his
book The Novel Now (see H51) and adds that SWF is "a
very important novel," though he finds GGB a "fake."

H171 Dolmetsch, Carl Richard. "'Camp' and Black Humor in Recent American Fiction." In Amerikanische Literatur im 20. Jahrhundert/ American Literature in the 20th Century. Ed. Alfred Weber and Deitmar Haack. Göttingen: Vandenhoeck & Ruprecht, 1971. Pp. 147-74. [pp. 151, 154, 160-63]

Dolmetsch argues that Barth, in SWF, presents history as "a Camp dream (or nightmare?) from which we all ought to try to awaken."

H172 Gindin, James. Harvest of a Quiet Eye: The Novel of Compassion. Bloomington: Indiana Univ. Press, 1971. [p. 340]

Gindin devotes a short paragraph to Barth's use of the fable in SWF and GGB.

H173 Glicksberg, Charles I. The Sexual Revolution in Modern American Literature. The Hague: Martinus Nijhoff, 1971. [pp. 186-87, 209-13, 229]

Glicksberg asserts that, in ER, the monogamic ideal of marriage is overtly flouted by Barth; Barth's book is "but one of a host of recent American novels which reflect a radical change of attitude" toward adultery.

H174 Grossman, Manuel L. Dada: Paradox, Mystification, and Ambiguity in European Literature. New York: Pegasus, 1971. [p. 157]

Barth, Beckett, and Burroughs are mentioned as contemporary writers "who have adopted the techniques, if not the spirit of the Dadas."

H175 Harris, Charles B. Contemporary American Novelists of the Absurd. New Haven: College & University Press, 1971. [pp. 7-10, 17-32 passim, 34, 100-20, 124, 129-30, 131, 134]

Harris' opening chapter "The Aesthetics of Absurdity," which contains an examination of the contemporary American novelists' use of parody and burlesque, provides an excellent introduction to the novel of the sixties. His chapter on Barth is primarily devoted to SWF and GGB, although Jacob Horner's remarks about putting experience into words are also discussed as is Todd Andrews' animalistic nature. Barth, through his use of burlesque, allows both SWF and GGB to "become paradigms of or metaphors for the absurdity he examines," and because the books imitate conventionally structured novels, "their reflection of absurdity becomes indirect"- the result being "inverted paradigms, ironic metaphors."

H176 Hassan, Ihab. The Dismemberment of Orpheus: Toward a Postmodern Literature. New York: Oxford Univ. Press, 1971.

[pp. 250-51]

Hassan discusses Barth's affinities with the literary tradition of silence, especially as they are evidenced in LF. Barth is, according to Hassan, the first American writer to make the dangers of silence explicit, yet when Barth, like West and Burroughs, gives himself over to parody and negation, he almost declares himself a "waiter upon transcendence."

H177 ----------. "Fiction and Future: An Extravaganza for Voice and Tape." In Liberations: New Essays on the Humanities in Revolution. Ed. Ihab Hassan. Middletown, Conn.: Wesleyan Univ. Press, 1971. Pp. 176-96. [pp. 180, 184, 190-91, 194]   Rpt. in Paracriticisms: Seven Speculations of the Times (Urbana: Univ. of Illinois Press, 1975), pp. 97-117. [pp. 101, 104-05, 111-12, 114]

Hassan points out that Barth, in SWF and GGB and especially in LF, turns the notion of the death of the novel "to enormous advantage."

H178 ----------. "POSTmodernISM: A Paracritical Bibliography." New Literary History, 3 (1971), 5-30. [pp. 12, 14, 15] Rpt. in Paracriticisms: Seven Speculations of the Times (Urbana: Univ. of Illinois Press, 1975), pp. 39-59. [pp. 44, 46]

Hassan mentions GGB, LF, and "The Literature of Exhaustion" in attempting to define post-Modernism.

H179 Hauck, Richard Boyd. A Cheerful Nihilism: Confidence and "The Absurd" in American Humorous Fiction. Bloomington and London: Indiana Univ. Press, 1971. [pp. xii, 8, 9, 13, 201-36, 244]

Hauck examines Barth's fictional aesthetics before launching into a discussion of LF, which he sees as "an exercise in the problems the absurd creator as storyteller faces." Most of his attention, in this section, is devoted to "Night-Sea Journey" and "Lost in the Funhouse." Hauck then turns to FO and ER. He focuses on the "artistic" temperament in Todd Andrews which allows Todd to accept the absurd and paradoxical nature of life; Hauck, when examining ER, discusses Jacob Horner's cosmopsis and his decision to "commit himself to the therapy of arbitrariness" rather than live a life of despair, Joe Morgan's "vicious" moral absolutism, and the Doctor's pragmatism. Analyses of SWF and GGB round out Hauck's chapter on Barth. Both books, Hauck feels, are comic epics, and both contain protagonists who gradually become "convinced that men operate in a vacuum, the Establisher of Ultimate Value being either nonexistent or unavailable."

H180 Heller, Joseph. "Work in Progress/ Joseph Heller: An Interview by James Shapiro." Intellectual Digest, 2, No. 4 (1971), 6, 8, 10-11. [p. 11]

Heller mentions that FO is one of the novels he recommends that students in his writing courses read.

H181 Karl, Frederick R. and Leo Hamalian. "Introduction." I: The Naked I: Fictions for the Seventies. Ed.-Frederic] R. Karl and Leo Hamalian. Greenwich, Conn.: Fawcett, 1971. Pp. 1-7. [pp. 4-5]

Karl and Hamalian assert that, because Barth's short fictions have a discontinuous design, they challenge us to pick up coherences and juxtapositions if we are to understand the works.

H182 Kattan, Naïm. "L'éclatement du mythe." La Quinzaine Littéraire, No. 126 (1971), p. 12.

Kattan contends that Barth not only plays with myths and archetypes but also questions them. His books dea: fantastically, rather than realistically, with the incoherent elements of American life; as a result, an artificial environment is created which is so strong that the reader's emotional and intellectual sensibilities are shattered.

H183 Kenedy, R. C. "John Barth." Art International, 15, No. 7 (1971), 26-30.

Kenedy feels that the major problem with Barth's protagonists is that they possess a changeless inner being, that they have no capacity for growth. Barth does not use artifice metaphorically; rather, he uses it to conceal the fact that he is unable to deal with metaphysical issues. GGB does not succeed as a fable because it creates intellectually imposed ambiguities rather than organically emotive ones. And SWF is a failed picaresque because Eben Cooke, unlike Don Quixote, is the victim of external forces: he has, after all, no inner being.

H184 Kiely, Benedict. "Afterword." In The Sounder Few: Essay from the Hollins Critic. Ed. R. H. W. Dillard, George Garrett, and John Rees Moore. Athens: Univ. of Georgia Press, 1971. Pp. 207-09.

Kiely praises LF. He especially likes "Menelaiad," a "gigantic joke" which nonetheless contains "universal truth." "Night-Sea Journey," he feels, reflects seriously on man's lot, whereas "Ambrose His Mark" and "Water-Message" are tales of "idyllic simplicity."

H185 Klein, James Robert. "The Tower and the Maze: A Study of the Novels of John Barth." Diss. University of Illinoi at Urbana-Champaign, 1971. [DAI, 32: 5794A]

All of Barth's protagonists (or, as Klein calls them, "satiric heroes") are "eirons and anti-novelists whose antagonists (often part of themselves) are alazons who cannot but see the world as a novel above which they tower in heroic perspective." The struggle between the orderly, self-assured, linear vision of the tower-affirming antagonists and the self-conscious, chaotic, funhouse vision of the maze-affirming protagonists creates a dramatic tension which is central to Barth's work. FO, ER, SWF, GGB, "Lost in the Funhouse," and "Night-Sea Journey" are examined in this context. Klein attempts to demonstrate that Barth's self-conscious, artificial narratives mirror realism's mimetic mirror in such a way that fiction is shown to be a funhouse rather than a tower.

H186 Lebowitz, Naomi. Humanism and the Absurd in the Modern Novel. Evanston: Northwestern Univ. Press, 1971. [pp. 123-24, 126]

Lebowitz feels that SWF attests to Barth's wit and intelligence, but she faults the novel for failing to translate "the epistemological problem into a moral one." An absurdist like Barth wishes to escape human limitations instead of using his talents in the service of contemporary life as does the humanist.

H187 Leff, Leonard J. "Utopia Reconstructed: Alienation in Vonnegut's God Bless You, Mr. Rosewater." Critique, 12, No. 3 (1971), 29-37. [pp. 29-30]

Leff feels that the theme of dislocation or alienation is one common to most contemporary American fiction. Malamud, in The Assistant, and Barth, in FO, focus on internal conflicts when dealing with alienation, whereas Vonnegut's focus is on external conflicts.

H188 Lindberg-Seyersted, Brita. "American Fiction Since 1950." Edda, 71 (1971), 193-203. [pp. 200-01]

Lindberg-Seyersted labels Barth a Black Humorist and praises SWF for its "marvelous story" and the philosophical and metaphysical discussions carried on by the characters in the book.

H189 Loughman, Celeste M. "Mirrors and Masks in the Novels of John Barth." Diss. University of Massachusetts, 1971. [DAI, 32: 1519A]

Loughman's discussions of FO, ER, SWF, and GGB center on Barth's use of masks, "human constructs which, while often inhibiting direct response to feeling, disguise and protect man from the uncertainty, mutability and disorder which lie beneath his masks," and mirrors, which "penetrate the masks by revealing hidden or submerged truths, at times salutary as well as destructive, about the characters and the nature of their lives." Actual mirrors, eyes, body language, and myth are among Barth's mirroring devices. Loughman concludes that FO and ER are interesting, if somewhat naïve, studies in existentialism and that GGB is inventive but lacking in vitality (she registers the same complaint about LF). SWF is clearly Barth's greatest work.

H190 Lutwack, Leonard. Heroic Fiction: The Epic Tradition and American Novels of the Twentieth Century. With a preface by Harry T. Moore. Carbondale and Edwardsville: Southern Illinois Univ. Press, 1971. [pp. 148-54]

Lutwack argues that, although SWF and GGB revel in irony and parody, "epic heroism does not altogether die in the novels; it is simply made to operate in the context of a world in which absurdity is felt with more than usual keenness and the chances of humanity prevailing are not thought to be very high."

†H191 May, John Richard. "Apocalypse in the American Novel." Diss. Emory University, 1971. [DAI, 32: 4009A-10A]

This dissertation served as the basis for H227.

H192 Mercer, Peter. "The Rhetoric of Giles Goat-Boy." Novel, 4 (1971), 147-58.

Mercer examines the structure, cadence, and diction of the prose in GGB and concludes that one can characterize the rhetoric under four headings: "academic" and "goatish" registers, "heroic" and "comic" styles. These four elements represent, respectively, the antithetical pairs rational/animal and heroic/bathetic. As a result, the four provide "a structural principle for the entire hierarchy of the book's moral allegory as well as the terms for the stages of the narrative allegory." Although Giles falls short of physical triumph within The Revised New Syllabus, he triumphs linguistically through his putative creation of the sacred book.

H193 Numasawa, Koji. "Rokuju-nendai Eibungaku to Black Humour." Eigo Seinen (The Rising Generation), 116 (1971), 823-24.

Barth is one of the thirteen contemporary Black Humor novelists examined by Numasawa, who focuses on the detached, ruthless comedy of these writers as well as their "negative cosmology."

H194 Paulson, Ronald. "What Is Modern in Eighteenth-Century Literature?" In The Modernity of the Eighteenth Century. Ed. Louis T. Milic. Cleveland and London: The Press of Case Western Reserve Univ. (Studies in Eighteenth-Century Culture, Vol. 1), 1971. Pp. 75-86.

Paulson argues that Barth, like many contemporary fiction writers and like many of the English novelists of the eighteenth century, uses self-consciousness in his novels to point out the difference between literature and Reality—but only to "return to something more expressive and immediate."

H195 Riche, James. "Pragmatism: A National Fascist Mode of Thought." Literature & Ideology, No. 9 (1971), pp. 37-44. [pp. 43-44]

Riche attacks Barth, Mailer, and Updike as "out and out fascists and enemies of the people." Citing ER as an example, Riche contends that the social relationships in Barth's works "are so blatantly centred around self-interest that even a gesture of generosity or the expression of a democratic sentiment is a surprise."

H196 Schmitz, Neil. "Donald Barthelme and the Emergence of Modern Satire." The Minnesota Review, NRP No. 1 (Fall 1971), pp. 109-18. [pp. 109-10, 111, 112-13, 114]

Schmitz argues that "Barthelme's innovative strategies—the summary abandonment of plot, his dismissal of traditional forms and ironic embrace of the 'world of society' in all its flux and waste—have managed to release him from the masochistic circularity of Lost in the Funhouse." Barth's fiction is cerebral, print-oriented, and academic, whereas Barthelme writes metafictions "that emanate from the world moving in time outside the province of literary tradition."

H197 Schulz, Max F. "The Unconfirmed Thesis: Kurt Vonnegut, Black Humor, and Contemporary Art." Critique, 12, No. 3 (1971), 5-28. [pp. 5-7, 14]

Schulz examines the plight of the novelist in a pluralistic world. He may attempt to write "omnibus parodies of knowledge," a strategy which, in practical terms, "is transparently impossible, as Barth's heroic efforts in this direction only too rapidly argue." A workable alternative is to hold a limited number of viewpoints in equipoise; Barth employs a radical version of this strategy in SWF, GGB, and some of the fictions in LF.

H198 Scott, Nathan A., Jr. Nathanael West: A Critical Essay. Grand Rapids, Mich.: William B. Eerdmans (Contemporary Writers in Christian Perspective Series), 1971. [pp. 7-8]

Scott asserts that SWF is among "the most impressive fictions of the present time" and that Nathanael West's legacy was "a major formative influence" on writers such as Barth.

H199 Shimura, Masao. "Barth to America Bungaku no Dento."

Eigo Seinen (The Rising Generation), 117 (1971), 414-16.

Shimura argues that "Night-Sea Journey" is rooted in America's literary past: Poe's Narrative of Arthur Gordon Pym, Melville's Moby-Dick, and the late works of Twain.

H200 ----------. "John Barth, The End of the Road, and the Tradition of American Fiction." Studies in English Literature (The English Literary Society of Japan), English No. (1971), pp. 73-87.

Shimura finds similarities between ER and a host of other American fictions: James' The Turn of the Screw, Faulkner's Wild Palms and Old Man, Hawthorne's The Scarlet Letter and "The Birthmark," and Hemingway's The Sun Also Rises. He adds that one may take FO as a parodic version of the Quentin episode in Faulkner's The Sound and the Fury. Shimura's comparisons are carried out in an attempt to distill those features which make Barth an American writer.

H201 Stern, Daniel. "The Mysterious New Novel." In Liberations: New Essays on the Humanities in Revolution. Ed. Ihab Hassan. Middletown, Conn.: Wesleyan Press, 1971. Pp. 22-37. [pp. 29-30]

Barth is a part of the post-Modernist "undercurrent" in contemporary fiction, according to Stern. The post-Modernists are all concerned, to some degree, with "a sense of the mysterious possibilities in the body or the will—against an increasingly totalitarian life—and the relationship of these possibilities to the religious sense."

H202 Tanner, Stephen L. "John Barth's Hamlet." Southwest Review, 56 (1971), 347-54.

Tanner feels that Todd Andrews of FO is a satiric figure because he gives in to philosophical rationality at the expense of human feelings. The book's two main themes, according to Tanner, are the conflict between the mind and the heart (which centers on the father-child relationships represented by Todd and his father, Todd and Jeannine Mack, and Colonel Morton and his son) and the to-be-or-not-to-be question (which is reflected in the novel's numerous references to Hamlet, Todd's father's suicide, Mr. Haecker's suicide, and Todd's attempted suicide).

H203 Tanner, Tony. City of Words: American Fiction 1950-1970. New York: Harper & Row, 1971. [pp. 47, 99, 141, 146-47, 180, 230-59, 265, 273, 370]

Tanner contends that "Barth starts with a sense of verbal play that precedes existence and essence" and that his fiction is rooted in the Wittgensteinian proposition that "the world is all that is the case." As a result, Barth's works produce "a mood or atmosphere of ambiguous freedom, both for the character in his situation and the author in his fiction-making." This thesis provides the basis for extended discussions of FO, ER, SWF, GGB, and LF.

H204 Tatham, Campbell. "John Barth and the Aesthetics of Artifice." Contemporary Literature, 12 (1971), 60-73.

An important article in which Tatham argues that, in Barth's fiction, aesthetic concerns take precedence over the moral imperative. He demonstrates his point by examining FO, SWF, and GGB. The novels, Tatham observes, are "commentaries on theories of the novel; insofar as novels are a part of life, Barth's novels are a commentary on a part of life." The result is not decadence, but "new human work."

†H205 TenBroeke, Patricia Anne Mullins. "The Shadow of Satan: A Study of the Devil Archetype in Selected American Novels from Hawthorne to the Present Day." Diss. The University of Texas at Austin, 1971. [DAI, 32: 6457A-58A]

The imagery of hell is used to describe the environment in SWF, argues TenBroeke, and the devil himself is personified in the character of Henry Burlingame III. Burlingame, who serves as a mouthpiece for Barth's existential philosophy, is a "constructive/destructive" figure who destroys Eben Cooke's faith in Christian/Platonic eternal essences prior to delivering new philosophical outlooks to the poet.

<1972>

H206 Anon. "Night-Sea Journey." In Teacher's Manual: Three Stances of Modern Fiction—A Critical Anthology of the Short Story. Ed. Stephen Minot and Robley Wilson, Jr. Cambridge, Mass.: Winthrop, 1972. Pp. 21-22.

A discussion of the ironic tone of "Night-Sea Journey" and the story's twin thematic concerns, the meaning of love and the overwhelming power of love.

H207 Blair, Walter. "'A Man's Voice, Speaking': A Continuum in American Humor." In Veins of Humor. Ed. Harry Levin. Cambridge, Mass.: Harvard Univ. Press (Harvard English Studies, No. 3), 1972. Pp. 185-204. [p. 195]

Blair feels that Barth, Bellow, Roth, and Vonnegut do not, as a rule, catch the quality of actual talk in

their first-person narratives, "because they use too
many Latinate words, because they characterize too
complexly, and because they scorn simple chronology."

†H208 Decker, Sharon Davie. "Passionate Virtuosity: The Fiction of John Barth." Diss. University of Virginia,
1972. [DAI, 33: 3639A]

Barth's fiction, according to Decker, explores two
thematic avenues of escape from meaninglessness, creative energy and love (i.e., involvement with others)
as well as two formal ones, technical creativity and
master storytelling. These formal and thematic value
are traced in FO, ER, SWF, GGB, and LF. Also explore
is a related set of problems: the ambivalence of language as a tool for ordering experience and, in the
later fiction, the ambivalent nature of reality itsel

H209 Gardner, John. "The Way We Write Now." The New York
Times Book Review, 9 July 1972, pp. 2, 32-33. [p. 2]

Gardner observes that the "reality" of SWF and GGB is
to be found in Barth's style rather than in the books
contents. He adds that Barth's themes are "the tradi
tional American themes."

H210 Gillespie, Gerald. "Rogues, Fools, and Satyrs: Ironic
Ghosts in American Fiction." In Modern American Fiction: Insights and Foreign Lights. Ed. Wolodymyr T.
Zyla and Wendell M. Aycock. Lubbock: Interdepart-
mental Committee on Comparative Literature, Texas Tec
Univ. (Proceedings of the Comparative Literature Symposium, Vol. 5), 1972. Pp. 89-106. [pp. 92, 99-106]

Gillespie demonstrates SWF's kinship with the master-
works of Rabelais, Cervantes, and Sterne and shows th
novel to be "full of that realism whose vis comica
permits—through comic control—a simultaneous review
and restructuring of myth." Gillespie feels that a
serious concern underlies SWF—namely, regeneration.

H211 Gilman, Richard. "The Idea of the Avant-Garde." Parti
san Review, 39 (1972), 382-96. [p. 386]

Gilman feels that attacks on writers such as Barth ar
symptomatic of the all-too-prevalent conservative cri
icism which distrusts the imaginative dimension of th
new fiction.

†H212 Golden, Daniel. "Shapes and Strategies: Forms of Moder
American Fiction in the Novels of Robert Penn Warren,
Saul Bellow, and John Barth." Diss. Indiana Universi
1972. [DAI, 33:2933A-34A]

Golden explores FO, ER, SWF, and GGB as anti-novels,
novels of self-parody. In FO and ER, the universe i
which Barth's protagonists find themselves is depicte

as chaotic and disordered, whereas, in SWF and GGB, Barth's elaborate parodies of fictional form and his mockery of the role of the artist parallel and amplify the cosmic chaos of the early novels. In the later novels, Barth reveals to us that the techniques as well as the subjects of narrative art have been exhausted.

H213 Greene, Maxine. "From Disjunction to Multiplicity." The Journal of Aesthetic Education, 6, Nos. 1-2 (1972), 161-78. [p. 177]

Greene praises ER for the way in which it discloses that "roles falsify the concreteness of persons" and that "rule-governed discourse, metaphor, and myth betray the 'raggedness' of things."

†H214 Gresham, James Thomas. "John Barth as Menippean Satirist." Diss. Michigan State University, 1972. [DAI, 33: 5176A]

Gresham defines the Menippean satiric genre as a prelude to discussing Barth's works in that generic context. The Menippean characteristics of extreme self-consciousness, literary parody, ambiguous ridicule of existentialism, the motif of minstrelsy, the doctrine of "exhaustion," and distrust of mimesis are examined in FO, ER, and LF. In discussing Barth's two "major" works, SWF and GGB, Gresham focuses on Barth's use of dialectical systems and structure.

H215 Hassan, Ihab. "Barth, John (Simmons)." In Contemporary Novelists. Ed. James Vinson, with a preface by Walter Allen. New York: St. Martin's Press, 1972. Pp. 87-89.

After sketching out some biographical and bibliographical information about Barth, Hassan goes on to discuss FO, ER, SWF, GGB, and LF; each receives a paragraph. Hassan's focus is Barth's use of parody and paradox; his comic skepticism; and his ability to push beyond Beckett, Borges, and Nabokov, the "virtuosos of 'exhaustion.'"

H216 Hirsch, David. "John Barth's Freedom Road." Mediterranean Review, 2, No. 3 (1972), 38-47.

Hirsch feels that Jacob Horner's search, in ER, "is not for values, but for that which may lie beyond values." Jacob's narrative is an exploration of the possibilities of absolute freedom: "He is, as it were, a Nietzschean superman cast into a non-heroic mold." But his quest, if one can call it that, ends with Jacob "tossed between the Scylla and Charybdis of meaningless freedom and strangulating form." ER marks the terminus of Barth's attempt to employ concise, well-ordered structures and serves as a prologue to

-133-

the author's attempt "to move into new modes of sensibility in which form has become subordinate to the artist's freedom to invent worlds of his own."

H217 Howard, Daniel F. "John Barth." In Manual to Accompany The Modern Tradition: An Anthology of Short Stories, Second Edition. Boston: Little, Brown, 1972. Pp. 51-53.

Notes and study questions designed to lead one to an understanding of "Lost in the Funhouse" and "Life-Story."

†H218 Janoff, Bruce Lee. "Beyond Satire: Black Humor in the Novels of John Barth and Joseph Heller." Diss. Ohio University, 1972. [DAI, 33: 1728A]

H219 is a distillation of this dissertation.

H219 ----------. "Black Humor: Beyond Satire." The Ohio Review, 14, No. 1 (1972), 5-20.

According to Janoff, Black Humorists, like satirists, employ laughter as a tool with which to engage the audience's attention. In doing so, they "run the gamut from wit (verbal cleverness) to humor (broad situational and psychological comedy)"; Barth is the most skilled handler of sheer wit. The Black Humorist seems to possess the firm moral-ethical motivation which is basic to the satiric impulse, although, unlike the satirist, the Black Humorist does not employ ridicule primarily for didactic reasons. Man's position in the universe is more properly the target of the Black Humorist than is any social institution. The wellspring of the Black Humorist's vision is to be found "in his perception of the ridiculousness of the human predicament," and he tends to be "too realistic—and consequently too pessimistic—to believe that his meager work might possibly change the world." The special achievement of the Black Humorist lies in "his ability to mute his rage and transform his despair into provocative, comically entertaining, transcendent literature" despite the fact that, as he understands it, the world is absurd. Janoff devotes a lot of attention to FO and ER.

H220 Jones, D. Allan. "The Game of the Name in Barth's The Sot-Weed Factor." Research Studies (Washington State Univ.), 40 (1972), 219-21.

Jones discusses the numerous puns which resonate with meaning in the name Henry Burlingame III.

H221 ----------. "John Barth and the Literature of Accentuated Artifice." Thesis, Western Carolina University, 1972.

Jones examines each of Barth's works from FO through LF

-134-

in terms of its thematic and structural artifices as well as the relationships between these artifices and Barth's fabulistic aesthetic, an aesthetic which develops gradually throughout Barth's career.

H222 Kort, Wesley A. Shriven Selves: Religious Problems in Recent American Fiction. Philadelphia: Fortress Press, 1972. [pp. 61, 139]

FO is referred to as a comic-absurdist novel, and Barth is mentioned along with Kerouac, Kesey, Percy, Coover, Vonnegut, and Brautigan as a writer more concerned with escape than with involvement and conflict.

H223 Kyle, Carol A. "The Unity of Anatomy: The Structure of Barth's Lost in the Funhouse." Critique, 13, No. 3 (1972), 31-43.

Kyle insists that LF can best be understood as an anatomy. The book begins with fictions that demonstrate the absurdity of metaphysical, creative, and sexual journeys before moving on to the Ambrose stories, which parody the American adolescent novel and bring the anatomy to its climax. The fictions following "Lost in the Funhouse" form the book's dénouement: this part of LF "approximates an anti-climax with two contrapuntal forms: parody of myth alternates with parody of art until the 'novel' talks itself to death."

†H224 LeClair, Thomas Edmund. "Final Words: Death and Comedy in the Fiction of Donleavy, Hawkes, Barth, Vonnegut, and Percy." Diss. Duke University, 1972. [DAI, 33: 5731A]

The Barth chapter in this dissertation served as the basis for H261.

H225 Lehtonen, Reijo. Preface. In Uiva ooppera by John Barth. Helsinki: Werner Söderström, 1972. Pp. 5-14.

Lehtonen, in his preface to the Finnish edition of FO, contends that Barth, in FO, shows a true understanding of the world when he has Todd Andrews deny the validity of universal truths and decide that each man must define his own reality. In examining the absurdist vision of FO, Lehtonen likens the book to Shakespeare's Macbeth, Eliot's "The Hollow Men," Pynchon's The Crying of Lot 49, and the novels of Kurt Vonnegut, Jr.

H226 Lutwack, Leonard. "Raintree County and the Epicising Poet in American Fiction." Ball State University Forum, 13, No. 1 (1972), 14-28. [p. 14]

Ross Lockridge's Raintree County, like Frank Norris' The Octopus and Barth's SWF, presents a poetaster who fails in his attempt to produce an epic poem about America. Each of the novelists, however, produces a successful epic novel.

H227 May, John R. Toward a New Earth: Apocalypse in the American Novel. Notre Dame and London: Univ. of Notre Dame Press, 1972. [pp. 34, 40, 172-80, 199-200, 207-08, 217-18, 229]

May examines ER as a novel of "humorous apocalypse," which depicts the end of the absolute worlds of Jacob Horner (who lives by "articulation") and Joe Morgan (who believes in "living coherently"). May feels that the Doctor is responsible for Jacob's "terminal" state and that the Negro "epitomizes the last loosing of Satan before the final cataclysm." May then goes on to contrast Barth with two other apocalyptic humorists, Pynchon and Vonnegut.

H228 McDonald, James L. "Barth's Syllabus: The Frame of Giles Goat-Boy." Critique, 13, No. 3 (1972), 5-10.

McDonald argues that the frame of GGB is "both functional and necessary," since it allows Barth to surround his narrative fable (the R.N.S.) with a literary commentary and an analysis of the fable's composition and its effect on the various readers and thus call attention to the book's existence as an artifact. Such artificial existence is what Barth, a writer committed to the reinvention of the world in his fiction, offers us as an alternative to the fragmentation and chaos of our everyday lives.

†H229 Miller, Norman. "The Self-Conscious Narrator-Protagonist in American Fiction Since World War II." Diss. The University of Wisconsin, 1972. [DAI, 32: 5798A]

Barth's FO is one of the ten novels examined in this study, in which Miller contends that, because the narrator-protagonist in post-World-War-II American fiction is both the subject and vehicle of his tale and because his aims are fundamentally rhetorical, he is, to some extent, unreliable. The reader, in order to determine the author's perspective, must perceive the irony which develops between the story the narrator relates and the "story" of his attempt to shape that tale to his own ends.

H230 Olderman, Raymond M. Beyond the Waste Land: A Study of the American Novel in the Nineteen-Sixties. New Haven and London: Yale Univ. Press, 1972. [pp. 16, 17, 20, 25, 27-28, 50, 72-93, 96, 104, 107, 146, 176-77]

Olderman briefly notes that Barth, in SWF, parodies man search for identity through his handling of the protean Henry Burlingame III. GGB receives the bulk of Olderman's attention. The book, according to Olderman, both seriously employs and consciously parodies Eliot's The

Waste Land. George Giles is a quester who, like Tiresias, "narrates his own failure and is transformed from Grail Knight to wounded Fisher King." Olderman also argues that George's life as a hero is a constructed mythology based on the works of Lord Raglan and Joseph Campbell and that Barth's use of the university as a metaphor for the waste land of existence is indisputably apt.

H231 Pinsker, Sanford. "The Graying of Black Humor." Studies in the Twentieth Century, No. 9 (1972), pp. 15-33.

The Black Humorists, Pinsker feels, have demonstrated an inability to deal with structure (the endings of their books, especially, are weak) and have chosen to attack the all-too-easily attackable. "Real satire is made of sterner stuff. It takes a hard look at the absurdities of life and even a harder one at human illusions." By contrast, Black Humor is predictable and soon teaches us "how to be comfortable with the most grotesque and/or irreverent news such an aesthetic has to offer."

H232 ----------. "John Barth: The Teller Who Swallowed His Tale." Studies in the Twentieth Century, No. 10 (1972), pp. 55-68.

Pinsker discusses the "ultra-reflexive" narrators of FO and LF and concludes that Barth's lexical skill is not enough to sustain what is essentially a weak narrative line: "In short, Barth is not so much the great destroyer of Modernism—exaggerating its faults through extended parody, etc.—as he is the devourer of his own Art."

†H233 Price, Jonathan Lee. "Black Humor: Form as Manipulation." Diss. Stanford University, 1972. [DAI, 33: 2390A]

Initially, Price feels, the Black Humorist forces his reader to detach himself from his stereotyped characters and their suffering; as a result, laughter is produced. But, eventually, Black Humor works take on such a painful, somber air that the reader is compelled to sympathize with the suffering of the protagonist. This manipulative technique is characteristic of Barth's work as well as that of many of his contemporaries.

H234 Rodrigues, Eusebio L. "The Living Sakhyan in Barth's Giles Goat-Boy." Notes on Contemporary Literature, 2, No. 4 (1972), 7-8.

Rodrigues points out that the character of The Living Sakhyan in GGB is based on the historical personage of the Dalai Lama, a bodhisattva or "sage whose being has achieved enlightenment but who has refused Nirvana in order to be a compassionate savior of all beings."

Although Giles shuns the Living Sakhyan upon meeting
him, the Goat-Boy ultimately "arrives at the fundamental
Sakhyan truth that life is an illusion." And it is due
to the Living Sakhyan's "compassionate silence" that
Giles is able to pass through the Commencement Gate.

H235 Slethaug, Gordon E. "Barth's Refutation of the Idea of
Progress." Critique, 13, No. 3 (1972), 11-29.

Eben Cooke, George Giles, and Ambrose, the protagonists
of SWF, GGB, and LF, begin as idealists but learn that
man's condition and his beliefs are not susceptible to
radically ameliorative change. They discover, Slethaug
asserts, that history, far from moving in an upward
linear progression, moves along a straight (or even
downward) continuum in a series of correspondingly
similar circles. GGB's Max Spielman expresses this
awareness in his "Law of Cyclology."

†H236 Tenenbaum, Elizabeth Brody. "Concepts of the Self in the
Modern Novel." Diss. Stanford University, 1972. [DAI,
32: 7010A]

Tenenbaum examines works by five novelists who have
challenged the traditional concept that the self is a
coherent, more or less stable entity which is the product of an inherent nature or essence. Barth, in ER,
denies the reality of the private self, showing identity
to be nothing more than a mask chosen at will, and, in
so doing, he repudiates the basis of psychological fiction.

H237 Tuttleton, James W. The Novel of Manners in America.
Chapel Hill: Univ. of North Carolina Press, 1972.
[p. 139]

Tuttleton refers to Barth as a writer of "romance parody"

H238 Ziolkowski, Theodore. Fictional Transfigurations of Jesus
Princeton: Princeton Univ. Press, 1972. [pp. 75n, 226,
228, 230-34, 250-51, 256-66, 270-98 passim]

Ziolkowski views SWF as preparatory for GGB, since in
SWF Barth employed the general myth of the wandering
hero before arriving as the more specific form of transfiguration, which he uses in Giles. GGB is a "Fifth
Gospel" of "moral neutralism" in which Barth "exploits
the Bible for the sheer aesthetic fun of structural
parody." The novel, Ziolkowski asserts, is not an allegory but an analogue, which parodies the Gospels, the
whole relationship between the Old Testament and the New
and the entire tradition of "higher criticism" of the
Bible. The comedy which results wears somewhat thin
after a hundred or so pages, however, and the novel
becomes quite tedious.

<1973>

H239 Aldiss, Brian W. Billion Year Spree: The True History of Science Fiction. Garden City, N.Y.: Doubleday, 1973. [pp. 256-57]

Aldiss mentions GGB as one of the "impressive array of novels" which approach the interests of science fiction.

†H240 Allen, Mary Inez. "The Necessary Blankness: Women in Major American Fiction of the Sixties." Diss. University of Maryland, 1973. [DAI, 34: 7736A]

Women, Allen feels, are generally treated in a reactionary way by Barth, Roth, Updike, and others. They are seldom granted significant activity outside the home, are devoid of identity, seldom dream, are often bitches, and are far more inclined to madness than are their male counterparts.

H241 "Barth, John 1930—." In Contemporary Literary Criticism: Excerpts from Criticism of the Works of Today's Novelists, Poets, Playwrights, and other Creative Writers. Ed. Carolyn Riley. Detroit: Gale Research Co., 1973. Pp. 17-18.

Excerpts from H62, H88, H145, H152, H204, I105, and I168.

H242 Bell, Pearl K. "American Fiction: Forgetting the Ordinary Truths." Dissent, 20 (1973), 26-34. [pp. 26-27]

Bell contends that Barth, in GGB and Chimera, "becomes so hopelessly tangled in his proliferating metaphorical ingenuities that in the end he seems a failed Houdini; sealed inside the magic barrel, he can't remember how he'd planned to get out."

H243 Bienstock, Beverly Gray. "Lingering on the Autognostic Verge: John Barth's Lost in the Funhouse." Modern Fiction Studies, 19 (1973), 69-78.

Bienstock examines the unifying thread of LF, the individual's search for identity; Barth's handling of Greek mythology, especially as it is evidenced in "Menelaiad"; and Ambrose, the narrator of "Lost in the Funhouse" and "a younger, pre-Helen Menelaus." Bienstock concludes her article by explaining Ambrose's relationship to Barth and Barth's relationship to all writers, followed by the writer's relationship, through his work of art, to all readers—an eternal, recurring cycle symbolized by the Moebius strip which begins the Funhouse book.

†H244 ----------. "The Self-Conscious Artist in Contemporary American Fiction." Diss. University of California, Los Angeles, 1973. [DAI, 34: 7219A]

One of Bienstock's four chapters is devoted to analyzing the role of the artist in FO, ER, SWF, GGB, LF, and Chimera. Although she emphasizes the later books, she makes it clear that, in all of Barth's work, he "simultaneously questions the power of the artist and reveals his own commitment to art."

H245 Christadler, Martin. "Einleitung: Kultur- und Literaturkritik." In Amerikanische Literatur der Gegenwart in Einzeldarstellungen. Ed. with an intro. by Martin Christadler. Stuttgart: Alfred Kröner, 1973. Pp. xi-l [pp. xxviii-xxix]

Christadler briefly considers Barth as a Black Humorist and a parodist, mentioning ER, SWF, and GGB.

†H246 Elgin, Donald Deane. "The Rogue Reappears: A Study of the Development of the Picaresque in Modern American Fiction." Diss. Vanderbilt University, 1973. [DAI, 34: 4256A-57A]

One chapter of Elgin's dissertation is given over to a detailed analysis of the ways in which SWF demonstrates a modification of the traditional picaresque: the traditional point of view has been altered, a mask tradition added, and a greater capacity for abstraction afforded the picaro.

H247 Ewell, Barbara C. "John Barth: The Artist of History." The Southern Literary Journal, 5, No. 2 (1973), 32-46.

According to Ewell, SWF provides "serious commentary both on the nature of history and ultimately on the nature of the real." Barth, through his handling of the character of Henry Burlingame III, points out that, although the past is always going to be unverifiable, man can face the utter terror of reality by making a "leap of faith that proclaims him aware of the flux of Being and still able to construct his own identity within and despite it." Thus, art and artifice become necessary if one is to erect structures capable of coping with "the overwhelming preposterousness of Being"—as Barth does in SWF.

†H248 Fogel, Stanley Howard. "Ludic Fiction—Metafiction: The Contemporary Experimental Novel in America." Diss. Purdue University, 1973. [DAI, 35: 447A]

Fogel enunciates the tenets of metafiction and applies them to the works of Barth, Barthelme, Brautigan, Coover and Gass before examining the theological, sociological philosophical, and literary constructs with which these writers experiment.

H249 Godshalk, W[illiam] L. "Cabell and Barth: Our Comic Athletes." In The Comic Imagination in American Literatur

-140-

Ed. Louis D. Rubin, Jr. New Brunswick, N.J.: Rutgers Univ. Press, 1973. Pp. 275-83.

Godshalk discusses ER, SWF, GGB, LF, and "Bellerophoniad" in sketching the similarities between Barth and James Branch Cabell: both approach the fact that their civilization is collapsing with a smile, and both are players of literary games (e.g., both make ironic use of apparently exhausted literary forms, and they make use of infinite regression in and out of the fictive and real worlds). But beneath the games' fun lies a deadly seriousness; ultimately, the games "are a conscious way of getting at an intellectual solution to the problems of man in a transitory world." Barth and Cabell, through their mocking use of history and myth, smile sardonically at man's exaggerated sense of self-importance and ask their readers to come to "a comic acceptance of reality followed by a stoical resignation" to their lot.

H250 Hansen, Arlen J. "The Celebration of Solipsism: A New Trend in American Fiction." Modern Fiction Studies, 19 (1973), 5-15. [pp. 14-15]

Hansen feels that Barth's is a major voice in the movement towards a new solipsism in American fiction and that the narrator of Barth's "Anonymiad" is a fictional new soplisist. Unlike such old solipsists as Emerson and Whitman, the new solipsists seek to establish a "creative adjustment to whatever the mind takes to be 'out there.'" In other words, theirs is a transcendentalism colored by determinism.

H251 Harmon, William. "'Anti-Fiction' in American Humor." In The Comic Imagination in American Literature. Ed. Louis D. Rubin, Jr. New Brunswick, N.J.: Rutgers Univ. Press, 1973. Pp. 373-84. [pp. 375, 384]

Many modern American prose writers, including Barth, are composing works which are fictive but which offer very little that would satisfy anyone's "old-fashioned ordinary concept of 'story.'" Such anti-novelistic writing tends to produce comedy. Many of these experiments are worthwhile, although Barth has gone too far in LF; "Menelaiad" is especially objectionable to Harmon.

H252 Hassan, Ihab. "American Literature." In World Literature Since 1945: Critical Surveys of the Contemporary Literatures of Europe and the Americas. Ed. Ivan Ivask and Gero von Wilpert. New York: Frederick Ungar, 1973. Pp. 1-64. [pp. 4-5, 16-17, 26, 61]

A shortened version of H253.

H253 ----------. Contemporary American Literature 1945-1972:

An Introduction. New York: Frederick Ungar, 1973.
[pp. 18, 24, 56-60, 81-82, 170-71]

Barth is one of the ten "prominent" post-World-War-II novelists examined by Hassan (as opposed to the "major" novelists Bellow and Mailer). Hassan focuses on Barth' formal experimentation, especially his use of parody. FO, ER, SWF, GGB, and LF are each discussed at some length; of the five, Hassan clearly prefers SWF.

H254 ----------. "Echoes of Dark Laughter: Notes on the Comic Sense in Contemporary American Fiction." Eigo Seinen (The Rising Generation), 118 (1973), 688-91.

Hassan's purpose in this essay "is to note a certain event in the modern imagination: the deflection of laughter toward anguish." Although Hassan regards Mailer as "the most significant American writer alive," he has some nice things to say about Barth's ER, LF, and Chimera, which he praises for their "profound intellectual irony."

H255 ----------. "The New Gnosticism: Speculations on an Aspect of the Postmodern Mind." Boundary 2, 1 (1973), 547-69. [pp. 564, 565] Rpt. in Paracriticisms: Seven Speculations of the Times (Urbana: Univ. of Illinois Press, 1975), pp. 121-47. [pp. 140, 141]

Hassan speaks of "the playful 'ultimacy'" of Chimera and the post-Modernist writer's "complex desire to dissolve the world—or at least recognize its dissolution—and to remake it as an absurd or decaying or parodic or private—and still imaginative—construct."

H256 Hinden, Michael. "Lost in the Funhouse: Barth's Use of the Recent Past." Twentieth Century Literature, 19 (1973), 107-18.

Hinden argues that LF involves "an elaborate parody, revival, and refutation" of Joyce's Portrait of the Artist as a Young Man—especially insofar as the Funhouse book "concerns the collapse of credibility of the artist-as-hero theme in modern literature and the question raised as to whether there is 'anything more tiresome, in fiction, than the problems of sensitive adolescents.'" The six fictions which follow "Frame-Tale" treat the growth of consciousness in a given mind and the next seven tell of the confusion resulting from attempting to transmute hyper-consciousness into art.

†H257 Johnstone, Douglas Blake. "Myth and Psychology in the Novels of John Barth." Diss. University of Oregon, 1973. [DAI, 34: 5973A]

The protagonists of FO, ER, SWF, GGB, and LF are "prodigal Oedipus" types who, feeling physically and emotionally cut off from their fathers, attempt to work out durable physical relationships with women, only to break off such relationships when the women prove to be intolerable shapes of the mother image. As a result, the protagonists relinquish sexually and, in most cases, effect a psychological reattachment to the father image; this leaves them painfully aware of their own inadequacies. Johnstone goes on to postulate that unconscious psychological imprints are the raw material of myth and, secondly, that literature is the modern mythology. These premises lead him, in turn, to the conclusion that the psychological crippling of Barth's protagonists serves as a metaphor for the inadequacies of contemporary life.

H258 Kazin, Alfred. Bright Book of Life: American Novelists and Storytellers from Hemingway to Mailer. Boston and Toronto: Little, Brown, 1973. [pp. 258n, 280-81]

Kazin cites pasages from FO and ER to demonstrate the excessive tendency to explain oneself which he feels plagues the writings of the American absurdists.

H259 Kiernan, Robert F. "John Barth's Artist in the Fun House." Studies in Short Fiction, 10 (1973), 373-80.

Kiernan contends that LF is a Künstlerroman. The key stories in the book are the Ambrose stories, which trace the growth of the boy's artistic vocation. The fictions that alternate with the Ambrose stories ("Night-Sea Journey," "Autobiography," and "Petition") "complement and develop" the book's Künstlerroman structure. "Echo," the seventh story, "serves to crystallize the vectors of the Künstlerroman at the point where the fictions with Ambrose as their explicit subject give way to experimental fictions with Ambrose as their implicit subject." In the second half of LF, the narrator of the stories (implicitly Ambrose) comes to feel disdain toward his early attempts "to understand and master the funhouse of fiction." He learns to relinquish his adolescent sensitivity and to concern himself simply with the actual productions of fictional art.

†H260 Kochanek, Patricia Sharpe. "In Pursuit of Proteus: A Piagetian Approach to the Structure of the Grotesque in American Fiction of the Fifties." Diss. The Pennsylvania State University, 1973. [DAI, 33: 5729A-30A]

Kochanek argues that previous critics, in attempting to deal with the concept of the grotesque as applied to American fiction of the fifties, have fallen back on the theories of the unconscious expounded by Freud and Jung. As a result, they failed to perceive that the grotesque was a distinct aesthetic embodying a coherent, though dynamic, non-cathartic configuration. It is in the light of this Piagetian approach that Kochanek examines the important American grotesque fiction of the fifties, including ER.

H261 LeClair, Thomas. "John Barth's The Floating Opera: Death and the Craft of Fiction." Texas Studies in Literature and Language, 14 (1973), 711-30.

This is an excellent article in which LeClair argues convincingly that Todd Andrews is an unreliable narrator, who is, nonetheless, capable of conning the unwary reader into accepting his accounts as factual by virtue of the earnest and innocent tone he assumes. Todd is an artist capable of manipulating the reader just as surely as he manipulates the law: "his approach to life and his approach to art interpenetrate, are one." This manipulative ability is shared by Barth and the author's subsequent aestheticians: Jacob Horner of ER, Henry Burlingame III of SWF, and GGB's Harold Bray. LF reflects back on the condition of the artisans who appear in the novels. To live the aesthetic life, outside the bounds of reality, may be a desperate strategy, but the modern novelist, like Barth's "avant-gardiste" Scheherazade, is involved in a life-and-death struggle for his very existence.

H262 Lehan, Richard. A Dangerous Crossing: French Literary Existentialism and the Modern American Novel. With a preface by Harry T. Moore. Carbondale and Edwardsville: Southern Illinois Univ. Press, 1973. [pp. 172-83]

Lehan discusses the existential implications of FO, ER, SWF, "Night-Sea Journey," "Lost in the Funhouse," and "Life-Story"; he focuses on the problems of value, identity, and exhaustion.

H263 McElroy, Joseph. "The N Factor." Saturday Review of the Arts, 1 (6 Jan. 1973), 34-35.

McElroy observes that "SWF would have happened anyhow—but surely one movement of fiction in the Sixties away from plainer modes and into parody, labyrinth, and self-conscious convolution of wit owed something to Nabokov."

H264 Mellard, James M. "Night-Sea Journey." In Instructor's Manual: Four Modes—A Rhetoric of Modern Fiction. New York: Macmillan, 1973. Pp. 32-33.

Mellard contends that "Night-Sea Journey" is not so much an "adventure" story as it is "a lyrical response to the meaning of the journey" by a persona cut off from the assurance one normally finds in the external world.

H265 Nabokov, Vladimir. "Inspiration." Saturday Review of the

<pre>   Arts, 1 (6 Jan. 1973), 30-32. [p. 32]
        Nabokov cites "Lost in the Funhouse" as one of his
        six favorite short stories.

H266   Packer, Nancy Huddleston. "Fiction's New Mode." The
        Southern Humanities Review, 7 (1973), 387-94.</pre>

The "new mode" of fiction can be subdivided into three categories: the put-on (whose finest practitioner is Barth), aestheticism, and the celebration of the absurd. Packer readily grants that the "new mode" is filled with wit and invention, but she is bothered by the fact that it ignores the reader's emotions and fails to provide the reader with any meaning through which he may enrich his life.

†H267   Plater, William Marmaduke. "Metamorphosis: An Examination of Communication and Community in Barth, Beckett and Pynchon." Diss. University of Illinois at Urbana-Champaign, 1973. [DAI, 34: 7776A]

Using LF as a representative example, Plater attempts to demonstrate the way in which Barth's fiction depicts language as a barrier to communication, rather than a vehicle for conveying experience. Turning experience into words is, as Jacob Horner insists, "always a betrayal of experience, . . . but only so betrayed can it be dealt with." Barth, by allowing his protagonists to employ a technique which Plater labels metamorphosis (i.e., turning language upon itself, using it as parody to attack language), presents us with heroes who are able to escape the linguistic maze.

H268   Rubin, Louis D., Jr. "'The Barber Kept on Shaving': The Two Perspectives of American Humor." The Sewanee Review, 81 (1973), 691-713. [pp. 707-08] Rpt. in The Comic Imagination in American Literature, ed. Louis D. Rubin, Jr. (New Brunswick, N.J.: Rutgers Univ. Press, 1973), pp. 385-405. [pp. 399-400]

Rubin devotes a paragraph to the humor in SWF: he observes that the comedy stems from Barth's spoofing of history and historians, his parodying of older writings, and his abundant use of sexual vulgarity.

H269   ----------. "The Great American Joke." The South Atlantic Quarterly, 72 (1973), 82-94. [p. 94] Rpt. in The Comic Imagination in American Literature, ed. Louis D. Rubin, Jr. (New Brunswick, N.J.: Rutgers Univ. Press, 1973), pp. 3-15. [p. 15]

The fact that Barth contrasts literary language and poetic description with vernacular fact and colloquial speech in SWF puts the book in a line of American humorous masterpieces that includes Byrd's Dividing

Line, Irving's History of New York, Twain's Connecticut Yankee, and Hemingway's Torrents of Spring.

H270 Scholes, Robert. "The Allegory of Exhaustion." fiction international, No. 1 (1973), pp. 106-08.

Scholes examines Chimera and, to some lesser degree, LF as "esthetic allegories," fictions which deal with the problems of art. Barth's books differ from the esthetic allegories of Henry James in that Barth ultimately places more faith in love than he does in art, since art in the 1970's "is simply another god that failed, and Barth can do no more than play at a comic black mass based on the old beliefs."

H271 Schulz, Dieter. "John Barth." In Amerikanische Literatu der Gegenwart in Einzeldarstellungen. Ed. with an intro. by Martin Christadler. Stuttgart: Alfred Kröner 1973. Pp. 371-90.

Schulz sketches Barth's biography and names his literar influences before launching into a critical examination of his fiction from FO to LF. He devotes most of his attention to SWF. Barth's books, according to Schulz, employ metaphor, allegory, and myth; are permeated by nihilism and existentialism; and are artistic, artful, and sometimes artificial. By operating from the premis that art is but an imitation of art, Barth has created a positive alternative to the French New Novel, even though this alternative is more convincing in theory than it is in practice. Despite the fact that Barth's books are frequently brilliant, their endings are disappointing, since his insistence on the fictiousness of life and literature is not persuasive. Still, Barth holds a significant and independent place in American literature. A sizable bibliography is appended to the essay.

H272 Schulz, Max F. Black Humor Fiction of the Sixties: A Pluralistic Definition of Man and His World. Athens: Ohio Univ. Press, 1973. [pp. ix-x, 3-44 passim, 51, 72, 87-89, 93-94, 104-05, 127-30]

Schulz feels that the term Black Humor cannot readily be understood "as a universal attitude of mind, periodically emerging in the history of literature"; it is more useful to regard Black Humor as "a phenomenon of the 1960's, comprising a group of writers who share a viewpoint and an aesthetics for pacing off the boundaries of a nuclear-technological world intrinsically without confinement." Since the Black Humorist sees life as a multiple, endless maze, he devises "enormously self-conscious" fictional forms which suggest "unbounded multiplicity." This is especially true of Barth's SWF, GGB, and LF, the book Schulz discusses mos thoroughly. The most interesting piece in the Funhouse collection, according to Schulz, is the title story, in which Barth combines "local color realism" with "Black Humor pluralism."

H273 ──────────. "Toward a Definition of Black Humor." The Southern Review, NS 9 (1973), 117-34.

This is a slightly altered version of pp. 3-6, 7-13, 17-19, 21-25, and 27-28 of H272.

†H274 Scofield, James Davis. "Absurd Man and the Esthetics of the Absurd: The Fiction of John Barth." Diss. Kent State University, 1973. [DAI, 34: 4285A]

Scofield feels that the concept of the absurd produces "a unified explanation" of the form and content of Barth's fiction, and he attempts to demonstrate this thesis by analyzing Barth's development as an absurdist writer. Whereas Barth's early novels incorporate certain absurdist assumptions about the human condition, his later work depicts the doubt and indecision faced by the artist whose parodic vision has become self-directed and who no longer has anything to express except his inability to create something meaningful.

H275 Scott, Nathan A., Jr. "History, Hope, and Literature." Boundary 2, 1 (1973), 577-603. [pp. 586-90, 594-95]

Scott comments on the extent to which one influential group of contemporary American novelists has shelved traditional literary commitments in favor of approaching the literary vocation as a game. FO typifies this trend: in that novel, Barth exchanges mimesis for "snap and buoyancy and analogical inventiveness."

H276 ──────────. "'New Heav'ns, New Earth'—the Landscape of Contemporary Apocalypse." The Journal of Religion, 53 (1973), 1-35. [pp. 24, 25, 26-27]

Scott alludes to Barth and his novel SWF in discussing representative contemporary apocalyptic writers.

H277 Seymour-Smith, Martin. Funk & Wagnalls Guide to Modern Literature. New York: Funk & Wagnalls, 1973. [pp. 142-43]

Seymour-Smith, focusing on GGB, praises Barth's handling of ideas, though he finds the author's use of language to be lacking in creativity.

†H278 Sherman, Marilyn Robertson. "'Point of View' and the Creative Process in the Novels of John Barth." Diss. The University of Florida, 1973. [DAI, 35: 1123A]

Sherman examines all six of Barth's books as she endeavors to chart his movement from the use of essentially realistic first-person narration in FO and ER to his use of highly imaginative forms of narration in his more recent work. Barth's shift from personal, intellectual inquiries into absolute truth to fantastical, cosmic meanderings which involve the paradoxical nature of the universe evidences his development as a literary artist and thinker searching for alternative forms of narrative expression.

H279 Shimura, Masao. "New Novelists." Eigo Seinen (The Rising Generation), 119 (1973), 520-21.

Shimura feels that the work of Barth, Barthelme, Brautigan, Pynchon, and Vonnegut, for all its apparent newness, is really derivative. Such books as SWF, GGB, LF, and Chimera are born out of the Romantic tradition of American fiction.

H280 Stevick, Philip. "Scheherazade Runs Out of Plots, Goes on Talking; The King, Puzzled, Listens: An Essay on New Fiction." TriQuarterly, No. 26 (1973), pp. 332-62. [pp. 336, 349-50, 354, 356, 358, 361, 362]

Stevick examines Barth's handling of myth in ER and LF, and in listing seven axioms which he hopes will define "an aesthetic of new fiction," Stevick makes frequent reference to Barth.

H281 Trachtenberg, Stanley. "Counterhumor: Comedy in Contemporary American Fiction." The Georgia Review, 27 (1973), 33-48.

References to Barth and two of his creations, ER and GGB, are made in this essay, in which Trachtenberg attempts to distinguish "the novel of the fifties" from "the novel of the sixties." Whereas the fifties' novelist compelled his characters to strive to establish their authenticity and self-identity against all odds, to proceed rationally in an irrational universe, the contemporary novelist refuses to put his characters through all that agony. The comic character who pervades the novel of the sixties affirms the synthetic in an attempt to avoid any final confrontation with universal principles. He is determined to hold off the pressures of the present "until such time as existence is ready to sustain life once more."

†H282 Urbanski, Kenneth John. "The Forming Artifice in John Barth's Fictions." Diss. University of Kansas, 1973. [DAI, 34: 7789A]

Urbanski offers a critical methodology and vocabulary for exploring the formal design of contemporary "irrealistic" fiction. His central term forming artifice refers to those fictional works in which form is, as much as anything else, the subject of the fiction. After a brief examination of the principles of process and articulation in FO and ER, Urbanski looks at SWF, the

-148-

work which initiates Barth's movement toward "irrealistic" fiction. Successive chapters are then devoted to each of Barth's forming artifices: GGB, LF, and Chimera.

H283 Vernon, John. The Garden and the Map: Schizophrenia in Twentieth-Century Literature and Culture. Urbana: Univ. of Illinois Press, 1973. [pp. ix, 15-16, 37-38, 41-42, 48, 63-69, 74-75, 85]

Vernon discusses the image of the labyrinth—which he interprets as an image of "an objective world that is wearing out and beginning to show, like a glove, the subjectivity that has always animated it, like a hand"—as it applies to SWF, GGB, and "Lost in the Funhouse." These fictions, by virtue of the labyrinthine images they project, demonstrate the schizophrenic aspect of "reality," which turns out to be a mental construct rather than the absolute Western civilization conventionally regards it as. This schizophrenia is given fictional embodiment in the character of the "dandy"—Henry Burlingame III in SWF, Harold Bray in GGB—a role player whose protean external existence masks his inner nothingness.

H284 Weber, Brom. "The Mode of 'Black Humor.'" In The Comic Imagination in American Literature. Ed. Louis D. Rubin, Jr. New Brunswick, N.J.: Rutgers Univ. Press, 1973. Pp. 361-71. [pp. 361-62, 364, 370, 371]

Weber argues that Black Humor is neither a new nor an American concept: it "functioned as a central doctrine of French surrealism almost from its inception in the 1920's." Though Black Humor can be traced further back than that, the surrealists cultivated the concept and had a strong influence on Nathanael West, the first American whose writing is predominantly in the Black Humor vein. Of the contemporary Black Humorists, only Thomas Berger and Walker Percy continue to write vital Black Humor. Barth, after writing the brilliant SWF, "has devoted himself to demonstrating that writing has no function and silence is preferable."

H285 Weixlmann, Joseph Norman, Jr. "Counter-Types and Anti-Myths: Black and Indian Characters in the Fiction of John Barth." Diss. Kansas State University, 1973. [DAI, 34: 3439A-40A]

Weixlmann contends that Barth's blacks and Indians usually function as counter-typical or as anti-mythologized figures. Counter-typing, the more prevalent of the novelist's two techniques, involves Barth's use of stereotypical figures who become forceful comedic characterizations via the hyperbole with which they are presented. Anti-mythologizing consists of his comedic exposé of the underlying "truth" which renders some of

America's most sacred myths apocryphal. Three of the six chapters of this study are devoted to SWF, and one each is given over to the blacks of FO and LF, the Negro Doctor of ER, and the blacks of GGB.

<1974>

†H286 Bailey, Dennis Lee. "The Modern Novel in the Presence of Myth." Diss. Purdue University, 1974. [DAI, 35: 7292A-93A]

Myth, according to Bailey, involves a mediation between the individual and his community. The healing of this binary opposition is examined in Mann's Joseph and His Brothers, Faulkner's A Fable, Fowles' The Magus, and Barth's GGB.

†H287 Begnal, Mary Kate. "Self-Mimesis in the Fiction of John Barth." Diss. The Pennsylvania State University, 1974. [DAI, 35: 7293A]

Begnal examines Barth's fictional techniques in FO, ER, SWF, GGB, LF, and Chimera and concludes that they are self-mimetic; the books tend toward an imitation of the artistic process and the artistic self. This parodic vision results in the destruction of the static and dead and produces an assertion of freedom and a declaration of the need to create value anew in art—and in life. Barth's artist figures are constantly torn between art and the world, but, at least in Barth's later fiction, the artist's life becomes synthetic as he learns to fuse art with love.

†H288 Billings, Philip Allan. "John Barth's Initial Trilogy: A Study of the Themes of Value and Identity in The Floating Opera, The End of the Road, and The Sot-Weed Factor." Diss. Michigan State University, 1974. [DAI, 35: 6129A-30A]

Billings argues that FO, ER, and SWF, when examined together, form a thematic trilogy. They demonstrate the possibility of modern man's achieving a sense of value and identity through the act of love and despite the fact that the universe in which man finds himself is irrational and nihilistic—at best, relativistic. This paradoxical synthesis of affirming the irrational yet real feeling of love (of acting innocently, as though absolute identity and value existed) is dramatized in SWF.

H289 Browning, Preston M., Jr. "The Quest for Being in Contemporary American Fiction." Forum (Univ. of Houston), 12, No. 1 (1974), 40-46. [pp. 42-43]

Browning mentions Barth as a representative Black Humorist, Black Humor being a relatively amorphous genre which is characterized by the way in which its practitioners cloud the distinction between fantasy and reality.

†H290 Cantrill, Dante Kenneth. "Told by an Idiot: Toward an Understanding of Modern Fiction through an Analysis of the Works of William Faulkner and John Barth." Diss. University of Washington, 1974. [DAI, 35: 4505A]

Cantrill uses Barth's and Faulkner's fiction to image and illustrate the concept that the "fiction-maker" (the author and, in a very real sense, the reader) creates a world which is neither more nor less fictional than the one in which he resides.

H291 Farwell, Harold. "John Barth's Tenuous Affirmation: 'The Absurd, Unending Possibility of Love.'" Georgia Review, 28 (1974), 290-306.

Farwell sketches Barth's complex attitude toward love from its first appearance in Shirt of Nessus, Barth's M.A. project, through the recently published "Dunyazadiad." LF—and especially "Menelaiad"—is examined with the greatest intensity. Farwell concludes that Barth's fiction, especially his most recent work, contains a decided affirmation of the possibility of love—not as an absolute value, but as a value which is precious because of its fragility and the inevitability of its loss.

H292 Firth, John. "Lost in the Funhouse." In Instructor's Manual for The Art of Fiction. 2nd ed. Ed. R. F. Dietrich and Roger H. Sundell. New York: Holt, Rinehart and Winston, 1974. Pp. 131-34.

Firth discusses the "submerged" plot of "Lost in the Funhouse," the story's characters (all of whom, except for Ambrose, are consciously created stereotypes), Barth's symbolic use of the funhouse, and Ambrose's struggle to control his own destiny (especially his sexual destiny). Ten study questions accompany the essay.

†H293 Fort, Deborah Charnley. "Contrast Epic: A Study of Joseph Heller's Catch-22 (1961), Günter Grass's The Tin Drum (Die Blechtrommel [1959]), John Barth's The Sot-Weed Factor (1960, Revised 1967), and Vladimir Nabokov's Pale Fire (1962)." Diss. University of Maryland, 1974. [DAI, 35: 3677A-78A]

In mock epics, an inglorious present is treated ironically in relation to a glorious past. In contrast epics, like SWF, past and present are also juxtaposed, but what we learn is that the heroic values of the past are actually pernicious and that these values have survived in the present, thus interfering with contemporary man's attempts to deal with the moral evils he is forced to confront. Fort's fourth chapter demonstrates how Barth rejects the epic past embodied in the Iliad, the Odyssey, the Aeneid, Hudibras, and Tom Jones in an effort to destroy the values those books uphold.

H294   Gresham, James T. "Giles Goat-Boy: Satyr, Satire, and Tragedy Twined." Genre, 7, No. 2 (1974), 148-63.

Gresham examines the elements of Menippean satire and paradox in GGB.

H295   Guerard, Albert J. "Notes on the Rhetoric of Anti-Realist Fiction." TriQuarterly, No. 30 (1974), pp. 3-50. [pp. 3-4, 7, 9, 19, 21-22, 25, 48]

Guerard alludes to FO, GGB, and "Life-Story" as he attempts to distinguish the work of "anti-realist" writers such as Barth, Hawkes, Nabokov, and West from that of "realists" such as Bellow, Capote, Styron, and Updike.

H296   Hassan, Ihab. "Fiction." In Literary History of the United States: History. 4th ed., rev. Ed. Robert E. Spiller, et al. New York: Macmillan, 1974. Pp. 1460-75. [pp. 1469, 1471]

Hassan contends that Barth was the first contemporary American fantasist to "recognize the post-modern crisis of fiction," and he applies Barth's notions of exhaustion and articulation to FO, ER, SWF, GGB, LF, and Chimera.

H297   ----------. "The New Consciousness." In Literary History of the United States: History. 4th ed., rev. Ed. Robert E. Spiller, et al. New York: Macmillan, 1974. Pp. 1415-25. [p. 1425]

Hassan observes that Barth is one of several contemporary authors who have demonstrated the ability to create "striking new languages" out of the apparent lexical exhaustion of literature.

H298   Hawkes, John. "The Floating Opera and Second Skin." Mosaic, 8, No. 1 (1974), 17-28.

Hawkes begins this intriguing essay by observing that he and Barth espouse closely related fictional aesthetics. But whereas wit (i.e., wordplay, verbal parody and the subtle ridicule of everything pretentious, banal, ignorant, and pedestrian) marks Barth's fiction, heavier cadences and a "dark" voice characterize Hawkes' work; Hawkes claims that he is, at heart, a "ruthless" moralist. He goes on to sketch the "conceptual" parallels between FO and his own Second Skin (the differences in concept—he avoids the word plot—come later). He then illustrates the structural dissimilarities between the two novels. He observes that FO is carefully arranged and produces a sense of total consciousness; the book is, in short, a work of "artifice." Second Skin, on the other hand, is a work of "vision" which proceeds through the use of association and which creates a dream-like atmosphere. Whereas Hawkes' purpose is almost purely emotive, Barth's is "to extend fiction into the realm of pure and lively and fearful paradox, to cloak abstractions of the human voice in the comic clothes of humanity, to reinvent the world's language."

H299   Henderson, Harry B., III. Versions of the Past: The Historical Imagination in American Fiction. New York: Oxford Univ. Press, 1974. [pp. 270, 277-78, 280-85, 286, 299, 302]

Henderson examines Barth's use of history, role playing, and parody in SWF as well as the book's apocalyptic vision, and he likens Barth's treatment of his subject matter in SWF to Pynchon's handling of historical materials in V..

H300   Johnsen, William A. "Toward a Redefinition of Modernism." Boundary 2, 2 (1974), 539-56. [pp. 542, 554, 556]

Johnsen feels that coincidence resides at the heart of of post-Modernist aesthetics, "ranging from a metaphysical attitude towards coincidence in Kesey and Burroughs, towards urbane acceptance in Burgess and Barth."

H301   Jones, D. Allan. "John Barth's 'Anonymiad.'" Studies in Short Fiction, 11 (1974), 361-66.

Jones sets out to demonstrate that Barth's "Anonymiad" is "at once a parodic epic, a pastoral romance, a history of literature, and a treatise on aesthetics." Barth's treatment of the dual themes of art and love is also discussed in considerable detail.

†H302   Jordan, Enoch Pope, III. "A Critical Study of the Textual Variants in John Barth's Novels: The Floating Opera, The End of the Road, and The Sot-Weed Factor." Diss. The University of Oklahoma, 1974. [DAI, 35: 2273A]

The original and revised editions of Barth's first three novels are compared by Jordan, and all the variant readings are listed. Jordan feels that the revisions evidence Barth's maturation as a fictional stylist; Barth becomes increasingly aware of the sound and structure of his prose, the effects produced by the narrative voice, and the necessity of maintaining a suitable narrative pace. The changes Barth made in FO are radical: the book's tone, structure, and theme are affected. SWF and especially ER underwent considerably less alteration.

†H303 Josenhans, Elinor Louise. "Form in the Fiction of John Barth." Diss. Fordham University, 1974. [DAI, 35: 2993A]

Josenhans contends that four basic attitudes govern the formal choices which underlie Barth's art: a dissatisfaction with realism because of the restrictions it places on the creative possibilities in art, the corresponding belief that fiction must acknowledge artifice, a desire to return to oral-aural forms to express contemporary experience, and a conviction that the reader must change from being a passive observer of fiction to becoming an active participant in the fictive process. FO, ER, SWF, GGB, LF, and Chimera are examined in this context.

H304 Ketterer, David. New Worlds for Old: The Apocalyptic Imagination, Science Fiction, and American Literature. Bloomington and London: Indiana Univ. Press, 1974. [pp. 9, 35-36]

Ketterer observes that Barth's vision can be termed apocalyptic, but he does not discuss Barth's fiction.

H305 Koelb, Clayton. "John Barth's 'Glossolalia.'" Comparative Literature, 26 (1974), 334-45.

Koelb closely examines the prose rhythms of "Glossolalia" not in order to illuminate the story as such, but to arrive at "a new understanding of the relationships that obtain in practice among the notions of meter, verse, and prose."

H306 Lyons, John O. "The College Novel in America: 1962-1974." Critique, 16, No. 2 (1974), 121-28.

Lyons notes that ER and GGB cannot truly be considered college novels, although the latter illustrates "the manner in which the college is now used as a setting for wild allegory."

H307 Rahv, Philip. "Foreword." In Modern Occasions 2: New Fiction, Criticism, Poetry. Ed. with an intro. by Philip Rahv. Port Washington, N.Y., and London: Kennikat Press, 1974. Pp. 3-7. [p. 4]

Rahv feels that Barth's "recent" fiction, LF and perhaps Chimera, is not truly experimental. Barth has merely been "fiddling with the fictional medium," and, in so doing, he has been indulging in what "is no more than a sterile and aberrant form of avant-gardism."

†H308 Reed, Pleasant Larus, III. "The Integrated Short-Story Collection: Studies of a Form of Nineteenth- and Twentieth-Century Fiction." Diss. Indiana University, 1974. [DAI, 35: 6730A]

Part of the avowed purpose of Reed's study, which actually goes no further than Faulkner, is to provide a context in which such works as LF may more readily be understood.

†H309 Reilly, Charles Edward. "The Ancient Roots of Modern Satiric Fiction: An Analysis of 'Petronian' and 'Apuleian' Elements in the Novels of John Barth, J. P. Donleavy, Joseph Heller, James Joyce, and Vladimir Nabokov." Diss. University of Delaware, 1974. [DAI: 35: 2293A-94A]

Reilly recounts Barth's debt to the satiric mode employed by Apuleius in his Metamorphoses. In Chimera, Barth considers the same problem which obsessed Apuleius, how man can find peace and meaning in an absurd and amoral world, and concludes by affirming the Apuleian idea that these qualities can only be attained by rejecting earthly attractions and pursuing ideal truths. Moreover, Chimera, like the "Cupid and Psyche" subplot in the Metamorphoses, contains an allegorical representation of the human mind as it rises above the agonies and moral chaos of everyday existence through the godlike act of literary creation.

†H310 Rice, Elaine Fritz. "The Satire of John Barth and Kurt Vonnegut, Jr.: The Menippean Tradition in the 1960's in America." Diss. Arizona State University, 1974. [DAI, 35: 7876A-77A]

Rice argues that the works of Barth and Vonnegut, far from signaling the advent of a new novelistic form, are well within an established prose tradition, that of Menippean satire. "Like their literary ancestors, these contemporary analyzers of the human condition depict in comic form, covered with overtones of didacticism and nihilism, man as a victim instead of a beneficiary of progress." Yet Barth and Vonnegut also differ from their predecessors, who were "usually conservatives with a belief in traditional morality."

†H311 St.Germain, Amos Joseph. "Religious Interpretation and Contemporary Literature: Kurt Vonnegut, Jr., Robert Coover and John Barth." Diss. The University of Iowa, 1974. [DAI, 35: 4552A]

St.Germain explores the possibilities of a "theological" criticism of literature and attempts to demonstrate the value of such a criticism to interdisciplinary studies by examining the writings of Vonnegut, Coover, and Barth. All three depict a world in which humanity is overwhelmed by alienation, but Barth's vision is clearly the bleakest. Only in his latest work does Barth back away from the view that philosophical and theological speculations, as well as all other intellectual and artistic activity, are utterly useless.

H312 Schulz, Max F. "Characters (Contra Characterization) in the Contemporary Novel." In The Theory of the Novel: New Essays. Ed. John Halperin. New York: Oxford Univ. Press, 1974. Pp. 141-54. [pp. 147-53]

Barth, Schulz argues, has developed "from a writer of traditional stories" (in FO and ER) to "a mythicist, parodist, artificer, and Black Humorist" (in SWF and GGB but, more notably, in LF and Chimera). Schulz gives the majority of his attention to LF, a book in which "the author-protagonist sees himself both in the serialized growth of his protagonist into a writer and in the archetypal dimensions of the eternal artist."

H313 Stark, John O. The Literature of Exhaustion: Borges, Nabokov, and Barth. Durham, N.C.: Duke Univ. Press, 1974. [pp. 1-12, 61, 118-78]

After establishing the common ground shared by Borges, Nabokov, and Barth, the essence of which is their fondness for artifice and their anti-realism, Stark examines each writer separately. The preponderance of his material on Barth concerns SWF, GGB, LF, and Chimera, although FO and ER are also discussed. Barth's use of Chinese boxes, the regressus in infinitum, paradox, allusion, metamorphosis, imagery (especially mirrors), and point of view are examined as are his unconventional handling of time, his treatment of the theme of love, and the autobiographical, social, political, psychological, and philosophical elements in Barth's fiction. Stark's focus is Barth's style, especially as it reinforces his themes, and the ways in which Barth sets the Real world in opposition to art.

†H314 Storms, Charles Gilbert, III. "Satire in the Fiction of John Barth." Diss. Rutgers University, 1974. [DAI, 35: 480A-81A]

Storms contends that Barth, unlike traditional satirists, whose satire tends to have a moral or social focus, examines the nature of reality itself, what people take reality to be, and the way in which reality is shaped by the structures people create. The artificiality and restrictiveness of personal masks and absolute values are ridiculed in FO, ER, SWF, and GGB. Moreover, SWF burlesques history, and GGB, LF, and Chimera parody the myth of the hero. Yet Barth's parody also reveals his deep feelings for the serious, tragic dimension of myth and the ability of literature to convey truth despite literature's artificiality.

H315 Tharpe, Jac. John Barth: The Comic Sublimity of Paradox. With a preface by Harry T. Moore. Carbondale and Edwardsville: Southern Illinois Univ. Press; London and Amsterdam: Feffer & Simons, 1974.

Chapters on the philosophical and aesthetic underpinnings of Barth's fiction frame six intermediate chapters, one devoted to each of Barth's books. Tharpe argues that, although the books, taken as a group, "comprise a history of philosophy," Barth is primarily an aesthetician; in fact, "form—form itself—is the content" of LF and Chimera. Nothing is heartily affirmed or denied in Barth's fiction—aside from the fact that nothing can be heartily affirmed or denied. "Barth's genius lies in his awareness of magnificent ironies and his ability to dramatize paradox"—the paradox of reproduction and decay, illusion and reality, the fabulous and the ridiculous. Tharpe feels that Barth's vision is "marvelous-[ly] carnal," yet the horror of this vision is nearly concealed by the author's expansive humor.

The implications of "performance" and the paradoxical Hamlet question dominate Tharpe's treatment of FO, whereas, in looking at ER, his primary concerns are cosmopsis and Barth's use of the Adamic myth. The Adamic myth also figures prominently in Tharpe's treatment of SWF. In that novel, the New Eden turns out to be the scene of all human ills; as much as anything else, SWF dramatizes "the plagues in Paradise." The moral and metaphysical implications of Eben Cooke's attempt to establish his identity in a universe of illusion and seemingly endless possibility as well as Barth's depiction of the complex feminine principle (in the person of Joan Toast) are also given considerable attention. Barth's abundant use of cyclology and paradox as well as his creation of a "phylogenic tragedy" highlight the GGB chapter. The twin themes of art and love, according to Tharpe, dominate LF, Barth's "portrait of the artist as hero." Unlike many critics, Tharpe sees "Echo" as the central story in the Funhouse collection. The brief chapter devoted to Chimera focuses on the autobiographical aspect of the book as well as its presentation of the "hero as artist" motif.

Tharpe's book is primarily directed toward the reader who knows his Barth. Anyone whose acquaintance with Barth's fiction is slight is likely to find Tharpe's volume to be of limited usefulness. On the other hand, the devoted Barthian should find the book to be a most valuable addition to the growing corpus of serious Barth criticism.

Reviews:

*H316   Anon. The Long Beach (Calif.) Independent Press Telegram, 4 Dec. 1974.

*H317   Burns, G. Frank. "Series Adds Barth and O'Connor." The (Nashville) Tennessean, 5 Jan. 1975.

H318   Isaacson, David. Library Journal, 100 (1 Feb. 1975), 298.

H319   Anon. Choice, 12 (Apr. 1975), 224.

-157-

H320 Detweiler, Robert. <u>Modern</u> <u>Fiction</u> <u>Studies</u>, 21 (Summer 1975), 292-93.

H321 Schoenberg, E. I. "A Little Bit of Luck." <u>Review</u> <u>of</u> <u>Books</u> <u>and</u> <u>Religion</u>, 4 (July-Aug. 1975), 8.

†H322 Turner, Theodore Baker, III. "Mind Forged Manacles: Images of the University in American Fiction of the Nineteen Sixties, A Study in Kesey, Mailer, Barth, Bellow, Nabokov, and Burroughs." Diss. The University of Iowa, 1974. [<u>DAI</u>, 35: 4566A-67A]

Turner examines the ways in which characters in the novels of Barth and five other contemporary American fictionalists endeavor to overcome the damaging effects of an educational system which stands as a threat to their selfhood. Barth's criticism of the university, like Bellow's and Nabokov's, has "an air of self-mocking, satirical disgust." However bleak the picture, each of the six authors expresses some optimism that the will and creativity of the individual can be restored and that better relationships with institutions can be developed.

†H323 Underwood, Jerry Lawrence. "The Fictional Universe of John Barth." Diss. State University of New York at Stony Brook, 1974. [<u>DAI</u>, 36: 895A]

Underwood feels that <u>FO</u>, <u>ER</u>, <u>SWF</u>, <u>GGB</u>, <u>LF</u>, and <u>Chimera</u> are unified by "two fundamental and interrelated quest motifs: the search for values in the <u>nada</u> universe and the search for fresh ways to write." Meaning and shape are given to Barth's fictional world by virtue of the fact that he and his characters are able to avoid silence and despair by "fill[ing] in the blank" presented by <u>nada</u> and the empty page.

H324 Weinstein, Arnold L. <u>Vision</u> <u>and</u> <u>Response</u> <u>in</u> <u>Modern</u> <u>Fiction</u>. Ithaca and London: Cornell Univ. Press, 1974. [p. 269n]

Weinstein argues that <u>LF</u>, like Butor's <u>Passing</u> <u>Time</u>, Simon's <u>The</u> <u>Flanders</u> <u>Road</u>, and Robbe-Grillet's <u>In</u> <u>the</u> <u>Labyrinth</u>, "records the breakdown and exhaustion of the mimetic, naturalistic tradition and announces the possibilities of a mythological solution."

<1975>

H325 Alter, Robert. "The Self-Conscious Moment: Reflections on the Aftermath of Modernism." <u>TriQuarterly</u>, No. 33 (1975), pp. 209-30. [pp. 210, 214, 215-18, 219]

Alter mentions Barth as an important writer of self-
conscious fiction but spends more time expressing his
uneasiness about Barth's "Literature of Exhaustion"
essay.

†H326 Brunette, Peter Clark, Jr. "Narrators and Narration in
the Fiction of John Barth." Diss. The University of
Wisconsin, Madison, 1975.

Brunette, through a close, formalistic reading of FO,
ER, SWF, and GGB, attempts to show that "the act of
creating language and more specifically, fiction,
functions as the primary matter" of Barth's novels.
Brunette is quick to add, however, that the books show
fiction finally to be "helpless in the face of death,
the only real story."

H327 Dickstein, Morris. "Fiction Hot and Kool: Dilemmas of
the Experimental Writer." TriQuarterly, No. 33 (1975),
pp. 257-72. [pp. 259, 262-68, 269]

Dickstein has some fondness for Barth's novels, especially SWF, which he feels helped to break down the
realistic conventions of novel writing in America. But
he is alienated by the self-conscious aestheticism of
Barth's short fiction, which he finds lacking in imagination, characterization, and emotion. Dickstein says
of Chimera: "Storytelling is rooted in wonder, in the
marvelous, in magical charm, enchantment, even posses-
sion. Barth's versions utterly lack vividness, let
alone the power to charm or possess. The stories
themselves are pallid and hard to follow, swamped by
digression and commentary."

H328 Fredericks, S. C. "Science Fiction and the World of Greek
Myths." Helios, NS 2 (1975), 1-22. [pp. 2-3, 18]

Fredericks cites GGB as a novel which exemplifies the
"prefigurative technique" of mythological fiction. Giles
carries out each phase of Joseph Campbell's heroic initiation pattern, "yet Barth's final message is that myths
in fact do not establish patterns of universal validity
for human action." And, in an aside, Fredericks observes
that it is instructive to compare William Tenn's A Lamp
for Medusa (1951), a humorous retelling of the Perseus
myth, with Barth's "Perseid" and "Bellerophoniad."

H329 Graff, Gerald. "Babbitt at the Abyss: The Social Context
of Postmodern American Fiction." TriQuarterly, No. 33
(1975), pp. 305-37. [p. 322]

Graff contends that, paradoxically, GGB is self-con-
sciously anti-realistic in method yet satiric in effect
and—to complicate matters still further—that the
novel might be regarded as a reductio ad absurdum of
both.

H330   Hassan, Ihab. Paracriticisms: Seven Speculations of the
        Times. Urbana: Univ. of Illinois Press, 1975. [pp. 22,
        44, 46, 82, 83, 85-86, 101, 104-05, 111-12, 114, 140,
        141]

        Barth's name comes up frequently (as do the following of
        his works: GGB, "The Literature of Exhaustion," and LF)
        as Hassan struggles with the problems of post-Modernist
        aesthetics.

H331   Kennard, Jean E. Number and Nightmare: Forms of Fantasy
        in Contemporary Fiction. Hamden, Conn.: Archon Books,
        1975. [pp. 11-12, 23, 25, 29, 32, 33, 37-38, 52, 57-
        82, 94, 96, 97, 100, 103, 110, 124, 127-28, 131, 132,
        156, 166, 204]

        Kennard's treatment of Barth involves a reworking and
        expansion of H148. FO, ER, SWF, GGB, and Chimera all
        illustrate a post-existentialist sensibility, though
        only the last three are what Kennard terms "novels of
        number"; that is, "dramatizations of man's alienation
        from his world" in a form that "takes the reader sys-
        tematically and logically towards nothing . . . by
        breaking down one by one his expectations of realism."

H332   Klinkowitz, Jerome. Literary Disruptions: The Making of
        a Post-Contemporary American Fiction. Urbana: Univer-
        sity of Illinois Press, 1975. [pp. ix, 4-11, 18, 19,
        22, 32, 58-59, 99-100, 101, 112, 136-37, 153, 165, 170,
        171, 173, 175, 189-90, 192]

        In arguing for the existence of a "post-contemporary"
        American fiction, Klinkowitz contends that Vonnegut,
        Barthelme, Kosinski, and others were demonstrating that
        fiction was alive and well at the very time Barth was
        in the process of formally accepting fiction's death—
        in his "Literature of Exhaustion" essay ("a literary
        suicide note") and his books LF and Chimera. Whereas
        Barth seems overwhelmed by existence and all too often
        leads his reader in the direction of frustrated in-
        articulation, the "literary disruptionists" are able to
        confront existence squarely and verbalize their ideas.
        The major problem with LF and Chimera, as Klinkowitz
        sees it, is that, in both books, Barth "confuses the
        product of art with the conditions of its inception";
        that is, he fails to integrate his aesthetic concerns
        with storytelling.

H333   Kostelanetz, Richard. "New Fiction in America." In Sur-
        fiction: Fiction Now . . . and Tomorrow. Ed. Raymond
        Federman. Chicago: Swallow Press, 1975. Pp. 85-100.
        [pp. 88, 93-94]

        Kostelanetz mentions that Barth has exploited non-
        literary materials in his fiction "by turning the forms
        and trappings of literary scholarship into fiction" (à

-160-

la Borges and Nabokov) and by employing a Moebius strip in "Frame-Tale."

H334 LeClair, Thomas. "Death and Black Humor." *Critique*, 17, No. 1 (1975), 5-40. [pp. 5-6, 17-19, 22, 28-30, 32-38]

"The theses of this essay are that the 'blackness' of Black Humor is primarily funereal, that the fact and awareness of death are the basic sources of the pessimism or nihilism of such fiction, that the presence of death in such fiction does much to explain the kinds of heroes presented, the strategies of selfhood they adopt, and the kinds of endings and forms the writers employ, and that the Black Humorists' ultimate concern with death gives their fiction both a philosophical ultimacy and an artistic rationale." LeClair, when discussing Barth's work, focuses on FO, but he also alludes to SWF, GGB, and Chimera.

H335 Litz, A. Walton. "The Short Story Today." In *Major American Short Stories*. Ed. A. Walton Litz. New York: Oxford Univ. Press, 1975. Pp. 713-19.

Nearly all of Litz's section on the contemporary American short story is devoted to Barth. Litz examines Barth's use of parody and burlesque, his reaffirmation of the vitality of narrative art, and his attempt, in LF, "to express the discontinuous nature of our technological society."

H336 McConnell, Frank. "The Corpse of the Dragon: Notes on Postromantic Fiction." *TriQuarterly*, No. 33 (1975), pp. 273-303. [pp. 275, 283-84, 285, 290, 295, 298-300, 301, 303]

McConnell praises "Menelaiad" and Chimera. He is especially taken with "Bellerophoniad," since he feels that it embodies "Barth's most indelible achievement, the discovery that monster and monster-slayer, civilizing hero and the perennial entropy undermining all civilizing quests, are not contradictory but contrary principles, allowing us to reassert values not in spite of but upon the basis of the fictiveness, the sham which we have found to underlie all human value systems."

H337 Morris, Christopher D. "Barth and Lacan: The World of the Moebius Strip." *Critique*, 17, No. 1 (1975), 69-77.

Morris contends that existential and phenomenological approaches to LF are, at best, inadequate, since selfhood is altogether ignored in the book "except as a farcical or sentimental entity, and the locus of the 'narrative' affliction is ultimately reduced to the linguistic problem of substitution."

H338 Pearce, Richard. 'Enter the Frame." In Surfiction: Fiction Now . . . and Tomorrow. Ed. Raymond Federman. Chicago: Swallow Press, 1975. Pp. 47-57. [p. 48]

Pearce feels that Barth and others have followed the lead of Samuel Beckett, the progenitor of "surfiction" (i.e., fiction in which the reader no longer sees "a clear picture contained within the narrator's purview, but an erratic image where the narrator, the subject, and the medium are brought into the same imaginative field of interaction, an image that is shattered, confused, self-contradictory but with an independent and individual life of its own").

H339 Said, Edward W. "Contemporary Fiction and Criticism." TriQuarterly, No. 33 (1975), pp. 231-56. [pp. 236-37, 238-39]

Said cites Barth's Chimera and his "Literature of Exhaustion" essay as examples of the school of writing which demonstrates that " . . . American fiction, more than fiction generally, is a particularly apt fictional extension of past fiction." Writers like Barth do not view fiction as an intervention into reality but as an intervention into other fiction.

H340 Scholes, Robert. Structural Fabulation: An Essay on Fiction of the Future. Notre Dame and London: Univ. of Notre Dame Press (Univ. of Notre Dame Ward-Phillips Lectures in English Language and Literature, Vol. 7), 1975. [pp. 8, 69]

Scholes discusses the metafictional aspect of LF and likens Paul Atreides, the protagonist of Frank Herbert's Dune, to "the comic-mythic heroes" of Chimera.

H341 Sukenick, Ronald. "The New Tradition in Fiction." In Surfiction: Fiction Now . . . and Tomorrow. Ed. Raymond Federman. Chicago: Swallow Press, 1975. Pp. 35-45. [pp. 39, 43]

Sukenick briefly discusses Barth as a writer who has experimented with the technological structure of fiction (in "Frame-Tale) and who has attempted to revitalize narrative art through "exhuberant invention."

H342 Tatham, Campbell. "Message [Concerning the Felt Ultimacies of One John Barth]." Boundary 2, 3 (1975), 259-87.

Tatham's is an unconventional article or, perhaps more accurately, an article of exhaustion, which examines a number of central Barthian paradoxes: that Todd Andrews of FO and Jacob Horner of ER fail to "feel . . . the ultimacies to which they assent analytically," that

-162-

turning experience into speech involves a necessary falsification of experience, that Barth's characters seek out something to affirm but fear that in so doing they will betray the complexity of existence, that Eben Cooke of <u>SWF</u> can accept the fact "that lives are stories" but finds <u>it</u> "unthinkable" that lives, like stories, end, <u>et cetera</u>. What, then, do Barth's novels <u>mean</u>? "Nothing, exactly," responds Tatham. "His fictions repeatedly demonstrate the various ways in which the intellectual operations initially immobilize the individual seeking certitude; but he simultaneously implies that intellectual anxiety must be allowed to run its full course, must be pressed to the <u>point</u> of exhaustion, before it can circle back on itself, in-itself a trace, a key, a <u>felt</u>-ultimacy—not only for the particular character spiralling through the jumble of letters, but for the reader as well. He meddles with the process of thought the better to weaken it and allow for a <u>different</u> mode of certitude, for renewed acting."

I. REVIEWS OF BOOKS BY JOHN BARTH

THE FLOATING OPERA

<Ala   Appleton-Century-Crofts, [1956]>

I1   Anon. Virginia Kirkus' Service, 24 (15 June 1956), 417.

I2   Adelman, George. Library Journal, 81 (Aug. 1956), 1789.

*I3 Anon. "First Novel Inspired by Famous Showboat." Springfield (Mass.) Sunday Republican, 12 Aug. 1956, Sec. C, p. 12.

I4   Anon. Los Angeles Mirror and Daily News, 20 Aug. 1956, Part 2, p. 2.

I5   [Werner, William L.] "It's a Real Good Year For Authors." State College and Bellefonte, Pa., Centre Daily Times, 21 Aug. 1956, p. 4.

I6   Mandel, Siegfried. "Gaudy Showboat." The New York Times Book Review, 26 Aug. 1956, p. 27.

I7   Myers, Art. "Life's But a Showboat Drifting by." The Washington Post and Times Herald, 26 Aug. 1956, p. E6.

I8   Rubin, Louis D., Jr. "Novels of The Eastern Shore and War." Baltimore Evening Sun, 27 Aug. 1956, p. 16.

*I9 Freedley, George. The (New York) Morning Telegraph, 28 Aug. 1956, p. 2.

I10 Hogan, William. "Life Is a Showboat, A Young Author Finds." San Francisco Chronicle, 28 Aug. 1956, p. 19.

I11 [Werner, William L.] "Warning Given Genteel Readers On New Novel." State College and Bellefonte, Pa., Centre Daily Times, 28 Aug. 1956, p. 4.

I12 Prescott, Orville. "Books of the Times." The New York Times, 3 Sept. 1956, p. 11.

I13 Ward, Lynn. "Barth Writes Novel On Suicide Theme." The (Pennsylvania State University) Daily Collegian, 2 Oct. 1956, p. 2.

I14   Cooper, Madison. "Chockfull of Curiosities." The Dallas Morning News, 14 Oct. 1956, Part 5, p. 15.

I15   Harding, Walter. "Needless Vulgarity in Novel." Chicago Sunday Tribune Magazine of Books, 21 Oct. 1956, p. 14.

I16   Schickel, Richard. "An 'Opera' Afloat." Milwaukee Journal, 30 Dec. 1956, Part 5, p. 4.

I17   Anon. "Comic Opera." Omaha World-Herald, 13 Jan. 1957, Sec. G, p. 29.

<Alb   Avon Books, [1965]>

I18   Hyman, Stanley Edgar. "John Barth's First Novel." The New Leader, 48 (12 Apr. 1965), 20-21.

I19   Hicks, Granville. "Doubt Without Skepticism." Saturday Review, 48 (3 July 1965), 23-24. Rpt. in Literary Horizons: A Quarter Century of American Fiction, with the assistance of Jack Alan Robbins (New York: New York Univ. Press, 1970), pp. 259-62.

<A6a   Doubleday & Company, 1967>

I20   Bannon, Barbara A. Publishers' Weekly, 191 (6 Mar. 1967), 73.

I21   Haney, Patrick. The Denver Quarterly, 2 (Summer 1967), 170-71.

I22   Hendin, Josephine. "John Barth's Fictions for Survival." Harper's, 247 (Sept. 1973), 102-06.

<A6b   Secker & Warburg, [1968]>

I23   Wall, Stephen. "The Horrors of Holovision." The (London) Observer Review, 29 Sept. 1968, p. 26.

I24   Price, R.G.G. "New Novels." Punch, 255 (2 Oct. 1968), 487.

I25   Graham, Kenneth. "Frayn's a Caution." The Listener, 80 (3 Oct. 1968), 449.

-166-

I26   Anon. "Liebestodd." The Times Literary Supplement, 10 Oct. 1968, p. 1161.

I27   Bradbury, Malcolm. "The Human Comedy." Manchester Guardian Weekly, 99 (10 Oct. 1968), 14.

<A6d   Bantam Books, [1972]>

I28   Petersen, Clarence. "Pick of the Paperbacks." Book World, 6 Aug. 1972, p. 13.

THE END OF THE ROAD

<A2a   Doubleday & Company, 1958>

I29   Anon. Virginia Kirkus' Service, 26 (15 May 1958), 362.

I30   Boatwright, Taliaferro. "Jacob Horner Came Out of His Corner, and Then—." New York Herald Tribune Book Review, 20 July 1958, p. 3.

I31   Anon. "A Study in Nihilism." Time, 72 (21 July 1958), 80.

I32   Pickrel, Paul. "Unlucky Jake." Harper's Magazine, 217 (Aug. 1958), 87.

I33   LaHaye, Judson. Best Sellers, 18 (1 Aug. 1958), 165.

I34   Wermuth, Paul C. Library Journal, 83 (1 Sept. 1958), 2319-20.

I35   Parker, Dorothy. "Dorothy Parker on Books." Esquire, 50 (Oct. 1958), 102-03. [p. 102]

I36   Kerner, David. "Psychodrama in Eden." Chicago Review, 13 (Winter-Spring 1959), 59-67.

I37   Bluestone, George. "John Wain and John Barth: The Angry and the Accurate." The Massachusetts Review, 1 (Spring 1960), 582-89.

<A2b   Avon Books, [1960]>

I38   Hicks, Granville. "Doubt Without Skepticism." Saturday Review, 48 (3 July 1965), 23-24.   Rpt. in Literary Horizons: A Quarter Century of American Fiction, with the assistance of Jack Alan Robbins (New York: New York Univ. Press, 1970), pp. 259-62.

<A2c   Secker & Warburg, 1962>

I39   Coleman, John. "Books." Queen, 221 (18 Sept. 1962), 27-28.

I40   Raven, Simon. "A Lemon for the Teacher." The Spectator, No. 7004 (21 Sept. 1962), p. 410.

I41   Richardson, Maurice. "Upper Crusts." New Statesman, 64 (21 Sept. 1962), 370.

I42   Anon. "Fiction by Tyndareus." John O'Londons, 7 (27 Sept. 1962), Pull-Out Guide to New Books, iv.

I43   Anon. "Strife and Struggle." The Times Literary Supplement, 28 Sept. 1962, p. 757.

I44   Bradbury, Malcolm. "New Novels." Punch, 243 (10 Oct. 1962), 540.

<A7a   Doubleday & Company, 1967>

I45   Bannon, Barbara A. Publishers' Weekly, 191 (26 June 1967), 64.

I46   Hendin, Josephine. "John Barth's Fictions for Survival." Harper's, 247 (Sept. 1973), 102-06.

THE SOT-WEED FACTOR

<A3a   Doubleday & Company, 1960>

I47   Anon. Virginia Kirkus' Service, 28 (15 June 1960), 462-63.

148 Fuller, Edmund. "The Joke Is on Mankind." The New York Times Book Review, 21 Aug. 1960, p. 4.

149 Harding, Walter. "An Historical Novel to End All Historical Novels." Chicago Sunday Tribune Magazine of Books, 21 Aug. 1960, p. 5.

150 Anon. "I' Faith, 'Tis Good." Newsweek, 56 (29 Aug. 1960), 88-89.

151 Werner, W[illiam] L. "Detailed Report on Bundle of Reading." State College and Bellefonte, Pa., Centre Daily Times, 30 Aug. 1960, p. 5.

152 Young, Philip. "Response Not Typical." State College & Bellefonte, Pa., Centre Daily Times, 2 Sept. 1960, p. 4.

153 Anon. "The Virgin Laureate." Time, 76 (5 Sept. 1960), 77.

154 Robie, Burton A. Library Journal, 85 (15 Sept. 1960), 3099.

155 Walsh, William J., S.J. Best Sellers, 20 (15 Sept. 1960), 200-01.

156 McLaughlin, Richard. "'The Sot-Weed Factor': Lengthy Historical Spoof, by John Barth, About 17th-Century London and Maryland." Springfield (Mass.) Sunday Republican, 25 Sept. 1960, p. 4D.

157 Southern, Terry. "New Trends and Old Hats." The Nation, 191 (19 Nov. 1960), 380-83. [p. 381]

158 Barker, Shirley. "History Is Still Good Fiction." Saturday Review, 43 (26 Nov. 1960), 21-22.

159 Sutcliffe, Denham. "Worth a Guilty Conscience." The Kenyon Review, 23 (Winter 1961), 181-84.

160 Werner, W[illiam] L. "Poetry Discussion, Work into a Novel." State College and Bellefonte, Pa., Centre Daily Times, 3 Jan. 1961, p. 2.

161 Arthur, Helen. "The Marathon Adventures of a 17th-Century Englishman." New York Herald Tribune Lively Arts and Book Review, 22 Jan. 1961, p. 30.

162 Fiedler, Leslie. "John Barth: An Eccentric Genius." The New Leader, 44 (13 Feb. 1961), 22-24. Rpt. in On Contemporary Literature, ed. with an intro. by Richard Kostelanetz (New York: Avon Books, 1964; expanded ed., 1969), pp. 238-43; also rpt. in The Collected Essays of Leslie Fiedler (New York: Stein and Day, 1971), II, 325-30.

<A3b>   Secker & Warburg, 1961>

I63   King, Francis. "Smog of the Spirit." New Statesman, 62
       (13 Oct. 1961), 524-25.

I64   Shrapnel, Norman. "Boy's Own Boccaccio." The (Manchester)
       Guardian, 13 Oct. 1961, p. 7.

I65   Anon. "Invitation to Escape." The Times Literary Supple-
       ment, 27 Oct. 1961, p. 765.

I66   Baines, Nancy. "Bawdy Frolic." The Cape Times (Capetown,
       So. Africa), 29 Nov. 1961, p. 12.

<A3c   Grosset & Dunlap Universal Library, [1964]>

I67   Hyman, Stanley Edgar. "The American Adam." The New
       Leader, 47 (2 Mar. 1964), 20-21. Rpt. in Standards:
       A Chronicle of Books for Our Time (New York: Horizon
       Press, 1966), pp. 204-08.

I68   Dientsfry, Harris. "Blended Especially for a Heady Smoke."
       Book Week, 15 Mar. 1964, p. 18.

I69   Hicks, Granville. "Doubt Without Skepticism." Saturday
       Review, 48 (3 July 1965), 23-24. Rpt. in Literary
       Horizons: A Quarter Century of American Fiction, with
       the assistance of Jack Alan Robbins (New York: New York
       Univ. Press, 1970), pp. 259-62.

I70   Bannon, Barbara A. Publishers' Weekly, 190 (14 Nov. 1966),
       111.

I71   Petersen, Clarence. "Paperbacks." Chicago Tribune Books
       Today, 8 Jan. 1967, p. 9.

<A3d   Panther Books, [1965]>

I72   Anon. "Paperbacks." The (London) Observer, 10 Oct. 1965,
       p. 22.

<A5a   Doubleday & Company, 1967>

I73   Anon. Choice, 4 (June 1967), 418.

-170-

I74   Hendin, Josephine. "John Barth's Fictions for Survival." Harper's, 247 (Sept. 1973), 102-06.

GILES GOAT-BOY

<A4a   Doubleday & Company, 1966>

I75   Anon. "Doubleday." Publishers' Weekly, 189 (25 Apr. 1966), 71.

I76   Kitching, Jessie. Publishers' Weekly, 189 (23 May 1966), 81.

I77   Anon. The Virginia Kirkus Service, 34 (1 June 1966), 550.

I78   Harding, Walter. "Satire with a Ba-a-a." Chicago Tribune Books Today, 31 July 1966, p. 3.

I79   ----------. Library Journal, 91 (Aug. 1966), 3762.

I80   Highet, Gilbert. Book-of-the-Month Club News, Aug. 1966, pp. 13-14.

I81   Davis, Douglas M. "Mr. Barth Is a Grand Tease In The Rippling and Rolling 'Giles.'" The National Observer, 1 Aug. 1966, p. 19.

I82   Fremont-Smith, Eliot. "The Surfacing of Mr. Barth [Laughter]." The New York Times, 3 Aug. 1966, p. 35.

I83   Anon. "New Barth Novel Widely Acclaimed." The (Pennsylvania State University) Daily Collegian, 4 Aug. 1966, p. 3.

I84   Maddocks, Melvin. "Should the Scapegoat Win a Sheepskin?" The Christian Science Monitor, 4 Aug. 1966, p. 5.

I85   Anon. "Black Bible." Time, 88 (5 Aug. 1966), 92.

I86   Hicks, Granville. "Crowned with the Shame of Men." Saturday Review, 49 (6 Aug. 1966), 21-23. Rpt. in Literary Horizons: A Quarter Century of American Fiction, with the assistance of Jack Alan Robbins (New York: New York Univ. Press, 1970), pp. 262-68.

I87   Poirier, Richard. "WESCAC and the Messiah: John Barth's Long, Brilliant Satire on the Labyrinthine Ways of

Mankind." *Book Week*, 7 Aug. 1966, pp. 1, 12. Rpt. in *The World of Black Humor: An Introductory Anthology of Writings and Criticism*, ed. Douglas M. Davis (New York: E.P. Dutton, 1967), pp. 324-28.

I88 Scholes, Robert. "'George is my name.'" *The New York Times Book Review*, 7 Aug. 1966, pp. 1, 22.

I89 Anon. "Heroic Comedy." *Newsweek*, 68 (8 Aug. 1966), 81-82.

I90 Fuller, Edmund. "A New Novel by Barth: Revelation or Scandal?" *The Wall Street Journal*, 9 Aug. 1966, p. 14.

I91 Schott, Webster. "A Black Comedy to Offend Everyone." *Life*, 61 (12 Aug. 1966), 10.

I92 Carruth, Hayden. "Barth's Good Goat-Boy Satire Stretched Too Far in 710 Pages." *Buffalo Evening News Magazine*, 13 Aug. 1966, p. B-10.

I93 Goldman, Albert. "*Giles Goat-Boy*, 'egghead omnibus.'" *Vogue*, 148 (15 Aug. 1966), 51.

I94 Anon. "Barth's New Novel." *Buffalo Evening News*, 17 Aug. 1966, p. 44.

I95 Donoghue, Denis. "Grand Old Opry." *The New York Review of Books*, 18 Aug. 1966, pp. 25-26.

I96 Anon. "Recent and Readable." *The National Observer*, 29 Aug. 1966, p. 17.

I97 Anon. "Books." *Playboy*, 13 (Sept. 1966), 32, 34.

I98 Featherstone, Joseph. "John Barth as Jonathan Swift." *The New Republic*, 155 (3 Sept. 1966), 17-18.

I99 Grosskurth, Phyllis. "Biting Themes and Bawdy Humor." *The (Toronto) Globe Magazine* (insert, *The Globe and Mail*), 3 Sept. 1966, p. 15.

I100 O'Connell, Shaun. "Goat Gambit at the University." *The Nation*, 203 (5 Sept. 1966), 193-95.

I101 Bannerman, James. "A Pan for Barth's Goat-Boy." *Maclean's*, 79 (17 Sept. 1966), 59.

I102 Corbett, Edward P.J. *America*, 115 (17 Sept. 1966), 290-91.

I103 Schlueter, Paul. "Puncturing the Gods." *The Christian Century*, 83 (21 Sept. 1966), 1149.

I104 Klein, Marcus. "Gods and Goats." *The Reporter*, 35 (22 Sept. 1966), 60-62.

I105 Byrd, Scott. "Giles Goat-Boy Visited." Critique, 9, No. 1 (Fall 1966), 108-12.

I106 McColm, Pearlmarie. "The Revised New Syllabus and the Unrevised Old." The Denver Quarterly, 1 (Autumn 1966), 136-41.

I107 Morse, J. Mitchell. "Fiction Chronicle." The Hudson Review, 19 (Autumn 1966), 507-14. [p. 512]

I108 Stuart, Dabney. "A Service to the University." Shenandoah, 18 (Autumn 1966), 96-99.

I109 Anon. Choice, 3 (Oct. 1966), 632.

I110 Arimond, John. "Revelation or Hoax?" Extension, 61 (Oct. 1966), 54.

I111 Shapiro, Joel L. Best Sellers, 26 (1 Oct. 1966), 231-32.

I112 Samuels, Charles Thomas. "John Barth: A Bouyant Denial of Relevance." Commonweal, 85 (21 Oct. 1966), 80-82.

I113 Munn, Ed. "Giles Goat-Boy: Satire Ad Infinitum." The (Pennsylvania State University) Daily Collegian, 28 Oct. 1966, p. 3.

I114 Anon. "Samplings." Teachers College Record, 68 (Nov. 1966), 185-86.

I115 Malin, Irving. "Son of a Computer." The Progressive, 30 (Nov. 1966), 43.

I116 Anon. The Booklist and Subscription Books Bulletin, 63 (15 Nov. 1966), 363.

I117 Hill, William B., S.J. America, 115 (26 Nov. 1966), 706-07.

I118 Malin, Irving. Commonweal, 85 (2 Dec. 1966), 270.

I119 Balliett, Whitney. "Rub-a-Dub-Dub." The New Yorker, 42 (10 Dec. 1966), 234-36. [p. 234]

I120 Anon. "Year of the Fact." Newsweek, 68 (19 Dec. 1966), 117-19. [pp. 117-18]

I121 Anon. The Virginia Quarterly Review, 43 (Winter 1967), viii.

I122 Merril, Judith. "Books." The Magazine of Fantasy and Science Fiction, 32 (Mar. 1967), 20-27.

I123 Lodge, David. "Goatscape with Figures." The Tablet, 221 (8 Apr. 1967), 383-84.

-173-

I124   Lifson, Hugh. "Giles Goat Bore." The North American Review, NS 4 (Nov. 1967), inside back cover.

I125   Harvey, David D. "Muddle-Browed Faction." The Southern Review, NS 5 (Jan. 1969), 259-72. [pp. 267-69]

I126   Hendin, Josephine. "John Barth's Fictions for Survival." Harper's, 247 (Sept. 1973), 102-06.

<A4d   Secker & Warburg, [1967]>

I127   Anon. "The Joker Is Wild." The Times Literary Supplement, 30 Mar. 1967, p. 261. Rpt. in T. L. S.: Essays and Reviews from The Times Literary Supplement, 1967 (London: Oxford Univ. Press, 1968), pp. 100-04.

I128   Corke, Hilary. "New Novels." The Listener, 77 (30 Mar. 1967), 437.

I129   Burgess, Anthony. "Caprine Messiah." The Spectator, No. 7240 (31 Mar. 1967), pp. 369-70.

I130   MacNamara, Desmond. "Scape Goat." New Statesman, 73 (31 Mar. 1967), 442.

I131   Johnson, B.S. "Giles FitzWESCAC FitzEnglit." Books and Bookmen, 12 (Apr. 1967), 60-61.

I132   Alvarez, A[lfred]. "By Computer, out of Virgin." The (London) Observer Review, 2 Apr. 1967, p. 27.

I133   Shuttleworth, Martin. "New Novels." Punch, 252 (5 Apr. 1967), 504.

I134   Green, Martin. "Acting the Goat." Manchester Guardian Weekly, 96 (6 Apr. 1967), 11.

I135   McGuiness, Frank. London Magazine, NS 7 (May 1967), 91-92.

I136   Brooks, Peter. "John Barth." Encounter, 28 (June 1967), 71-75.

<A4f   Fawcett Publications, [1967]>

I137   Fleischer, Leonore. Publishers' Weekly, 191 (26 June 1967), 68.

I138 Petersen, Clarence. "Paperbacks." Chicago Tribune Books Today, 20 Aug. 1967, p. 13.

I139 Levitas, Gloria. "City Blights." Book World, 17 Sept. 1967, p. 15.

I140 Anon. Saturday Review, 50 (30 Sept. 1967), 47.

LOST IN THE FUNHOUSE

<A8a   Doubleday & Company, 1968>

I141 Bannon, Barbara A. Publishers' Weekly, 194 (29 July 1968), 56.

I142 Anon. The Kirkus Service, 36 (1 Aug. 1968), 836.

I143 Cassill, R[onald] V. "The Artist as Art." Chicago Tribune Book World, 15 Sept. 1968, p. 16.

I144 Harding, Walter. Library Journal, 93 (15 Sept. 1968), 3153.

I145 Davis, Douglas M. "The End Is a Beginning for Barth's 'Funhouse.'" The National Observer, 16 Sept. 1968, p. 19.

I146 Wolf, Geoffrey. "Latter-Day Scheherazade." The Washington Post and Times Herald, 26 Sept. 1968, p. A23.

I147 Anon. "Fables for People Who Can Hear with Their Eyes." Time, 92 (27 Sept. 1968), 100.

I148 Welch, Bill. "Moebius Twist For 'Funhouse.'" State College and Bellefonte, Pa., Centre Daily Times, 27 Sept. 1968, p. 4.

I149 Hicks, Granville. "The Up-to-Date Looking Glass." Saturday Review, 51 (28 Sept. 1968), 31-32. Rpt. in Literary Horizons: A Quarter Century of American Fiction, with the assistance of Jack Alan Robbins (New York: New York Univ. Press, 1970), pp. 268-71.

I150 Axthelm, Pete. "Tiny Odyssey." Newsweek, 72 (30 Sept. 1968), 106, 108.

I151 Roberts, R.E. Book-of-the-Month Club News, Fall 1968, p. 12.

I152 Adams, Phoebe. The Atlantic, 222 (Oct. 1968), 150.

I153 Carruth, Hayden. "Barth's 'Lost in the Funhouse': Reality's Essence Explored In Unconventional 'Fictions.'" The Philadelphia Inquirer, 6 Oct. 1968, Sec. 7, p. 7.

I154 Murray, John J. Best Sellers, 28 (15 Oct. 1968), 282.

I155 Fremont-Smith, Eliot. "Make It New!" The New York Times, 16 Oct. 1968, p. 45.

I156 Schott, Webster. "One Baffled Barth in Search of a Book. Life, 65 (18 Oct. 1968), 8.

I157 Davenport, Guy. "Like Nothing Nameable." The New York Times Book Review, 20 Oct. 1968, pp. 4, 63.

I158 Appel, Alfred, Jr. "The Art of Artifice." The Nation, 207 (28 Oct. 1968), 441-42.

I159 Anon. "Books." Playboy, 15 (Nov. 1968), 26, 30.

I160 Richardson, Jack. "Amusement and Revelation." The New Republic, 159 (23 Nov. 1968), 30, 34-35.

I161 Hill, William B., S.J. America, 119 (30 Nov. 1968), 563-64.

I162 Ardery, P.P. National Review, 20 (3 Dec. 1968), 1230-31.

I163 Hjortsberg, William. "John Barth in the Global Village." The Catholic World, 208 (Jan. 1969), 188.

I164 Garis, Robert. "Fiction Chronicle." Hudson Review, 22 (Spring 1969), 148-64. [pp. 163-64]

I165 Tanner, Tony. "No Exit." Partisan Review, 36 (Spring 1969), 293-95, 297-99.

I166 Lemon, Lee T. "Barth's Good Book." Prarie Schooner, 43 (Summer 1969), 231-32.

I167 Anon. The Virginia Quarterly Review, 45 (Autumn 1969), cxxviii.

I168 Harper, Howard M., Jr. "Trends in Recent American Fiction." Contemporary Literature, 12 (Spring 1971), 204-30. [pp. 206-07, 210-11]

I169 Davidson, Richard A. Studies in Short Fiction, 8 (Fall 1971), 659.

I170 Hendin, Josephine. "John Barth's Fictions for Survival." Harper's, 247 (Sept. 1973), 102-06.

<A8e   Secker & Warburg, [1969]>

I171   Anon. "Just for the Record." The Times Literary Supplement, 18 Sept. 1969, p. 1017.

I172   Hood, Stuart. "Silver-Age Fun." The Listener, 82 (18 Sept. 1969), 385.

I173   Fenton, James. "Bàrthist." New Statesman, 78 (19 Sept. 1969), 384-85. [p. 384]

I174   Tube, Henry. "Vivifiction." The Spectator, No. 7369 (20 Sept. 1969), pp. 374-75. [p. 375]

I175   Bailey, Paul. London Magazine, NS 9 (Dec. 1969), 111-12.

CHIMERA

<A9b   Random House, [1972]>

I176   Anon. Kirkus Reviews, 40 (15 July 1972), 813.

I177   Anon. Publishers' Weekly, 202 (31 July 1972), 67-68.

I178   Allen, Bruce. Library Journal, 97 (Aug. 1972), 2638.

I179   Green, Alan. "Trade Winds." Saturday Review, 55 (9 Sept. 1972), 81-82, 86. [p. 81]

I180   H[owes], V[ictor]. "Lost in the Barth-house." Christian Science Monitor, 20 Sept. 1972, p. 10.

I181   Lehmann-Haupt, Christopher. "Found in the Funhouse." The New York Times, 20 Sept. 1972, p. 45.

I182   Michaels, Leonard. "Chimera." The New York Times Book Review, 24 Sept. 1972, pp. 35-37.

I183   Anon. The New Yorker, 48 (30 Sept. 1972), 125.

I184   Adams, Phoebe. The Atlantic Monthly, 230 (Oct. 1972), 135.

I185   Anon. Playboy, 19 (Oct. 1972), 26.

I186   Sheppard, R.Z. "Scheherazade & Friend." Time, 100 (2 Oct. 1972), 80.

I187   Brady, Charles A. "Ancient Tales Retold In Modern Melange." Buffalo Evening News Magazine, 7 Oct. 1972, p. B-8.

I188   Breslin, John B. "A Prospect of Books." America, 127 (7 Oct. 1972), 265-69. [p. 265]

I189   Perkins, Bill. "In One of Three, Barth Seems Not So Parched and Plucked After All." The National Observer, 7 Oct. 1972, p. 21.

I190   Prescott, Peter S. "Heroes Over the Hill." Newsweek, 80 (9 Oct. 1972), 108, 110.

I191   Crinklaw, Don. "One Low Voice in Wild Company." National Review, 24 (13 Oct. 1972), 1136-37.

I192   Wood, Michael. "New Fall Fiction." The New York Review of Books, 19 Oct. 1972, pp. 33-37. [pp. 34-35]

I193   Russ, Margaret. "John Barth: Master of Retold Myth." Buffalo Courier-Express Focus, 22 Oct. 1972, p. 17.

I194   Anon. The Booklist, 69 (15 Nov. 1972), 274.

I195   Hill, William B., S.J. "Fiction." America, 127 (18 Nov. 1972), 420, 422-23. [p. 422]

I196   Anon. Choice, 9 (Dec. 1972), 1288, 1290.

I197   Anon. The New York Times Book Review, 3 Dec. 1972, p. 74

I198   Bryant, Jerry H. "The Novel Looks at Itself—Again." The Nation, 215 (18 Dec. 1972), 631-33.

I199   Anon. The Virginia Quarterly Review, 49 (Winter 1973), viii.

I200   O'Connell, Shaun. "American Fiction, 1972: The Void in the Mirror." The Massachusetts Review, 14 (Winter 1973 190-207. [p. 201]

I201   Sale, Roger. "Enemies, Foreigners, and Friends." The Hudson Review, 25 (Winter 1972-73), 703-14. [pp. 705-0

I202   Anon. Psychology Today, 6 (Jan. 1973), 20.

I203   Prescott, Peter S. "Readout: The Year in Books." Newsweek, 81 (1 Jan. 1973), 53-54. [p. 53]

I204   Ellmann, Mary. "Recent Novels." The Yale Review, 62 (Spring 1973), 461-68. [p. 468]

I205   Meyer, Arlin G. "Form, Fluidity, and Flexibility in

Recent American Fiction." Cresset, 36 (Apr. 1973), 11-15. [pp. 13-14]

I206 Hendin, Josephine. "John Barth's Fictions for Survival." Harper's, 247 (Sept. 1973), 102-06.

I207 Klinkowitz, Jerome. "How Fiction Survives the Seventies." The North American Review, NS 10 (Fall 1973), 69-73. [p. 69]

I208 Rovit, Earl. "Some Shapes in Recent American Fiction." Contemporary Literature, 15 (Autumn 1974), 539-61. [pp. 543-44]

<A9c   Fawcett Publications, [1973]>

I209 Anon. Publishers' Weekly, 204 (13 Aug. 1973), 57.

I210 Anon. "Fiction." Best Sellers, 33 (1 Nov. 1973), 355.

I211 McLellan, Joseph. "Paperbacks." Book World, 18 Nov. 1973, p. 5.

<A9d   Andre Deutsch, [1974]>

I212 Cunningham, Valentine. "Bag of Tricks." New Statesman, 88 (19 July 1974), 90.

I213 Ackroyd, Peter. "Chinese Boxes and Othel Novels." The Spectator, No. 7621 (20 July 1974), pp. 86-87. [p. 86]

I214 Sage, Lorna. "Low Life on Olympus." The (London) Observer Review, 21 July 1974, p. 27.

I215 Anon. "The Narrative Springs." The Times Literary Supplement, 26 July 1974, p. 783.

I216 Shrapnel, Norman. "Myth-Making with a Rib-Tickler." The (Manchester) Guardian Weekly, 111 (26 July 1974), 21.

J. BIBLIOGRAPHIES OF JOHN BARTH

J1 Anon. "Books by John Barth." In The Sounder Few: Essays from the Hollins Critic. Ed. R. H. W. Dillard, George Garrett, and John Rees Moore. Athens: Univ. of Georgia Press, 1971. P. 210.

Lists the editions of Barth's first five books.

J2 Bryer, Jackson. "Two Bibliographies." Critique, 6, No. 2 (1963), 86-94. [pp. 86-89]

Bryer lists the editions and reviews of Barth's first three novels, his short fiction and non-fiction, and the critiques of his works.

J3 B[urns], M[ildred] B[lair]. "Books by John Barth." The Hollins Critic, 3 (Dec. 1966), 7.

Burns lists the editions of Barth's four novels.

J4 Morrell, David Bernard. "Bibliography." In "John Barth: An Introduction." Diss. The Pennsylvania State University, 1970. Pp. 226-38.

Morrell attempts to catalogue all of the works by and about John Barth through 1970.

J5 Weixlmann, Joseph N. "John Barth: A Bibliography." Critique, 13, No. 3 (1972), 45-55.

Weixlmann lists the editions of Barth's first five books, his published short fiction and non-fiction, tape and disc recordings of his work, biographical and critical studies of his fiction (including selected reviews), and previously published bibliographies.

SUBJECT INDEX

[The subject entries are based on the annotations in the body of the bibliography and are by no means exhaustive. The title entries, however, are thorough—or nearly so.]

absurdism H12, H23-H25, H30,
   H60, H103, H122, H124, H137,
   H144, H159, H163-H164, H168,
   H175, H179, H186, H190,
   H218-H219, H222-H223, H225,
   H231, H255, H258, H274,
   H309.
academic fiction H13-H14,
   H109, H113-H114, H157, H192,
   H306, H322.
The Adventures of Roderick
   Random B1.
"Afterword" to Roderick Random B1, E35.
allegory F6, H9, H29, H46,
   H59, H89, H97, H104, H109-
   H110, H115, H126, H140,
   H143, H155, H192, H238,
   H270-H271, H306, H309.
Ambrose H102, H111, H145,
   H165, H185, H232, H235,
   H243, H257, H259, H292 [see
   also "Ambrose His Mark,"
   "Lost in the Funhouse," LF,
   and "Water-Message"].
"Ambrose His Mark" A8a-A8f,
   C4, D1, E27-E28, E67, H48,
   H184, H259 [see also LF].
Anastasia H58 [see also GGB].
Andrews, Todd H8, H10, H33,
   H53, H58, H63-H64, H76-H77,
   H102-H104, H109, H112, H117,
   H127, H129, H137, H145,
   H151, H154, H175, H179,
   H185, H202, H224-H225, H229,
   H232, H257, H261, H342 [see
   also FO].
"Anonymiad" A8a-A8f, E67,
   H165, H250, H301 [see also
   LF].
anti-heroes H4, H52, H74,
   H216.

anti-novels H77, H85, H212.
apocalyptic fiction H26, H31,
   H58, H157, H191, H227, H276,
   H304.
"Autobiography" A8a-A8f, C9,
   D2-D4, E62, E64, E67, E76,
   G3, G74, G89 [see also LF].
Az ut Vége A2a.
"Bellerophoniad" A9a-A9d, C13,
   H249, H328, H336 [see also
   Chimera].
"Biographical Sketch" of
   Smollett B1, E34.
black humor C17, F7, F19,
   H15, H19, H21, H30, H35,
   H47, H53, H57-H58, H60, H65,
   H68, H71, H78, H86, H104,
   H118, H121, H147, H188, H193,
   H218-H219, H231, H233, H245,
   H272-H273, H284, H289, H312,
   H334.
Bray, Harold H58, H224, H261,
   H283 [see also GGB]
burlesque H23, H25, H65, H133,
   H137, H175, H285, H314, H335.
Burlingame, Henry, III H7, H10,
   H26, H58, H84, H98, H106,
   H114, H205, H220, H224, H230,
   H247, H261, H283 [see also
   SWF].
Chimera A9a-A9d, A10, F19, F21-
   F23, G20, G26, G31, G46, G50,
   G65, G71, G88, G99-G100, H242,
   H244, H254-H255, H270, H279,
   H282, H287, H296, H303, H307,
   H309, H312-H315, H323, H327,
   H331-H332, H334, H336, H339-
   H340, I176-I216.
compared to:
   Aristophenes H47, H59
   Atreides, Paul H340
   Barthelme, Donald H131, H196

-183-

Beckett, Samuel H174
Borges, Jorge Luis H7, H313, H333
Burroughs, William H174, H176
Butor, Michel H324
Cervantes, Miguel de H47, H59, H165, H210
Coover, Robert H131
Dostoevsky, Fyodor H60
Durrell, Lawrence H7
Eliot, T. S. H225, H230
Faulkner, William H200
Fielding, Henry H165
Hawthorne, Nathaniel H200
Heller, Joseph H24, H157
Hemingway, Ernest H200
James, Henry H200, H270
Joyce, James H87, H256
Kafka, Franz H164
Melville, Herman H199
Nabokov, Vladimir H7, H313, H333
Poe, Edgar Allan H199
Pynchon, Thomas H24, H157, H191, H225, H227, H299
Rabelais, Francois H47, H59, H210
Robbe-Grillet F6, H324
Shakespeare, William H165, H225
Simon, Claude H324
Sterne, Laurence H210
Swift, Jonathan H47, H59
Twain, Mark H26, H199
Voltaire H47, H59
Vonnegut, Kurt, Jr. H187, H191, H225, H227
West, Nathanael H26, H60, H176
Cooke, Anna H42, H84 [see also SWF].
Cooke, Ebenezer H10, H33, H42, H58, H60, H63-H64, H69, H76-H77, H98, H102-H104, H106, H112, H129, H137, H141, H145, H154, H175, H179, H183, H185, H205, H226, H235, H257, H342 [see also SWF].
cosmopsis F22, H10, H32, H53, H103, H152, H154, H179, H315.
Dadaism H83, H174.

departmental file, Pennsylvani State University E74.
Der Tabakhändler A3a.
dissertations G96, H12, H28, H58, H63, H81, H92, H97-H99, H114, H127, H130, H135, H137 H138, H144, H149, H153, H169 H185, H189, H191, H205, H208 H212, H214, H218, H224, H229 H233, H236, H240, H244, H246 H248, H257, H260, H267, H274 H278, H282, H285-H288, H290, H293, H302-H303, H308-H311, H314, H322-H323, H326, J4.
Doctor H10, H75, H129, H169, H191, H227, H285 [see also ER].
"Dorchester Tales" E14-E16, G80, H153.
double H97, H145, H189.
"Dunyazadiad" A9a-A9d, C12, G8, G109, H291 [see also Chimera].
"Echo" A8a-A8f, E64, E67, G3, G74, G89, H315 [see also LF]
The End of the Road A2a-A2f, A7a-A7c, D5-D6, E4-E6, E48, E58, F6, F14-F15, F19, F21-F22, G5-G7, G9, G20, G35, G40, G50, G69, G75, G80, G8: G88, G97, G105, G107, G111, H1, H4, H6, H9-H11, H13-H14 H23, H26-H29, H32-H33, H39-H42, H44, H46, H48-H49, H54 H57-H58, H60, H62-H64, H67, H70, H74-H77, H79, H81, H88 H91, H94-H95, H97, H102-H10! H108-H109, H112-H113, H115, H120-H121, H127-H130, H135, H137, H145, H148-H149, H151 H154, H156, H163-H164, H169 H173, H175, H179, H185, H18 H191, H195, H200, H203, H20 H212-H216, H218-H219, H221, H224, H227, H236, H244-H245 H249, H252-H254, H257-H258, H260-H262, H271, H274, H278 H280-H282, H285, H287-H288, H291, H296, H302-H303, H306 H312-H315, H323, H326, H331 H342, I29-I46.
entropy H118, H161, H336.
existentialism H1, H4, H6, H H81, H94, H103-H104, H135-

H136, H144, H148, H189,
H205, H214, H262, H271,
H281, H331, H337.
fable and fabulation G85,
H10, H59, H145, H221.
Fine della strada A2a.
The Floating Opera A1a-A1b,
  A6a-A6d, D7-D8, E1-E3, E44-
  E47, F6, F14-F15, F19, F21-
  F22, G5-G7, G20, G35, G40,
  G50, G75, G80, G82, G88,
  G97, G105, G107, G111, H3,
  H7-H8, H10-H11, H23, H27,
  H32-H33, H37, H39, H41,
  H44, H46, H48, H53-H54,
  H56-H58, H62-H64, H66, H70,
  H74, H76-H77, H81, H94,
  H97, H102-H104, H108-H109,
  H112, H117, H120-H121,
  H127, H129-H130, H137,
  H145, H148-H149, H151,
  H153-H154, H159, H163,
  H175, H179-H180, H185,
  H187, H189, H200, H202-
  H204, H208, H212, H214-
  H215, H218-H219, H221-
  H222, H224-H225, H229,
  H232, H244, H252-H253,
  H257-H258, H261-H262,
  H271, H274-H275, H278,
  H282, H285, H287-H288,
  H291, H295-H296, H298,
  H302-H303, H312-H315,
  H323, H326, H331, H334,
  H342, I1-I28, I37.
Foreword to Western Wind,
  Eastern Shore B4.
"For my first ten years
  . . . " B3a-B3b.
"Fox-Island Incident"
  Preface, H153 (de-
  scribed in).
"Frame-Tale" A8a-A8f, E67,
  H165, H243, H333, H341
  [see also LF].
French New Novel F6, F14,
  H271, H324.
"A Gift of Books" C18,
  E55-E56.
Giles, George H33, H58, H63-
  H64, H77, H102, H104, H112,
  H114, H129, H137, H140,
  H145, H155, H162, H175,
  H179, H185, H230, H234-
  H235, H257 [see also GGB].
Giles Goat-Boy A4a-A4f, E25-
  E26, E30-E33, E38-E42, E49-
  E51, E54, E72, F1, F6, F8-
  F9, F11, F14-F15, F18-F19,
  F21, G7, G20, G35, G50, G60,
  G75-G76, G88, G105, G107,
  G111, H23, H32-H33, H36, H39,
  H41, H50, H54-H59, H61-H64,
  H66, H68, H77, H81, H85, H87,
  H90, H93-H94, H96-H97, H99,
  H102, H104, H107-H110, H112-
  H115, H121, H125-H126, H128-
  H130, H137, H140, H143, H145,
  H148-H149, H151, H153, H155,
  H157, H162-H164, H167, H170,
  H172, H175, H177-H179, H183,
  H185, H189-H190, H192, H197,
  H203-H204, H208-H209, H212,
  H214-H215, H221, H224, H228,
  H230, H234-H235, H238-H239,
  H242, H244-H245, H249, H252-
  H253, H257, H261, H271-H272,
  H274, H277, H279, H281-H283,
  H285-H287, H291, H294-H296,
  H303, H306, H312-H315, H323,
  H326, H328-H331, H334, H342,
  I75-I140.
"Glossolalia" A8a-A8f, E67,
  H305 [see also LF].
Greene, Peter H104 [see also
  GGB].
grotesque H12, H157, H260.
Haecker, Mr. H202 [see also
  FO].
"Help" C11, G7.
hero, myth of the F6, F8, F14,
  H114, H162-H163, H230, H238,
  H314, H328.
history, use of F15, H23-H24,
  H51, H69, H80, H83, H123,
  H134, H157, H171, H235, H247,
  H249, H268, H299, H314.
Horner, Jacob F15, H4, H9-H10,
  H33, H42, H58, H60, H63-H64,
  H67, H74-H77, H79, H88, H102-
  H105, H109, H112, H115, H127,
  H129, H137, H145, H151-H152,
  H154, H169, H175, H179, H185,
  H191, H216, H224, H227, H257,
  H261, H342 [see also ER].
identity, theme of H4, H10,
  H33, H48, H54, H64, H76, H102,
  H106, H114, H149, H152, H154,

H230, H236, H240, H243, H247, H262, H281, H288, H315.
Il coltivatore del Maryland A3a.
innocence, theme of G97, H10, H84, H129, H149, H154.
"Introduction for Library of Congress Reading" E62.
"Intro. for Buffalo" E57.
"Intro. for Harvard Reading" E64.
"Intro. for Petition and Life-Story Reading" E66.
"Intro. for U. of Md. Reading" E63.
"John Updike—Introduction" E60.
Jones, Captain Osborne H58 [see also FO]
"Jorge Luis Borges: Introduction" E65.
"Joseph Heller—Introduction" E59.
"Landscape: The Eastern Shore" C3, E14, E16.
L'Enfant-Bouc ou Version revue et corrigée du Nouveau Syllabus A4a.
Letters to:
  Bluestone, George I37
  Contemporary Authors G12
  The Dorchester News C20, G83, G112
  Doubleday editor E44
  Freedgood, Anne E54
  Hills, Rust E28
  Kilmer, Robert H149
  Kostelanetz, Richard H23
  Library Journal G80
  Mann, Charles W. E73, E75
  Tatham, Campbell H97
  Wensburg, Mr. E61
"Life-Story" A8a-A8f, D9-D11, E67, H217, H262, H295 [see also LF].
"Lilith and the Lion" C1, H54, H153.
"The Literature of Exhaustion" and the theme of literary exhaustion C19, D39-D41, E52-E53, E57, F8, F13, F20, H13, H102, H121, H177-H178, H214-H215, H249, H262, H296-H297, H324-H325, H330, H332, H339, H342.
The Living Sakhyan H234 [see also GGB]
L'Opéra flottant A6a.
L'opera galleggiante A6a.
"Lost in the Funhouse" A8a-A8f, B3a-B3b, C7, D12-D22, E63, E67, G30, H100, H111, H179, H185, H217, H243, H259 H262, H265, H272, H283, H292 [see also LF].
Lost in the Funhouse A8a-A8f, E67-E70, F4, F14-F16, F18, F20, F22, G20, G23, G68, G75 H102, H109, H115, H121, H131 H138-H139, H143, H145, H150-H151, H153, H157-H158, H165, H176-H179, H181, H184, H196-H197, H203, H208, H214-H215, H221, H223-H224, H232, H235, H243-H244, H249, H251-H254, H256-H257, H259, H261, H267, H270-H272, H274, H279-H280, H282, H284-H285, H287, H291, H296, H303, H307-H308, H312-H315, H323-H324, H330, H332, H335, H337, H340, H342, I141 I175.
love, theme of H206, H208, H287-H288, H291, H301, H315.
love triangle F14, H9, H120, H145.
Mack, Jeannine H202 [see also FO].
Magda H111 [see also "Lost in the Funhouse" and LF]
manuscripts E1-E77, G27, G56-G58, G91.
mask-assuming and role-playing H7, H26, H33, H62, H112, H152, H154, H189, H203, H213 H236, H246, H283, H299, H314
Matkan pää A2a.
"Menelaiad" A8a-A8f, D23, E67 F22, G55, G62-G63, G77, H82, H102, H142, H184, H243, H251 H291, H336 [see also LF].
metafiction H158, H196, H248, H340.
mirrors H189, H203.
mock-epic H43, H293.
Modern Occasions B2a-B2c.

-186-

Morgan, Joe   F15, H129, H152,
   H156, H179, H191, H227 [see
   also ER].
Morgan, Rennie   H42, H58,
   H156 [see also ER].
Morton, Colonel   H202 [see
   also FO].
"Muse, Spare Me"   C17, D42-
   D43, E36-E37.
"My Two Muses"   C15.
mythology, classical   F20,
   H138, H142, H223, H243,
   H249, H271, H280, H324,
   H328, H340.
Mythotherapy   H75, H123,
   H213, H280.
narrative technique   H88,
   H97, H104, H111, H127,
   H130, H149, H152, H278,
   H302, H313, H326.
National Book Award, 1969
   G23, G68.
National Book Award, 1973
   A10, F23, G26, G46, G65,
   G71, G99-G100.
"National Book Award . . .
   Acceptance Remarks"   A10.
"Night-Sea Journey"   A8a-A8f,
   C6, D24-D33, E67, G29, H79,
   H109, H165, H179, H184-
   H185, H199, H206, H262,
   H264 [see also LF].
nihilism   H1, H4, H12, H19,
   H36, H44, H54, H70, H94,
   H108, H119-H120, H144,
   H193, H271, H310-H311,
   H334.
paradox   H12, H77, H179,
   H215, H288, H298, H315,
   H342.
"Parnassus Approached"
   Preface, H153 (described
   in).
parody   F15, F20, H7, H9,
   H36, H40, H42, H44, H51,
   H55, H58, H65, H70, H87,
   H114, H133, H137, H140,
   H145, H152, H162, H175-
   H176, H190, H197, H212,
   H214-H215, H223, H230,
   H232, H237-H238, H245,
   H252-H253, H255-H256, H263,
   H268, H274, H287, H298-
   H299, H301, H312, H314,
   H335.
Perdido no túnel do terror   A8a.
Perdu dans le Labyrinthe   A8a.
"Perseid"   A9a-A9d, C14, G36,
   G67, G72, G102, H328 [see
   also Chimera].
Peter   H111 [see also "Lost in
   the Funhouse" and LF].
"Petition"   A8a-A8f, C10, E66-
   E67 [see also LF].
picaresque   H7, H65, H98, H147,
   H183, H246.
Pocahontas myth   H5, H37, H72,
   H106, H285 [see also SWF].
post-Modernism   F21, H45, H107,
   H123, H159, H178, H201, H255,
   H296, H300, H330.
proof copies of novels   A3a,
   A4a, A7a, A8a, E24, E51, E58,
   E70.
Rankin, Peggy   H42 [see also
   ER].
rationalism   H12, H149, H192.
"Reading Your Own"   E61, F11.
"The Remobilization of Jacob
   Horner"   C2, D5-D6.
"The Revolving Bookstand"   C16.
"Sams' Son Agonistes"   E71.
satire   H7, H30, H35, H117,
   H119, H155, H202, H214, H218-
   H219, H231, H294, H309-H310,
   H314, H329.
science fiction   H20, H107,
   H239.
"Shirt of Nessus"   E77, H153,
   H291.
The Sot-Weed Factor   A3a-A3e,
   A5a-A5b, D34-D37, E7-E13, E15,
   E17-E21, E24, E43, F6, F14-
   F15, F19-F22, G5-G7, G20, G35,
   G50, G75, G80, G82, G88, G97,
   G105, G107, G111, H5, H7, H10-
   H11, H13, H15-H19, H23-H29,
   H31-H34, H36-H37, H39-H44,
   H46, H48, H51, H54-H66, H69-
   H70, H72, H76-H77, H80-H81,
   H83-H84, H88, H90-H91, H94,
   H97-H98, H102-H104, H106-H108,
   H112-H114, H116, H119-H121,
   H125, H128-H132, H134, H137,
   H141, H145, H147-H149, H151,
   H153-H154, H157, H159, H163-
   H164, H166-H167, H170-H172,
   H175, H177, H179, H183, H185-

H186, H188-H190, H197-H198,
H203-H205, H208-H210, H212,
H214-H215, H220-H221, H224,
H226, H230, H235, H238,
H244-H247, H249, H252-H253,
H257, H261-H263, H268-H269,
H271-H272, H274, H276, H279,
H282-H285, H287-H288, H291,
H293, H296, H299, H302-H303,
H312-H315, H323, H326-H327,
H331, H334, H342, I47-I74.
Stoker, Maurice   H104 [see
   also GGB].
"Test Borings"   B2a-B2c, E29,
   E31-E33, E72, F3.
textual revisions   F12, H302.
theses, M.A.   H30, H42, H49,
   H52, H54, H64, H76, H85,
   H94, H102, H104, H108-H109,
   H112, H119, H154, H221.
"Title"   A8a-A8f, C8, D38,
   E62, E64, E67, G3, G74, G89,
   H77 [see also LF].
Toast, Joan   H42, H58, H315
   [see also SWF].

translations of novels   A1a,
   A2a, A3a, A4a, A6a, A8a.
"A Tribute to John Hawkes"
   C22.
A Tribute to Vladimir Nabokov
   C21.
"Two Meditations"   A8a-A8f,
   E67 [see also LF].
Uiva ooppera   A1a.
Uncle Karl   H111 [see also
   "Lost in the Funhouse" and
   LF].
value, theme of   H39, H44, H48,
   H54, H58, H64, H76, H102,
   H129, H145, H149, H152, H154,
   H179, H208, H216, H262, H287-
   H288, H291, H293, H314, H323,
   H336.
"Water-Message"   A8a-A8f, C5,
   E22-E23, E67, G28, H165,
   H184, H259 [see also LF].
Western Wind, Eastern Shore
   B4.
"What One Person Can Do"   C23.
Writer's Choice   B3a-B3b.

-188-

AUTHOR INDEX

[All commentators, editors, and translators are indexed below.]

Abrahams, William D20, H100
Ackroyd, Peter I213
Adams, Phoebe I152, I184
Adelman, George I2
Aldiss, Brian W. H239
Aldrich, Terence O. H30
Aldridge, John H65
Alkmin, Edilson A8a
Allen, Bruce I178
Allen, Mary I. H240
Allen, Walter H215
Alter, Robert H31, H325
Altieri, Charles H165
Alvarez, Alfred I132
Anselment, Carol D2, G39
Appel, Alfred, Jr. C21, I158
Ardery, P. P. I162
Arimond, John I110
Arthur, Helen I61
Asselineau, Roger H146
Axthelm, Pete I150
Aycock, Wendell M. H210
Bailey, Dennis L. H286
Bailey, Paul I175
Baines, Nancy I66
Baldwin, Neil G73
Balliett, Whitney I119
Banks, Ann F25
Banks, Russell H126
Bannerman, James I101
Bannon, Anthony G74
Bannon, Barbara A. I20, I45, I70, I141
Barker, Shirley I58
Barnes, Hazel E. H1
Bazzanella, Dominic J. H127
Beagle, Peter S. H32
Bean, John C. H166
Beatty, Richard C. D13, G50
Begnal, Mary K. H287
Bell, Pearl K. H242
Bellamy, Joe David F19-20
Bennett, Joseph T. D15, G52

Bergonzi, Bernard H128
Berthoff, Warner H167
Bianciardi, Luciano A3a
Bienstock, Beverly Gray H243-H244
Bier, Jesse H66
Billings Philip A. H288
Binni, Francesco H33
Blair, Walter D17, G95, H207
Bluestone, George I37
Boatwright, Taliaferro I30
Bowden, Mark F24
Bowker, Stanley A., Jr. H102
Boyers, Robert H67
Bradbury, John M. H103
Bradbury, Malcolm G75, H168, I27, I44
Bradley, Sculley D13, G50
Brady, Charles A. I187
Brady, Karen F10, G76-G77
Breslin, John B. I188
Brooks, Cleanth D36, G48
Brooks, Peter I136
Browning, Preston M., Jr. H289
Brunette, Peter C., Jr. H326
Bryant, Jerry H. H129, I198
Bryer, Jackson J2
Bufithis, Philip H. H169
Burgess, Anthony H34, H51, H170, I129
Burhans, Clinton S., Jr. D43
Burnett, David G28-G30
Burns, G. Frank H317
Burns, Mildred Blair J3
Buzzi, Aldo A2a
Byrd, Scott H68, I105
Cantrill, Dante K. H290
Carlisle, E. Fred D24, G49
Carpenter, Jack D26
Carruth, Hayden H126, I92, I153
Cassill, R. V. I143
Charyn, Jerome D7

-189-

Chiasson, Sharon D.   H104
Christadler, Martin   H245, H271
Churchill, Thomas   H170
Ciancio, Ralph A.   H12
Clare, Warren L.   D34
Clark, Mary L.   H52
Clauss, Anne R.   H130
Coleman, John   I39
Collins, Elizabeth Tunstall   G78
Cooper, Arthur   F7
Cooper, Madison   I14
Corbett, Edward P. J.   I102
Core, George   H116
Corke, Hilary   I128
Crews, Frederick C.   H18
Crinklaw, Don   I191
Cunningham, Valentine   I212
Curley, Dorothy Nyren   H101
Davenport, Guy   I157
Davidson, Richard A.   I169
Davis, Douglas M.   D8, F16, H15, H19, H25, H35, H53, I81, I87, I145
Davis, Robert Murray   H105
Decker, Sharon Davie   H208
DeGast, Robert   B4
Dembo, L. S.   F6
denHollander, A. N. J.   H168
Detweiler, Robert   H320
Dickstein, Morris   H131, H327
Dientsfry, Harris   I68
Dietrich, R. F.   D14, G51, H292
Dillard, R. H. W.   G1, H184, J1
Dippie, Brian W.   H106
Diser, Philip E.   H69
Dolan, Paul J.   D15, D42, G52
Dolmetsch, Carl R.   H171
Donoghue, Denis   I95
Elgin, Donald D.   H246
Elkin, Stanley   D23
Elliott, George P.   H36, H70
Ellmann, Mary   I204
Enck, John J.   F6
Epstein, Leslie   H132
Ericksen, Kenneth J.   D34
Ethridge, James M.   G12, G21
Ewell, Barbara C.   H247
Falk, Robert   D24, G49
Farwell, Harold   H291

Featherstone, Joseph   I98
Federman, Raymond   D40, G79, H333, H338, H341
Feldman, Burton   H71
Fenton, James   I173
Fiedler, Leslie A.   H2-H3, H13-H14, H20, H37, H72-H73, H107, H133, I62
Firth, John   H292
Fleischer, Leonore   I137
Foerster, Norman   D24, G49
Fogel, Stanley H.   H248
Foley, Martha   G28-G30
Fort, Deborah C.   H293
Franco, Jean   G75
Fredericks, S. C.   H328
Freedley, George   I9
Fremont-Smith, Eliot   I82, I155
French, Michael R.   H74
Friedman, Bruce Jay   D35, H21
Friedman, Melvin J.   H159
Fuller, Edmund   I48, I90
Furst, Henry   A6a
Gado, Frank   F22
Galloway, David D.   H38, H134
Gardner, John   H209
Garis, Robert   H39, H61, I164
Garrett, George   G1, H184, J1
Giachetti, Romano   F15
Gibson, Donald B.   D2, G39
Gillespie, Gerald   H210
Gilman, Richard   H211
Gindin, James   H172
Gingrich, Arnold   D5, G40
Glicksberg, Charles I.   H173
Godshalk, William L.   H249
Goldberg, Howard   H61
Golden, Daniel   H212
Goldman, Albert   I93
Golwyn, Judith   G80
Gourevitch, Mary Turzillo   H135
Grabo, Norman S.   D24, G49
Graff, Gerald E.   H75, H329
Graham, Kenneth   I25
Green, Alan   I179
Green, Martin   I134
Greene, Maxine   H213
Greene, Michael T.   H76
Gresham, James T.   H214, H294
Gross, Beverly   H77
Grosskurth, Phyllis   I99
Grossman, Manuel L.   H174
Guerard, Albert J.   H295

Gulassa, Cyril M.   D27, G81
Haack, Deitmar   H171
Hall, James   H136
Hamalian, Leo   D1, G42, H181
Haney, Patrick   I21
Hansen, Arlen J.   H250
Harding, Walter   I15, I49,
   I78-I79, I144
Harmon, William   H251
Harper, Howard M., Jr.   I168
Harris, Charles B.   H137,
   H175
Harris, Eugenie   H138
Hart, James D.   G82
Harte, Barbara   G21
Harvey, David D.   I125
Hassan, Ihab   H4, H6, H40,
   H139, H176-H178, H201,
   H215, H252-H255, H296-
   H297, H330
Hauck, Richard B.   H140, H179
Hawkes, John   F3, H22, H298
Heilman, Robert B.   H141
Heller, Joseph   H180
Henderson, Harry B., III
   H299
Hendin, Josephine   I22, I46,
   I74, I126, I170, I206
Henkle, Roger   F25, H142
Hesse, Josette   H23
Hicks, Granville   H143, I19,
   I38, I69, I86, I149
Hicks, Walter J.   H54
Highet, Gilbert   I80
Hill, Hamlin   H78
Hill, William B., S.J.   I117,
   I161, I195
Hills, Penny Chapin   D6, D29,
   H79
Hills, Rust   B3a-B3b, D5-D6,
   D22, D29, G40, H79
Hinden, Michael   H256
Hirsch, Michael   H216
Hjortsberg, William   I163
Hogan, William   I10
Holder, Alan   H80
Homan, Richard   G83
Hood, Stuart   I172
Hornberger, Theodore   D17,
   G95
Howard, Daniel F.   D11, D19,
   G84, H217
Howes, Victor   I180
Hughes, Douglas A.   D32, G85

Hunt, Sandra A.   H108
Hyman, Stanley Edgar   I18, I67
Intrater, Roseline   H144
Isaacson, David   H318
Janoff, Bruce L.   H218-H219
Johnsen, William A.   H300
Johnson, B. S.   I131
Johnstone, Douglas B.   H257
Jones, D. Allan   H220-H221,
   H301
Jordan, Enoch P., III   H302
Josenhans, Elinor L.   H303
Joseph, Gerhard   H145
Kalter, Marjorie H.   H109
Kaplan, Charles   D10, G86
Karl, Frederick R.   D1, G42,
   H181
Katona, Anna   H147
Kattan, Naïm   H182
Kaufman, Michael T.   F17
Kazin, Alfred   H258
Kenedy, R. C.   H183
Kennard, Jean E.   H81, H148,
   H331
Kennedy, Mopsy S.   G87
Kerner, David   I36
Ketterer, David   H304
Kiely, Benedict   H41, H184
Kiernan, Robert F.   H259
Kilmer, Robert C.   H149
King, Francis   I63
Kitching, Jessie   I76
Klein, James R.   H185
Klein, Marcus   D31, D39, G44,
   H71, H82, H110, I104
Klinkowitz, Jerome   D3, H332,
   I207
Knapp, Edgar H.   H111
Knickerbocker, Conrad   H15
Knoll, Elizabeth   G88
Kochanek, Patricia Sharpe   H260
Koelb, Clayton   H305
Kopala, Barbara   G21
Kort, Wesley A.   H222
Kostelanetz, Richard   D37, H23-
   H25, H55, H83, H333, I62
Kramer, Elaine Fialka   H101
Kramer, Maurice   H101
Krim, Seymour   H132
Krupnick, Mark L.   H150
Kyle, Carol A.   H223
LaHaye, Judson   I33
Lambert, Beverly Allen   H112
Lask, Thomas   F2, G89

Lawton, Harry   H61
Lebowitz, Naomi   H186
LeClair, Thomas E.   H224,
    H261, H334
Lee, L. L.   H84
Leff, Leonard J.   H187
Lehan, Richard   H262
Lehmann-Haupt, Christopher
    I181
Lehtonen, Reijo Ala, H151,
    H225
Leighton, Wallace R.   H42
Lemon, Lee T.   I166
Leonard, Lionel R., Jr.   H85
Levin, Harry   H207
Levine, Paul   H56
Levitas, Gloria   I139
Lewis, R. W. B.   D36, G48,
    H26
Lichtenstein, Gene   D5, G40
Lifson, Hugh   I124
Lindberg-Seyersted, Brita
    H188
Litz, A. Walton   D18, G90,
    H335
Lodge, David   I123
Long, E. Hudson   D13, G50
Loughman, Celeste M.   H189
Lutwack, Leonard   H190, H226
Lyons, John O.   H306
MacNamara, Desmond   I130
Madden, David   H133, H141
Maddocks, Melvin   I84
Majdiak, Daniel   H152
Malin, Irving   I115, I118
Mandel, Siegfried   I6
Marsland, Sheila   H113
Mason, Julian D.   G91
May, John R.   H191, H227
McColm, Pearlmarie   I106
McConnell, Frank   H336
McDonald, James L.   H228
McElroy, Joseph   H263
McGuinness, Frank   I135
McKenzie, Barbara   D21, D30,
    G92, H111
McLaughlin, Richard   I56
McLellan, Joseph   I211
McMichael, George   D25, G93
Mellard, James M.   D28, H264
Meras, Phyllis   F8
Mercer, Peter   H192
Merril, Judith   I122

Meyer, Arlin G.   I205
Meyer, Dorothy C.   G94
Michaels, Leonard   I182
Michaels, Rochelle   F5
Milic, Louis T.   H194
Miller, James E., Jr.   D17,
    G95, H57
Miller, Norman   H229
Miller, Russell H.   H43
Minot, Stephen   D33, H206
Moore, Harry T.   H29, H133,
    H141, H190, H262, H315
Moore, John Rees   G1, H184, J1
Morrell, David B.   G96, H153,
    J4
Morris, Christopher D.   H337
Morse, J. Mitchell   I107
Mottram, Eric   G75
Munn, Ed   I113
Murphy, Richard W.   G97
Murray, John J.   I154
Myers, Art   I7
Nabokov, Vladimir   G98, H265
Neumeyer, Peter   D26
Newman, Charles   C21
Noland, Richard W.   H44
Numasawa, Koji   H86, H193
Nye, Russel B.   D24, G49
Oates, Joyce Carol   D4
O'Connell, Shaun   I100, I200
Olderman, Raymond M.   H114,
    H230
Pace, Eric   G99-G100
Pack, Robert   D31, G44
Packer, Nancy Huddleston   H266
Parker, Dorothy   I35
Paulson, Ronald   H194
Pearce, Richard   H338
Perkins, Bill   I189
Perkins, George   D13, G50
Petersen, Clarence   I28, I71,
    I138
Pickering, James H.   D38, G101
Pickrel, Paul   I32
Pinsker, Sanford   H231-H232
Plater, William M.   H267
Poirier, Richard   D12, G10,
    H87, H115, I87
Pollard, Arthur   G107
Pondrom, Cyrena N.   F6
Powers, Dennis A.   H154
Prescott, Orville   I12
Prescott, Peter S.   I190, I203

-192-

Price, Jonathan L.   H233
Price, R. G. G.   I24
Prince, Alan   F14
Putman, Thomas   G102
Quinn, Edward   D42
Raban, Jonathan   H88
Rademacher, Susanna   A3a
Rahv, Philip   B2a-B2c, G103, H307
Rambaud, Maurice   A4a, A8a, H155
Raven, Simon   I40
Reed, Pleasant L., III   H308
Reich, Charles A.   H156
Reilly, Charles E.   H309
Rice, Elaine Fritz   H310
Rice, Joseph A.   H58
Richardson, Jack   I60
Richardson, Kenneth   H113
Richardson, Maurice   I41
Riche, James   H195
Riley, Carolyn   G21, H241
Robbins, Jack A.   H143, I19, I38, I69, I86, I149
Roberts, R. E.   I151
Robie, Burton A.   I54
Robillot, Henri   A6a
Rodrigues, Eusebio L.
Rogers, Thomas   G104
Rovit, Earl   H7, I208
Rubin, Louis D., Jr.   H27, H45, H116, H249, H251, H268-H269, H284, I8
Russ, Margaret   I193
Ryan, Marjorie   H117
Saarikoski, Pentti   Ala
Sage, Lorna   I214
Said, Edward W.   H339
St. Germain, Amos J.   H311
Sale, Roger   I201
Samuels, Charles T.   I112
Saporta, Marc   H157
Schickel, Richard   H8, I16
Schlueter, Paul   I103
Schmitz, Neil   H196
Schoenberg, E. I.   H321
Scholes, Robert   H46-H47, H59, H89, H142, H158, H270, H340, I88
Schorer, Mark   D16, G105
Schott, Webster   I91, I156
Schulz, Dieter   H271
Schulz, Max F.   H90, H118, H197, H272-H273, H312

Scofield, James D.   H274
Scott, Nathan A., Jr.   H159, H198, H275-H276
Seymour-Smith, Martin   H277
Shafer, Ronald G.   G106
Shapiro, James   H180
Shapiro, Joel L.   I111
Shapiro, Stephen A.   H28, H91
Shenker, Israel   F21, F27
Sheppard, R. Z.   I186
Sherman, Marilyn Robertson   H278
Sherman, William D.   G107, H92
Shimura, Masao   H199-H200, H279
Shore, William A.   H119
Shrapnel, Norman   I64, I216
Shuttleworth, Martin   I133
Simon, Jeff   F23, G108-G109
Skerrett, Joseph T., Jr.   H60
Slethaug, Gordon E.   H235
Smith, H. Katherine   F13
Smith, Harry   H93
Smith, Herbert F.   H9
Solotaroff, Theodore   H160
Solow, Martin   H61
Somer, John   D3
Sommavilla, Guido   H120
Southern, Terry   I57
Spackey, James A.   H94
Spiller, Robert E.   H6, H296-H297
Stark, John O.   H313
Stern, Daniel   H201
Stevick, Philip   D9, G110, H280
Stewart, Randall   D17, G95
Storms, Charles Gilbert, III   H314
Stuart, Dabney   I108
Stubbs, John C.   H48
Sugiura, Ginsaku   H95, H121
Sukenick, Ronald   H341
Sundell, Roger H.   D14, G51, H292
Sutcliffe, Denham   I59
Sutton, Henry   H96
Tanner, Stephen L.   H202
Tanner, Tony   H62, H161, H203, I165
Tatham, Campbell   H97, H162, H204, H342
Tellér, Guyla   A2a
Tempest, Timothy   F18
TenBroeke, Patricia A. M.   H205
Tenenbaum, Elizabeth Brody   H236

-193-

Tharpe, Jac H315
Thomas, Jesse J. H63
Tilton, John W. H163
Tiusanen, Antero A2a
Tobin, Allan J. H61
Trachtenberg, Alan H10
Trachtenberg, Stanley H281
Tube, Henry I174
Turner, Theodore B., III
  H322
Tuttleton, James W. H237
Underwood, Jerry L. H323
Urbanski, Kenneth J. H282
Valencia, Willa F. H98
Vance, William L. D12, G10
Vernon, John H283
Vickery, John B. H159
Vinson, James H215
Vonnegut, Kurt, Jr. H142
von Wilpert, Gero H252
Wager, Willis G111
Wakeman, John G20
Waldmeir, Joseph J. H122
Wall, Stephen I23
Walsh, William J., S.J.
  I55
Ward, Lynn I13

Warren, Lucian C. G112
Warren, Robert Penn D36, G48
Wasson, Richard H123
Weber, Alfred H171
Weber, Brom H284
Weinberg, Helen H164
Weinstein, Arnold L. H324
Weixlmann, Joseph N., Jr.
  H285, J5
Welch, Bill I148
Wells, Daniel A. H64
Wermuth, Paul C. I34
Werner, William L. I5, I11,
  I51, I60
West, Paul H11
Widmer, Kingsley H29
Wilson, George R., Jr. H99
Wilson, Robley, Jr. D33, H206
Willett, Ralph G107
Wolf, Geoffrey I146
Wood, Michael I192
Wylder, Delbert E. H124
Young, Philip H5, I52
Young, Raymond C. H49
Zall, Paul H125
Ziolkowski, Theodore H238
Zyla, Wolodymr T. H210

TITLE INDEX

[See the subject index for the titles of primary works.]

"About John Barth"   G1
"About the Authors"   G110
Absurd Hero in American Fiction, The   H38, H134
"Absurd Insurrection: The Barth-Percy Affair"   H103
"Absurd Man and the Esthetics of the Absurd: The Fiction of John Barth"   H274
"Acquisition Notes"   G91
"Acting the Goat"   I134
After the Tradition: Essays on Modern Jewish Writing   H31
"Afterword"   H143, H184
"Agony in the Essence Chamber: John Barth's First Three Novels"   H76
"Algebra and Fire: An Interview with John Barth"   F19
"Allegory of Exhaustion, The"   H270
"Ambivalent Animal: Man in the Contemporary British and American Novel, The"   H28, H91
"American Absurd Novel (1965), The"   H25
"American Adam, The"   I67
American Dreams, American Nightmares   H133, H141
"American Fiction: Forgetting the Ordinary Truths"   H242
"American Fiction, 1972: The Void in the Mirror"   I200
"American Fiction Since 1950"   H188
"American Fiction: The Postwar Years, 1945-65"   H16
American Literature   D12, G10
"American Literature"   H252
American Literature: A World View   G111
American Literature: The Makers and the Making   D36, G48
"American Novel in the Sixties, The"   H74
"American Novelist as Entropologist, The"   H161
American Novel Since World War II, The   D39, H71, H110
American Poetry and Prose   D24, G49
American Tradition in Literature, The   D13, G50
Amerikanische Literatur der Gegenwart in Einzeldarstellungen   H245, H271
Amerikanische Literatur im 20. Jahrhundert/ American Literature in the 20th Century   H171
"Amusement and Revelation"   I160
"Anatomy of Black Humor"   H71
"Ancient Roots of Modern Satiric Fiction, The"   H309
"Ancient Tales Retold In Modern Melange"   I187
"And Up Pops the 'Pop Novel,' or Black Humor Without a Sting"   H35
Anniversary Notes   G98
Anthology of American Literature   D25, G93
"'Anti-Fiction' in American Humor"   H251
"Anti-Novels of John Barth, The"   H77
Anti-Story: An Anthology of Experimental Fiction   D9, G110
"Apocalypse in the American Novel"   H191
"Apocalyptic Temper, The"   H31
"Art Is Artifice in Barth Reading"   G89
"Artist as Art, The"   I143
"Artist's Fight for Art, The"   H169

-195-

"Art of Artifice, The" I158
Art of Fiction, The D14, G51
"Art of Novel Writing, 1945-1970, The" H168
"At Home When Writing Here" G108
"Attitudes toward Sex in American 'High Culture'" H67
"Attrition of the Self in Some Contemporary Novels, The" H144
"Author John Barth Leaving UB Staff" G2
"Authors Barth, Fiedler Appointed To UB Endowed Chairs in English" G4
"Author Talks to Self in 'Oral Literature'" G3
"Babbitt at the Abyss: The Social Context in Postmodern American Fiction" H329
"Backstage with Esquire" G5-G8
"Bag of Tricks" I212
"'Barber Kept on Shaving': The Two Perpsectives of American Humor, 'The'" H268
"Barth" G101
"Barth and Hawkes: Two Fabulists" H10
"Barth and Lacan: The World of the Moebius Strip" H337
"Barth and the Representation of Life" H152
"Barth Authors 'End of Road'" G9
"Barth Blasts 'Perversion of Authority' in Cambridge" G83
Barth Chronology, 1930-68, A G10
"Barth Defended" H61
"Barth Enjoys Teaching Youth; Finds Buffalo Culturally Alive" F10
"Barth Helps Orient Audience" G88
"Barthist" I173
"Barth, John" G11
"Barth, John 1930—" G12, H241

"Barth, John (1930—)" G75, G82, G107, H101, H113
"Barth, John Simmons" G14-G19
"Barth, John (Simmons)" G13, G20, H215
"Barth, John (Simmons) 1930—" G21
"Barth Makes Literature of Tapes" G74
"Barth Resigning Aug. 31 From UB English Dept." G22
"Barth, Rogers Nominated for Book Award" G23
"Barth's Endless Road" H9
"Barth's Good Book" I166
"Barth's Good Goat-Boy Satire Stretched Too Far in 710 Pages" I92
"Barth's 'Lost in the Funhouse': Reality's Essence Explored In Unconventional 'Fictions'" I153
"Barth's New Novel" I94
"Barth's Refutation of the Idea of Progress" H235
"Barth's Syllabus: The Frame of Giles Goat-Boy" H228
"Barth's Work Goes to Library of Congress" G27
"Barth Taking Leave To Teach at Boston" G24
"Barth to Amerika Bungaku no Dento" H199
"Barth To Spend Terms in Spain" G25
"Barth Valedictory: 'Chimera' Readings, A" G109
"Barth Wins National Book Award" G26
"Barth Writes Novel On Suicide Theme" I13
"Bawdy Frolic" I66
Best American Short Stories, The G28-G30
"Bestsellers Nobody Reads" H93
"Beyond Satire: Black Humor in the Novels of John Barth and Joseph Heller" H218
Beyond the Waste Land: A Study of the American Novel in the Nineteen-Sixties H230
"Beyond the Waste Land: A Study of the American Novel in the Nineteen-Sixties" H114

-196-

"Bibliography" J4
Billion Year Spree: The True
  History of Science Fiction
  H239
"Biographical Notes" G81
"Biting Themes and Bawdy
  Humor" I99
Black and White: Stories of
  American Life D2, G39
"Black Bible" I85
"Black Comedy to Offend Every-
  one, A" I91
Black Humor D35, H21
"Black Humor: A Comic Vision
  of the World" H42
"Black Humor: An American
  Aspect" H86
"Black Humor: Beyond Satire"
  H219
Black Humor Fiction of the
  Sixties H272-H273
"Black Humor: Form as Manipu-
  lation" H233
"Black Humorists, The" H17
"Black Humor: Its Cause and
  Cure" H78
"Blended Especially for a
  Heady Smoke" I68
Blueprint for a Bestseller
  H50
"Books" I39, I97, I122, I159
"Books About to Be" G31
"Books by John Barth" J1, J3
"Books of the Times" I12
"Boy's Own Boccaccio" I64
"Brandeis Awards 10th Arts
  Prizes" G32
Bright Book of Life: American
  Novelists and Storytellers
  from Hemingway to Mailer
  H258
"Buffalo Area Alive With Au-
  thors; Many Well Known, All
  Are Busy" G76
"Buffalo Strike: High Spirits
  and Cloudy Issues, The" F17
"By Computer, out of Virgin"
  I132
"Cabell and Barth: Our Comic
  Athletes" H249
"'Camp' and Black Humor in
  Recent American Fiction"
  H171
"Caprine Messiah" I129

"Celebration of Solipsism: A
  New Trend in American Fiction,
  The" H250
"Censorship—1967: A Series of
  Symposia" F12
"Characters (Contra Characteriza-
  tion) in the Contemporary Novel"
  H312
Cheerful Nihilism: Confidence and
  "The Absurd" in American Hu-
  morous Fiction, A H179
"Chimera" I182
"Chinese Boxes and Other Novels"
  I213
"Chockfull of Curiosities" I14
"Christine Barth Engaged" G33
"City Blights" I139
"City Life" H131
City of Words: American Fiction
  1950-1970 H161, H203
Collected Essays of Leslie Fied-
  ler, The H2, H20, H73, H107,
  I62
"College Novel in America: 1962-
  1974, The" H306
"Comic Christ and the Modern
  Reader, The" H140
Comic Imagination in American
  Literature, The H249, H251,
  H268-H269, H284
"Comic Opera" I17
"Complicated Simple Things" F21
"Concepts of the Self in the
  Modern Novel" H236
"'Conscience' of the New Litera-
  ture, The" H159
Contemporary American Literature
  1945-1972 H253
"Contemporary American Novel:
  Beyond Comic Anarchy, The"
  H92
Contemporary American Novelists
  of the Absurd H175
"Contemporary American Novelists
  of the Absurd" H137
Contemporary Authors G12, G21
"Contemporary Fiction and Criti-
  cism" H339
"Contemporary Fiction and Mass
  Culture" H65
Contemporary Literary Criticism
  H241
Contemporary Novelists H215
Contemporary Writer, The F6

"Contrast Epic: A Study of Joseph Heller's Catch-22, Günter Grass's The Tin Drum, John Barth's The Sot-Weed Factor, and Vladimir Nabokov's Pale Fire" H293
"Contributors" G79
"Conversation with John Barth, A" F22
"Corpse of the Dragon: Notes on Postromantic Fiction, The" H336
"Counterhumor: Comedy in Contemporary American Fiction" H281
"Counter-Types and Anti-Myths: Black and Indian Characters in the Fiction of John Barth" H285
"Critical Study of the Textual Variants in John Barth's Novels, A" H302
"Cross the Border, Close the Gap" H107
"Crowned with the Shame of Men" I86
Curious Death of the Novel, The H45
"Curious Death of the Novel, The" H45
Current Biography Yearbook 1969 G13
"Dada and the Future of Fiction" H83
Dada: Paradox, Mystification, and Ambiguity in European Literature H174
Dangerous Crossing: French Literary Existentialism and the Modern American Novel, A H262
"Death and Black Humor" H334
"Destroyers, Defilers, and Confusers of Men" H70
"Detailed Report on Bundle of Reading" I51
"Dial and Recent American Fiction, The" H40
"Dialectic and Demonstration in Black Humor" H30
"Digression as Narrative Technique in Contemporary Fiction" H130
"Disciple of Scheherazade" H46
Dismemberment of Orpheus: Toward a Postmodern Literature, The H176
Diverging Parallels: A Comparison of American and European Thought and Action H168
"Donald Barthelme and the Emergence of Modern Satire" H196
"Dorothy Parker on Books" I35
"Dostoievsky, Nathanael West, and Some Contemporary American Fiction" H60
"Doubleday" I75
"Doubt Without Skepticism" I19, I38, I69
"Dream Metaphor, The" H141
"Dream of the New, The" H133
"Echoes of Dark Laughter: Notes on the Comic Sense in Contemporary American Fiction" H254
"Einleitung: Kultur- und Literaturkritik" H245
Elements of Fiction H89
Elements of Fiction: Introduction to the Short Story D26
"End Is a Beginning for Barth's 'Funhouse,' The" F16, I145
"Enemies, Foreigners, and Friends" I201
"Enter the Frame" H338
Esquire Reader, The D5, G40
"Events in the Offing" G34
"Exclusive Interview with John Barth" F19
"The Exemplary Narratives of John Barth" H149
"Existentialist Comedian" G35
"Existential Novel, The" H4
"Fables for People Who Can Hear with Their Eyes" I147
Fabulators, The H47, H59
Fact of Fiction: Social Relevance in the Short Story, The D27, G81
"Fiction" H296, I195, I210
Fictional Transfigurations of Jesus H238
"Fictional Universe of John Barth, The" H323
"Fiction and Future: An Extravaganza for Voice and Tape" H177
"Fiction by Tyndareus" I42
"Fiction Chronicle" I107, I164

-198-

"Fiction Hot and Kool: Dilemmas of the Experimental Writer" H327
Fiction 100: An Anthology of Short Stories D38, G101
Fictions and Events G167
"Fiction's New Mode" H266
"Final Words: Death and Comedy in the Fiction of Donleavy, Hawkes, Barth, Vonnegut, and Percy" H224
"First Novel Inspired by Famous Showboat" I3
First Person: Conversations on Writers & Writing F22
"Flash of Darkness: Black Humor in the Contemporary American Novel" H58
"Floating Opera, The" H8
"Floating Opera and Second Skin, The" H298
"Foreword" H21, H307
"Form, Fluidity, and Flexibility in Recent American Fiction" I205
"Forming Artifice in John Barth's Fiction, The" H282
"Form in the Fiction of John Barth" H303
"Foss to Participate in UB Project" G36
"Found in the Barthhouse: Novelist as Savior" H111
"Found in the Funhouse" I181
"Four Contemporary Satires and the Problem of Norms" H117
Four Modes: A Rhetoric of Modern Fiction D28
"Frayn's a caution" I25
"From Disjunction to Multiplicity" H213
"Frontiers of Criticism: Metaphors of Silence" H139
Funk & Wagnalls Guide to Modern Literature H277
"Game of the Name in Barth's The Sot-Weed Factor, The" H220
Garden and the Map: Schizophrenia in Twentieth-Century Literature and Culture, The H283
"Gaudy Showboat" I6

"'George is my name'" I88
"Giles FitzWESCAC FitzEnglit" I131
"Giles Goat Bore" I124
"Giles Goat-Boy: An Interpretation" H163
"Giles Goat-Boy, 'egghead omnibus'" I93
"Giles Goat-Boy: Satire Ad Infinitum" I113
"Giles Goat-Boy: Satyr, Satire, and Tragedy Twined" H294
"Giles Goat-Boy Visited" I105
"Gilesian Monomyth: Some Remarks on The Structure of Giles Goat-Boy, The" H162
"Goat Gambit at the University" I100
"Goatscape with Figures" I123
"Gods and Goats" I104
"Grand Old Opry" I95
"Graying of Black Humor, The" H231
"Great American Joke, The" H269
Greening of America, The H156
"Grotesque in Modern American Fiction, The" H12
"Group of Scholars Gathers by Eggplant For . . . Yes. Well, Wow" G106
Harvest of a Quiet Eye: The Novel of Compassion H172
"Having It Both Ways: A Conversation between John Barth and Joe David Bellamy" F20
"Heroes Over the Hill" I190
"Heroic Comedy" F9, I89
Heroic Fiction: The Epic Tradition and American Novels of the Twentieth Century H190
Histoire du roman américain H157
"Historical Ebenezer Cooke, The" H69
"Historical Novel to End All Historical Novels, An" I49
"History, Hope, and Literature" H275
"History Is Still Good Fiction" I58
"'His Visage Wild; His Form Erotick': Indian Themes and Cultural Guilt in John Barth's

"The Sot-Weed Factor" H106
"Hoax That Joke Bilked, The" H62
"Homebound John Barth" G37
"Horrors of Holovision, The" I23
"How Fiction Survives the Seventies" I207
How We Live: Contemporary Life in Contemporary Fiction D6, D29, H79
"Human Comedy, The" I27
Humanism and the Absurd in the Modern Novel H186
"Humor With a Mortal Sting" H15
"Idea of the Avant-Garde, The" H211
"I' Faith, 'Tis Good" I50
"Il cinismo cosmico di John Barth" H120
"Image of man in the Literary Heroes of Jean-Paul Sartre and Three American Novelists: Saul Bellow, John Barth, and Ken Kesey, The" H63
"Imitations-of-Novels: John Barth no Shosetsu" H121
"In-Depth Interview With: John Barth, An" F7
"Inhuman Comedy: The Nihilism of John Barth" H94
Innovative Fiction: Stories for the Seventies D3
"In One of Three, Barth Seems Not So Parched and Plucked After All" I189
"In Print: John Barth" G97
"In Pursuit of Proteus: A Piagetian Approach to the Structure of the Grotesque in American Fiction of the Fifties" H260
"Inspiration" H265
Instructor's Manual for The Art of Fiction H292
Instructor's Manual: Four Modes—A Rhetoric of Modern Fiction H264
"Integrated Short-Story Collection: Studies of a Form of Nineteenth- and Twentieth-Century Fiction, The"

H308
"Intemperate Zone: The Climate of Contemporary American Fiction, The" H56
International Poetry Forum, The G53
"Interview with Anthony Burgess, An" H170
"Interview With John Barth, An" F14
"Introduction" H110, H181
"Introduction: No! in Thunder" H2
"Introduction: Prize Stories 1969" H100
Introduction to Fiction D15, G52
"Invitation to Escape" I65
"It's a Real Good Year For Authors" I5
"Jacob Horner Came Out of His Corner, and Then—" I30
"J. Barth" G98
John Barth G38, H145
"John Barth G41, H82
"John Barth" G39-G42, G78, G92, H63, H183, H217, H271, I136
"John Barth" G41, H82
"John Barth: A Bibliography" J5
"John Barth: A Bouyant Denial of Relevance" I112
"John Barth: A Contemporary Satirist" H119
"John Barth Among 11 Named to Arts and Letters Body" G43
"John Barth and Attitudes toward Reality" H64
"John Barth and Festive Comedy: The Failure of Imagination in The Sot-Weed Factor" H166
"John Barth and the Aesthetics of Artifice" H204
"John Barth and The End of the Road: An Aspect of American Literature in the '50's" H95
"John Barth and the Literature of Accentuated Artifice" H221
"John Barth and the Literature of Exhaustion" H102
"John Barth and the Novel of Comic Nihilism" H44
"John Barth: An Eccentric Genius"

-200-

"John Barth: An Interview"
    F6
"John Barth: An Introduction"
    G96, H153, J4
"John Barth: A Profile" G104
"John Barth As a Novelist of
    Ideas: The Themes of Value
    and Identity" H48
"John Barth as Jonathan Swift"
    I98
"John Barth as Menippean
    Satirist" H214
"John Barth: A Truffle No
    Longer" F8
"John Barth b. 1930" G84
"John Barth (b. 1930)" G44
"John Barth Dissects 'Prosaic'"
    F26
"John Barth e il romanzo di
    società" H33
"John Barth 1st Speaker on
    University Lecture Series"
    G45
"John Barth: From Anti-Hero
    to Hero" H52
"John Barth Gets Award For
    Fiction" G46
"John Barth: Goat-Boy's Father"
    G47
"John Barth: Imitations of
    Imitations" H148
"John Barth in Chiaroscuro,
    1969" G96
"John Barth in the Global
    Village" I163
"John Barth: Long Reach, Near
    Miss" H32
"John Barth: Master of Retold
    Myth" I193
"John Barth (1930)" G85
"John Barth 1930—" G51-G52,
    G93
"John Barth (1930—)" G48,
    G50, G86, G90
"John Barth [1930—]" G49
"John Barth: 'Poet in Prose'"
    G53
John Barth Reads from Giles
    Goat-Boy F1
"John Barth's 'Anonymiad'"
    H301
"John Barth's Artist in the
    Fun House" H259
"John Barth's Early Novels"
    H54
"John Barth's Fictions for
    Survival" I22, I46, I74,
    I126, I170, I206
"John Barth's First Novel" I18
"John Barth Freedom Road" H216
"John Barth's 'Glossolalia'"
    H305
"John Barth's Hamlet" H202
"John Barth's Initial Trilogy:
    A Study of the Themes of Value
    and Identity" H288
"John Barth's Tenuous Affirma-
    tion: 'The Absurd, Unending
    Possibility of Love'" H291
"John Barth's The Floating Opera:
    Death and the Craft of Fiction"
    H261
"John Barth: The Artist of His-
    tory" H247
John Barth: The Comic Sublimity
    of Paradox H315
"John Barth, The End of the
    Road, and the Tradition of
    American Fiction" H200
"John Barth: The Novel of Fic-
    tion" H108
"John Barth: The Teller Who
    Swallowed His Tale" H232
"John S. Barth, English Teacher,
    Author Featured" G94
"John [Simmons] Barth (1930—)"
    G105
"John Wain and John Barth: The
    Angry and the Accurate" I37
"Joke Is on Mankind, The" I48
"Joker Is Wild, The" I127
"Just for the Record" I171
"Kennan Announces 9 Literary
    Awards" G54
"Latest Barth Book Is 'Untaped
    Print'" F18
"Latter-Day Scheherazade" I146
"L'éclatement du mythe" H182
"Lecturing Novelist Acclaimed
    as One Of Decade's Best" G55
"Lemon for the Teacher, A" I40
Liberations: New Essays on the
    Humanities in Revolution
    H177, H201
Library of Literary Criticism,
    A H101
"Liebestodd" I26

"Life Is a Showboat, A Young Author Finds" I10
"Life's But a Showboat Drifting by" I7
"Like Nothing Nameable" I157
"Lingering on the Autognostic Verge: John Barth's Lost in the Funhouse" H243
"Literary and Cultural History" G56
Literary Disruptions: The Making of a Post-Contemporary American Fiction H332
Literary History of the United States: History H6, H296-H297
Literary Horizons: A Quarter Century of American Fiction H143, I19, I38, I69, I86, I149
Literary Rebel, The H29
Literature in America: The Modern Age D10, G86
Literature of America: Twentieth Century, The D16, G105
Literature of Exhaustion: Borges, Nabokov, and Barth, The H313
"Literature of Law and Order, The" H115
Literature of Possibility: A Study in Humanistic Existentialism, The H1
Literature of the United States, The D17, G95
"Little Bit of Luck, A" H321
"Living Sakhyan in Barth's Giles Goat-Boy, The" H234
"L'ombra di Sheherazade: Conversazione con John Barth" F15
"Lost in the Barth-house" I180
"Lost in the Funhouse" H292
"Lost in the Funhouse: Barth's Use of the Recent Past" H256
Love and Death in the American Novel H3, H37
"Low Life on Olympus" I214
"Ludic Fiction—Metafiction: The Contemporary Experimental Novel in America" H248
"Mad Narrator in Contemporary Fiction, The" H127

Major American Short Stories D18, G90, H335
"Make It New!" I155
"'Man's Voice, Speaking': A Continuum in American Humor, 'A'" H207
Manual to Accompany The Modern Tradition H217
"Manuscript Division Acquisitions, 1968" G57
"Manuscript Division Acquisitions, 1970" G58
"Marathon Adventures of a 17th-Century Englishman, The" I61
"Master Chef Barth Spices Homer's Myth for a 7-Layer Treat" G77
"'Menelaiad'" H82
"Message [Concerning the Felt Ultimacies of One John Barth]" H342
"Metafiction" H158
"Metamorphosis: An Examination of Communication and Community in Barth, Beckett and Pynchon" H267
"Mind Forged Manacles: Images of the University in American Fiction of the Nineteen Sixties" H322
"Mirrors and Masks in the Novels of John Barth" H189
"Mr. Barth Is a Grand Tease In The Rippling and Rolling 'Giles'" I81
"'Mithridates, he died old': Black Humor and Kurt Vonnegut, Jr." H47
"Mode of Black Humor, The" H284
Modern American Fiction: Insights and Foreign Lights H210
Modernity of the Eighteenth Century, The H194
Modern Novel, The H11
"Modern Novel in the Presence of Myth, The" H286
Modern Occasions G103
Modern Occasions 2 H307
"Modern Satire: A Mini-Symposium" H125
Modern Tradition: An Anthology of Short Stories, The D11, D19, G84

"Moebius Twist For 'Funhouse'" I148
"Mother Charges Son With Harrassment" G59
"Mother of Us All: Pocahontas Reconsidered, The" H5
"Muddle-Browed Faction" I125
Multimediate: Multi Media and the Art of Writing D34
"Mysterious New Novel, The" H201
"Myth and Psychology in the Novels of John Barth" H257
"Myth-Making with a Rib-Tickler" I216
"Mythotherapy and Modern Poetics" H75
Naked I: Fictions for the Seventies, The D1, G42, H181
"Narrative Springs, The" I215
"Narrators and Narration in the Fiction of John Barth" H326
Nathanael West: A Critical Essay H198
"National Book Award in Fiction: A Curious Case, The" G99
"Necassary Blankness: Women in Major American Fiction of the Sixties, The" H240
"Needless Vulgarity in Novel" I15
New American Arts, The H23
"New American Fiction, The" H23
"'New American Fiction' Reconsidered" H55
"New Barth Novel Widely Acclaimed" I83
"New Barth Novel Wins Wide Critical Acclaim" G60
"New Consciousness, The" H297
"New Creative Writers" G80
"New Fall Fiction" I192
"New Fiction in America" H333
New Fiction: Interviews with Innovative American Writers, The F20
"New Gnosticism: Speculations on an Aspect of the Postmodern Mind, The" H255

"'New Heav'ns, New Earth'—the Landscape of Contemporary Apocalypse" H276
"'New Mood': An Obsession With the Absurd,'The'" H19
"New Mutants, The" H20
"New Novel by Barth: Revelation or Scandal?" I90
New Novel in America: The Kafkan Mode in Contemporary Fiction, The H164
"New Novelists" H279
"New Novels" I24, I44, I128, I133
"New Pleasures of the Imagination, The" H136
"New Tradition in Fiction, The" H341
"New Trends and Old Hats" I57
New Worlds for Old: The Apocalyptic Imagination, Science Fiction, and American Literature H304
"N Factor, The" H263
"Night-Sea Journey" H264
"900 Hear Barth, Foss In 'Words and Music'" G102
"1930— John Barth" G95
"No Exit" I165
No! in Thunder H2
"Notes from the Funhouse" H150
"Notes on a New Sensibility" H123
"Notes on Contributors" G103
"Notes on the American Short Story Today" H24
"Notes on the Literary Scene: Their Own Language" H27
"Notes on the Rhetoric of Anti-Realist Fiction" H295
"Notes toward the Destitution of Culture" H96
"Nothing Game, The" H36
"Novel as Critique of the Novel, The" H138
"Novel as Parody: John Barth, The" H7
"Novelist Barth Scolds Cambridge" G112
"Novelist John Barth To Join Johns Hopkins Faculty" G61
"Novelist To Give Opening Lecture" G62

"Novelist to Present Work In Concert-Like Reading" G63
"Novel Looks at Itself—Again, The" I198
Novel Now: A Student's Guide to Contemporary Fiction, The H51
Novel of Manners in America, The H237
"Novels of John Barth: An Introduction, The" H97
"Novels of The Eastern Shore and War" I8
Number and Nightmare: Forms of Fantasy in Contemporary Fiction H331
"Of Making Many Books" G64
"Old Office Mates Share 2nd Honor" G65
On Contemporary Literature H23, H55, I62
"One Baffled Barth in Search of a Book" I156
"One Low Voice in Wild Company" I191
"Only an Occasional Rutabaga: American Fiction Since 1945" H122
Open Decision: The Contemporary American Novel and its Intellectual Background, The H129
"'Opera' Afloat, An" I16
"Organic and Humanist Models in Some English Bildungsroman" H165
"Our Literati in Residence" G73
Oxford Companion to American Literature, The G82
"Pan for Barth's Goat-Boy, A" I101
"Paperbacks" I71-I72, I138, I211
Paracriticisms: Seven Speculations of the Times H139, H177-H178, H255, H330
"Passionate Virtuosity: The Fiction of John Barth" H208
Penguin Companion to American Literature, The G75
Performing Self: Compositions and Decompositions in the Languages of Contemporary Life, The H87, H115
"Personal Matters" G66
"Philharmonic to Play Today, Tuesday" G67
"Picaresque Satires in Modern American Fiction" H147
"Picaresque Tradition in the Contemporary English and American Novel, The" H98
"Pick of the Paperbacks" I28
"Poetry Discussion, Work into a Novel" I60
"Point Is That Life Doesn't Have Any Point, The" H25
"'Point of View' and the Creative Process in the Novels of John Barth" H278
"Politics of Self-Parody, The" H87
"Pop, Op, and Black Humor" H90
"POSTmodernISM: A Paracritical Bibliography" H178
"Postwar American Novel, The" H34
"Pragmatism: A National Fascist Mode of Thought" H195
"Préface" to L'Enfant-Bouc H155
Preface to Matkan pää H151
Preface to Uiva ooppera H225
Prize Stories 1969: The O. Henry Awards D20, H100
"Prize-Winning Writer Reflects on Buffalo" F23
Process of Fiction: Contemporary Stories and Criticism, The D21, D30, G92, H111
"Professor Welcomes Winter— Then He Writes" F13
"Profs Given Book Award" G68
Prose Readings by John Barth F3
"Prospect of Books, A" I188
"Psychodrama in Eden" I36
"Puncturing the Gods" I103
"Quest for Being in Contemporary American Fiction, The" H289
"Quest Romance in Contemporary Fiction, The" H99
Quests Surd and Absurd: Essays in American Literature H57
Radical Sophistication: Studies in Contemporary Jewish-American

-204-

Novelists" H118
"Raintree County and the Epi-
   cizing Poet in American Fic-
   tion" H226
"Rake, Saint, and Cynic: John
   Barth's Masks" H112
"Readout: The Year in Books"
   I203
"Recent and Readable" I96
"Recent Novels" I204
Red Hot Vacuum and Other
   Pieces on the Writing of
   the Sixties, The H160
"Religious Interpretation and
   Contemporary Literature:
   Kurt Vonnegut, Jr., Robert
   Coover and John Barth" H311
"Response Not Typical" I52
"Return of The Native" F24
Return of the Vanishing Amer-
   ican, The H72
"Revelation or Hoax?" I110
"Revised New Syllabus and the
   Unrevised Old, The" I106
"Revolving Bookstand, The"
   H22
"Rhetoric of Giles Goat-Boy,
   The" H192
"Ripeness Was Not All: John
   Barth's Giles Goat-Boy" H41
Rise and Fall of American Hu-
   mor, The H66
"Rogue Reappears: A Study of
   the Development of the Pica-
   resque in Modern American
   Fiction, The" H246
"Rogues, Fools, and Satyrs:
   Ironic Ghosts in American
   Fiction" H210
"Rokuju-nendai Eibungaku to
   Black Humour" H193
"Roots of An Author" G87
"Rub-a-Dub-Dub" I119
"Samplings" I114
"Satire in the Fiction of
   John Barth" H314
"Satire of John Barth and Kurt
   Vonnegut, Jr., The" H310
"Satire with a Ba-a-a" I78
"Scape Goat" I130
Scenes from American Life:
   Contemporary Short Fiction
   D4
"Scheherazade & Friend" I186

"Scheherazade Runs Out of Plots,
   Goes on Talking; The King,
   Puzzled, Listens: An Essay on
   New Fiction" H280
"Science Fiction and the World
   of Greek Myths" H328
"Second Thoughts on the Old
   Gray Mare: The Continuing
   Relevance of Southern Literary
   Issues" H116
"Self-Conscious Artist in Contem-
   porary American Fiction, The" H244
"Self-Conscious Moment: Reflec-
   tions on the Aftermath of
   Modernism, The" H325
"Self-Conscious Narrator-Pro-
   tagonist in American Fiction
   Since World War II, The"
   H229
"Self-Mimesis in the Fiction
   of John Barth" H287
Sense of the Sixties, The D42,
   H21
"Separate War: Camp and Black
   Humor in Recent American Fic-
   tion, A" H68
"Series Adds Barth, O'Connor"
   H317
"Service to the University, A"
   I108
Sexual Revolution in Modern
   American Literature, The H173
"Shadow of Satan: A Study of
   the Devil Archetype in Selected
   American Novels from Hawthorne
   to the Present Day, The" H205
Shaken Realist, The H159
"Shapes and Strategies: Forms
   of Modern American Fiction in
   the Novels of Robert Penn
   Warren, Saul Bellow, and
   John Barth" H212
Short Stories: Classic, Modern,
   Contemporary D31, G44
"Short Story Today, The" H335
"Should the Scapegoat Win a
   Sheepskin?" I84
"Shrinking Garden and New Exits:
   The Comic-Satiric Novel in the
   Twentieth Century, The" H105
Shriven Selves: Religious Prob-
   lems in Recent American Fic-
   tion H222
"Silver-Age Fun" I172

"Since 1945"   H6
Single Voice: An Anthology of Contemporary Fiction, The   D7
Situation of the Novel, The   H128
"Smog of the Spirit"   I63
"Some Notes on the Jewish Novel in English or Looking Backward from Exile"   H73
"Some Shapes in Recent American Fiction"   I208
"Some Uses of Finnegans Wake in John Barth's the Sot-Weed"   H84
"Son of a Computer"   I115
"Sot-Weed Factor: A Contemporary Mock-Epic, The"   H43
"'Sot-Weed Factor': Lengthy Historical Spoof, by John Barth, About 17th-Century London and Maryland, 'The'"   I56
Sounder Few: Essays from the Hollins Critic, The   G1, H41, H47, H184, J1
Southern Fiction Today: Renascence and Beyond   H116
Standards: A Chronicle of Books for Our Time   I67
Stories from the Sixties   D23
"Strife and Struggle"   I43
Structural Fabulation: An Essay on Fiction of the Future   H340
Studies in Short Fiction: Five Short Novels & Thirty Stories   D32, G85
"Study in Nihilism, A"   I31
"Study of John Barth's Giles Goat-Boy as an 'Anatomy,' A"   H85
"Surfacing of Mr. Barth [Laughter], The"   I82
Surfiction: Fiction Now . . . and Tomorrow   D40, G79, H333, H338, H341
"Survey of John Barth's Narrative Art, With Emphasis upon Giles Goat-Boy, A"   H104
"Symposium Highlights: Wrestling (American Style) with Proteus"   F25, H142
"Symposium Sidelights"   F25

Teacher's Manual: Three Stances of Modern Fiction   H206
"Teaching Next Best To Rich Wife—Barth"   F5
Technique of Modern Fiction, The   H88
"Themes of Identity through Value in John Barth's Novels, The"   H154
Theory of the Novel, The   H312
"They're Mannerists, Not Moralists"   H18
"30's and the 60's—A Parallel, The"   F2
"Thomas Berger's Little Big Man as Literature"   H124
"Those Clowns of Conscience"   H21
Three Stances of Modern Fiction: A Critical Anthology of the Short Story   D33
"Time Gives Key Spot to Barth Novel"   G69
"Tiny Odyssey"   I150
T.L.S.: Essays and Reviews from The Times Literary Supplement, 1967   I127
"Told by an Idiot: Toward an Understanding of Modern Fiction through an Analysis of the Works of William Faulkner and John Barth"   H290
"Toward a Definition of Black Humor"   H273
Toward a New Earth: Apocalypse in the American Novel   H227
"Toward a Redefinition of Modernism"   H300
"Towards a Novel of the Absurd: A Study of the Relationship Between the Concept of the Absurd as Defined in the Works of Sartre and Camus and Ideas and Form in the Fiction of John Barth, Samuel Beckett, Nigel Dennis, Joseph Heller, and James Purdy"   H81
"Tower and the Maze: A Study of the Novels of John Barth, The"   H185
"Trade Winds"   I179
"Trends in Recent American Fiction"   I168
Trials of the Word: Essays in

-206-

American Literature and the Humanistic Tradition H26
12 from the Sixties D37, H24
Twentieth Century Writing: A Reader's Guide to Contemporary Literature H113
"Two Bibliographies" J2
"2 Book Awards Split for First Time" G100
200 Contemporary Authors G21
Two Narratives for Tape and Live Voice F4
"UB Chairs Go to Barth and Fiedler" G70
"UB's Barth Is Cited For Fiction" G71
"Unanswered Man: A Comparative Study of John Barth, The End of the Road; Samuel Beckett, Molloy; Albert Camus, The Stranger; Hermann Hesse, Steppenwolf; and Eugene O'Neill, The Iceman Cometh, The" H49
"Unconfirmed Thesis: Kurt Vonnegut, Black Humor, and Contemporary Art, The" H197
"Unity of Anatomy: The Structure of Barth's Lost in the Funhouse, The" H223
"Unlucky Jake" I32
"Upper Crusts" I41
"Up-to-Date Looking Glass, The" I149
"Use of Metaphor in the Novels and Short Fiction of John Barth, The" H109
"Utopia Reconstructed: Alienation in Vonnegut's God Bless You, Mr. Rosewater" H187
Veins of Humor H207
Versions of the Past: The Historical Imagination in American Fiction H299
"Virgin Laureate, The" I53
Vision and Response in Modern Fiction H324
"Vivifiction" I174
Waiting for the End H13-H14
"War Against the Academy, The" H14
"Warning Given Genteel Readers On New Novel" I11
"Way We Write Now, The" H209

Webster's New World Companion to English and American Literature G107
"WESCAC and the Messiah: John Barth's Long, Brilliant Satire on the Labytinthine Ways of Mankind" I87
"What Happened to John Barth?" H39
"What Is Modern in Eighteenth-Century Literature?" H194
"'What Marvelous Plot . . . Was Afoot?' History in Barth's The Sot-Weed Factor" H80
"Whither the Short Story (Or Is It Wither)?" F27
Who's Who in America G14-G18
Who's Who in the East G11, G19
"Will Take Part in Benefit Show" G72
"Work in Progress/ Joseph Heller: An Interview by James Shapiro" H180
World Authors, 1950-1970 G20
World Literature Since 1945 H252
World of Black Humor: An Introductory Anthology of Selections and Criticism, The D8, H15, H25, H53, I87
"Worth a Guilty Conscience" I59
Would-Be Writer, The D43
"Writer as Double Agent: Essay on the Conspiratorial Mode in Contemporary Fiction, The" H135
Writer's Choice D22
"Writer's Situation, The" H126
"Writer's Situation: II, The" H132
Writer's Yearbook '72 F19
"Year of the Fact" I120

PERIODICAL INDEX

Acta Litteraria Academiae Scientiarum Hungaricae H147
America I102, I117, I161, I188, I195
American Quarterly H80, H106
American Scholar, The C16, H22, H34
Amerika Bungaku H95
Annals of the American Academy of Political and Social Science, The H67
Art International H183
Arts in Society F12
Atlantic Monthly, The C7, C19, H70, I152, I184
Ball State University Forum H226
Baltimore Evening Sun I8
Best Sellers I33, I55, I111, I154, I210
Biography News F24
Booklist, The I116, I194
Books and Bookmen I131
Book Week C17, G104, H16, H18, H21, H36, I68, I87
Book World I28, I139, I143, I211
Boundary 2 H255, H275, H300, H342
Bucknell Review H163
Buffalo Courier-Express F13, G2-G3, G36, G59, G70-G71, G102, G112
Buffalo Courier-Express Focus F18, G67, I193
Buffalo Courier-Express Sunday Magazine G73
Buffalo Evening News F23, F26, G4, G22, G24, G26-G27, G37, G63-G64, G72, G74, G77, G109, I94
Buffalo Evening News Magazine F10, G76, G108, I92, I187
Cape Times, The I66
Catholic World, The I163

CEA Critic, The H40
Centennial Review, The H91
Centre Daily Times, State College and Bellefonte, Pa. G9, G23, G25, G33, G45-G46, G55, G60, G62, G65, G69, G94, G106, I5, I11, I51-I52, I60, I148
Chicago Review H77, I36
Chicago Sunday Tribune Magazine of Books I15, I49
Chicago Tribune Books Today I71, I78, I138
Choice H319, I73, I109, I196
Christian Century, The I103
Christian Science Monitor, The I84, I180
College English H90, H140
Colorado Quarterly, The H78
Commentary H31, H39, H61
Commonweal I112, I118
Comparative Literature H305
Contemporary Literature F6, H14, H44, H204, I168, I208
Cresset I205
Criticism H152
Critique H7-H10, H43, H48, H69, H187, H197, H223, H228, H235, H306, H334, H337, I105, J2, J5
Current Biography G13
Daily Collegian, The (Pennsylvania State University) F5, G68, I13, I83, I113
Dallas Morning News, The I14
Denver Quarterly, The I21, I106
Dissent H71, H242
Dorchester News, The C20
Edda H188
Eigo Seinen (The Rising Generation) H121, H193, H199, H254, H279
Encounter I136
Esquire C2, C4, C6, C10-C12, G5-G8, I35
Études Anglaises H146

Extension I110
Faculty Bulletin, The Pennsyl-
   vania State University G66
Falcon, The F19
Fiction C13
fiction international H270
Forum H289
Genre H162, H294
Georgia Review, The H281,
   H291
Globe Magazine, The (Toronto)
   I99
Guardian, The (Manchester)
   I64
Guardian Weekly, Manchester
   I27, I134, I216
Harper's Magazine C14, H27,
   I22, I32, I46, I74, I126,
   I170, I206
Harvard Advocate, The C22
Helios H328
Holiday C18, H32
Hollins Critic, The G78,
   H41, H47, J3
Hopkins Review, The C1
Horizon G97
Hudson Review, The I107,
   I164, I201
Idol, The F22
Intellectual Digest H180
Iowa Review, The H158
James Joyce Quarterly H84
John O'Londons I42
Johns Hopkins Gazette, The
   G61
Johns Hopkins Journal G61
Johns Hopkins Magazine, The
   C15
Journal of Aesthetic Educa-
   tion, The H213
Journal of General Education,
   The H165
Journal of Religion, The
   H276
Kansas Quarterly H105
Kenyon Review, The C3, H5,
   H45, H96, I59
Kirkus Reviews I1, I29, I47,
   I77, I142, I176
Kirkus Service, The [see
   Kirkus Reviews]
La Fiera Letteraria F15
Language Quarterly H68
La Quinzaine Littéraire H182

Les Temps Modernes H23
Letture H120
Library Journal G80, H318, I2,
   I34, I54, I79, I144, I178
Library of Congress Information
   Bulletin G34, G91
Life I91, I156
Listener, The I25, I128, I172
Literature & Ideology H195
London Magazine H161, I135,
   I175
Long Beach Independent Press
   Telegram, The H316
Los Angeles Mirror and Daily
   News I4
Maclean's I101
Magazine of Fantasy and Science
   Fiction, The I122
Malahat Review H170
Massachusetts Review, The H4,
   H56, I37, I200
Mediterranean Review H216
Midwest Quarterly, The H74
Milwaukee Journal I16
Minnesota Review, The H24,
   H196
Modern Fiction Studies H111,
   H122, H243, H250, H320
Modern Occasions H150
Morning Telegraph, The (New
   York) I9
Mosaic H148, H298
Nation, The I57, I100, I158,
   I198
National Observer, The F16,
   H19, H35, I81, I96, I145,
   I189
National Review I162, I191
New American Review C9, F20,
   H126, H132
New Leader, The I18, I62,
   I67
New Literary History H178
New Orleans Review, The H65
New Republic, The I98, I160
News, Book-of-the-Month Club
   I80, I151
New Society D41
New Statesman I41, I63, I130,
   I173, I212
Newsweek F9, I50, I89, I120,
   I150, I190, I203
New Yorker, The I119, I183
New York Herald Tribune Book

-210-

Review [see New York Herald Tribune Lively Arts and Book Review]
New York Herald Tribune Lively Arts and Book Review I30, I61
New York Review of Books, The I95, I192
New York Times, The F2, F17, F27, G32, G43, G54, G89, G100, I12, I82, I155, I181
New York Times Book Review, The F8, F11, F21, G31, G99, H15, H25, H46, H131, H209, I6, I48, I88, I157, I182, I197
North American Review, The I124, I207
Notes on Contemporary Literature H234
Novel F25, H142, H192
Observer Review, The (London) I23, I72, I132, I214
Ohio Review, The H219
Omaha World-Herald I17
Partisan Review H20, H62, H87, H115, H123, H211, I165
Patriot, The (Harrisburg, Pa.) F7
Philadelphia Inquirer, The I153
Playboy G47, H107, I97, I159, I185
Prarie Schooner I166
Prism F14
Progressive, The I115
Psychology Today I202
Publishers' Weekly I20, I45, I70, I75-I76, I137, I141, I177, I209
Punch I24, I44, I133
Quarterly Journal of the Library of Congress, The G56-G58
Queen I39
Ramparts H23
Reporter, The I104
Research Studies H220
Review of Books and Religion H321
Running Man, The H73
San Francisco Chronicle I10
Satire Newsletter H117, H125

Saturday Review I19, I38, I58, I69, I86, I140, I149, I179
Saturday Review of the Arts H263, H265
Scotsman, The H23
Sewanee Review, The H268
Shenandoah I108
Smith, The H93
South Atlantic Quarterly, The H103, H269
Southern Humanities Review, The H266
Southern Literary Journal, The H247
Southern Review, The H273, I125
Southwest Review C5, H202
Spectator, The I40, I129, I174, I213
Springfield (Mass.) Sunday Republican I3, I56
Student Life, Washington University G88
Studi Americani H33
Studies in English Literature (The English Literary Society of Japan) H86, H200
Studies in Short Fiction H259, H301, I169
Studies in the Twentieth Century H231-H232
Tablet, The I123
Teachers College Record I114
Tennessean, The (Nashville) H317
Texas Studies in Literature and Language H261
Time G35, H17, I31, I53, I85, I147, I186
Times Literary Supplement, The (London) I26, I43, I65, I127, I171, I215
TriQuarterly C21, G98, H55, H75, H280, H295, H325, H327, H329, H336, H339
Twentieth Century Literature H256
University of Dayton Review, The H60
Virginia Kirkus' Service [see Kirkus Reviews]
Virginia Quarterly Review, The H136, H139, I121, I167, I199
Vogue I93

-211-

Wall Street Journal, The G106, I90
Washington Post and Times Herald, The G83, I7, I146
Washington Post Potomac, The G87
Western American Literature H124

Wisconsin Studies in Contemporary Literature [see Contemporary Literature]
Works H83
World C23
Xavier University Studies H166
Yale Review, The C8, I204

PUBLISHER INDEX

Anchor Books D23
Appleton-Century-Crofts Ala
Archon Books H331
Arnold, Edward H88
Atheneum H160
Avon Books Alb, A2b, A2f,
  H23, H55, I62
Bantam Books A5b, A6d, A7c,
  A8d, D35, H21
Beacon Press H2
Brill, E. J. H168
Brown,Watson Ltd. A2d
Brown, William C. D26
Canfield Press D27, G81
Carnegie Library G53
Case Western Reserve Univ.,
  The Press of H194
Chicago Press, Univ. of H57
College & University Press
  H175
Cornell Univ. Press H164,
  H324
Criterion Books H3
Dell Publishing D3, D37, H24
Deutsch, Andre A9d
Dial Press D5, G40
Doubleday & Company A2a, A3a,
  A4a-A4c, A5a, A6a, A7a, A8a-
  A8b, D20, D23, H100, H239
Duke Univ. Press H313
Dutton, E. P. D8, H15, H25,
  H53, H167, I87
Eerdmans, William B. H198
Európa Kiadó A2a
F and W Publishing F19
Faber & Faber H51
Farrar, Straus & Giroux B2a,
  G103
Fawcett Publications A4f,
  A9c, D1, D39, G42, H71,
  H110, H181
Feffer & Simons H315
Fortress Press H222
Free Press, The D9-D10, D42,
  G86, G110, H21, H129
Funk & Wagnalls H277
Gale Research Company G12,

G21, H241
Gallimard A4a, A6a, A8a, H155
Georgia Press, Univ. of G1,
  H41, H47, H116, H184, J1
Grosset & Dunlap A3c, A3e,
  A7b, A8c, D13, G50
Harcourt Brace Jovanovich D21,
  D30, G92, H111
Harper & Row H161, H203
Harvard Univ. Press H207
Holt, Rinehart and Winston
  D14, D32, G51, G85, H66, H292
Horizon Press H23, I67
Houghton Mifflin D24, G29-G30,
  G49
Hutchinson & Company H11
Illinois Press, Univ. of F20,
  H139, H177-H178, H283, H330,
  H332
Indiana Univ. Press H172, H179,
  H304
Johns Hopkins Univ. Press B4
Kennikat Press H307
Kröner, Alfred H245, H271
Lidador A8a
Literary Guild A4c
Little, Brown and Company D11-
  D12, D19, D31, G10, G44, G84,
  H217, H258
Longanesi A6a
Louisiana State Univ. Press
  H45, H159
Macmillan D6-D7, D25, D28-D29,
  D38, G93, G101, H6, H79,
  H264, H296-H297
Marquis G11, G14-G19
McGraw-Hill D16, G75, G105
McKay, David A3a-A3b, D22
Minnesota Press, Univ. of H145
Nebraska Press, Univ. of H1
Newnes Books H113
New York Univ. Press G111,
  H143, I19, I38, I69, I86,
  I149
Nijhoff, Martinus H173
Noonday Press B2b
North Carolina Press, Univ. of

-213-

H237
Northwestern Univ. Press   C21,
   G98, H186
Notre Dame Press, Univ. of
   H227, H340
Ohio Univ. Press   H118, H272
Oxford Univ. Press   D18, G82,
   G90, H47, H59, H87, H89,
   H115, H176, H299, H312,
   H335, I127
Panther Books   A3d
Pegasus Books   H174
Penguin Books   A2e, A4e, A6c,
   A8f
Pennsylvania State Univ.   G41,
   H82
Pittsburg Press, Univ. of
   H128
Poetry Center, The   G38
Princeton Univ. Press   H238
Privately printed   A10
Random House   A9a-A9b, D4,
   D34, H156
Riverside Press, The   G28
Rizzoli   A2a, A3a
Rowohlt   A3a
Rutgers Univ. Press   H249,
   H251, H268-H269, H284
St. Martin's Press   D36, G48,
   H215
Scott, Foresman   D17, G95
Secker & Warburg   A2c, A3b,
   A4d, A6b, A8e, H50

Seghers   H157
Signet Books   B1
Söderström, Werner   A1a, A2a,
   H151, H225
Southern Illinois Univ. Press
   H29, H133, H141, H190, H262,
   H315
Stein and Day   H2, H13, H20,
   H37, H72-H73, H107, I62
Swallow Press   D40, G79, H333,
   H338, H341
Texas Press, Univ. of   H38,
   H134
Texas Tech Univ.   H210
Ungar, Frederick   H101, H252-
   H253
Union College Press   F22
Vandenhoeck & Ruprecht   H171
Washington Square Press   D2,
   G39
Weidenfeld and Nicolson   B2c
Wesleyan Univ. Press   H177,
   H201
Wiley and Sons, John   D15,
   G52
Wilson, H. W.   G13, G20
Winthrop   D33, H206
Wisconsin Press, Univ. of   F6
Wisconsin-Parkside, Univ. of
   G41, H82
World Publishing   G107
Xerox College Publishing   D43
Yale Univ. Press   H26, H230